DIFFICULT DECISIONS:

Closing and Merging Academic Libraries

Edited by
Sara Holder and
Amber Butler Lannon

Association of College and Research Libraries
A division of the American Library Association
Chicago, Illinois 2015

The paper used in this publication meets the minimum requirements of American National Standard for Information Sciences–Permanence of Paper for Printed Library Materials, ANSI Z39.48-1992. ∞

Library of Congress Cataloging-in-Publication Data

Difficult decisions : closing and merging academic libraries / edited by Sara Holder and Amber Lannon.
    pages cm
 Includes bibliographical references and index.
 ISBN 978-0-8389-8791-9 (pbk. : alk. paper) -- ISBN 978-0-8389-8793-3 (epub) -- ISBN 978-0-8389-8792-6 (pdf) -- ISBN 978-0-8389-8794-0 (kindle) 1. Academic libraries--Mergers. 2. Academic libraries--Departmental libraries. 3. Libraries--Reorganization. 4. Academic libraries--Administration--Decision making. 5. Academic libraries--United States--Administration--Case studies. 6. Academic libraries--Canada--Administration--Case studies. I. Holder, Sara, 1967- editor. II. Lannon, Amber, editor.
 Z675.U5D5155 2015
 027.7--dc23

2015022975

Table of Contents

Acknowledgments

The editors would like to acknowledge the assistance of the following individuals and institutions that have provided support throughout this project: the McGill Library, Kathryn Deiss and the Association of College and Research Libraries, Robin Canuel, Sean Forbes, Joseph Hafner, Dawn McKinnon, Christina Sylka, Sarah Severson, Natalie Waters, the chapter authors, and our families—Gil and Jack, Chris, Moreen, and Clare.

Introduction

Amber Butler Lannon and Sara Holder

UNIVERSITY LIBRARIES ACROSS North America are restructuring their systems to include fewer branches and redesigning their spaces to include fewer service points. The flood of recent closures and consolidations are most certainly a sign of the times—budgetary pressure combined with the move to using more digital resources means that libraries can serve users information needs more efficiently and with fewer physical locations.

Merging libraries is a complex task for librarians, particularly if there are constraints around time and budget. Operationally, moving staff, services, and collections requires detailed planning and careful execution. Quite often, this work is complicated by the considerable care that has to be taken to ensure that excellence in service to the faculties and departments that the branches were dedicated to serving are maintained. For both staff and users of branch libraries, a library closure can be a very emotional event; this must be taken into account throughout the process. Additionally challenging is the fact that the news about library closures can be widely distributed online, and user groups can provide feedback about these closures more easily via social media. Considerable thought must be given to communication and consultation.

At McGill University in Montreal, Quebec, three library branches have been consolidated into larger branches in the last three years (the case study in Chapter 8 describes and compares these mergers). The Management Library and Education Library were merged into the main Humanities and Social Sciences Library, and the Life Sciences Library was merged into the Science and Engineering Library. We, the editors of this book, played leadership roles in all of these mergers as former heads of the now closed libraries and as current heads of the newly restructured libraries: the Humanities and Social Sciences Library and the Schulich Library of Science and Engineering. Throughout the consolidation process, we sought advice and best practices from the literature and colleagues and found that while many librarians have led mergers, few had shared their experiences and the lessons learned through publication.

A call went out to librarians across North America for case studies, commentary, and research on academic library branch restructuring, and the result is this publication. In this work, there are case studies and chapters that explore some aspect of library closures in detail. Throughout the book are a number of recurring issues that librarians undertaking the work of restructuring and consolidation must give careful consideration to: communicating with faculty, students, and staff; making decisions about collections; managing large collections moves; and maintaining access to highly used services and collections such as course reserves, librarian assistance, and interlibrary loan. Also included are in-depth chapters on how to use data to make collections decisions in a merger, consolidate library websites, cross-train staff, create staff buy-in, and navigate culture.

The New Service Model (NSM) program at the University of Illinois at Urbana-Champaign (U of I) is the basis for the first group of case studies. Chapter 1 provides an overarching description of its multiyear program aimed to move the U of I libraries from a decentralized departmental library system to a design more aligned with 21st-century library services. This overview provides an example of how, even in the case of a large-scale restructuring of services, libraries can develop a responsive plan and engage library and campus stakeholders at all stages. Chapter 2 uses a historical view of area studies at Illinois to examine the International and Area Studies Library consolidation as part of the NSM program. Drawing on their experience from this project, the authors provide insights into recent changes in academia and the continuing evolution of library services and collections. Chapter 3 describes the NSM program initiative that merged the Applied Health Sciences Library, Education and Social Science Library, and other social science library services into the Social Sciences, Health, and Education Library. This chapter focuses on tasks that were instrumental in achieving this merger, in particular, the nuances of preparing collections for merging, the importance of creating a robust and inclusive web presence, the extensive training required during and after the implementation, and the importance of celebration as a way to bring closure to the process.

The case studies continue with Chapter 4, a descriptive and qualitative analysis of two academic libraries undergoing transition, one through downsizing and the other through consolidation. The author provides a comparison of the two situations, focusing on the strategies that were used for making decisions during the transition period. This analysis contains useful information for all libraries, but it is especially insightful for libraries faced with making big decisions that will have long-term consequences for their future operations. Chapter 5 tells the story of the transformation of the Welch Medical Library on the medical campus of Johns Hopkins University. The authors describe how library services and expectations evolved in the context of changing technology and the staffing and financial issues that accompanied this evolution. They provide a model for collaboration and alignment of strategic directions between the library and its stakeholder groups that increases and clarifies return on investment of the library and its services.

The study in Chapter 6 highlights a 10-year period during which Purdue Libraries reorganized from a decentralized system of 15 specialized libraries and other units to an organizational structure loosely arranged around four broad subject areas. The chapter primarily focuses on the redesign of the business library; the subsequent merger of the Hicks Undergraduate Library and the Humanities, Social Sciences and Education Library; and the new service models that contributed to, as well as emerged from, the changes. Chapter 7 describes Columbia University's creation of a science and engineering library that consolidated seven of its science libraries. The authors concentrate on the changes in staffing; services; and relationships with faculty, researchers, and students that have emerged from this migration away from departmental librarianship toward a team-based, service-oriented approach to outreach and research support.

The final case study, Chapter 9, covers the months leading to the closure of the Scripps Institution of Oceanography Library and the consolidation of its collections and staff into the University of California, San Diego's Geisel Library. The author explains how the changing academic and research environment influenced her decisions regarding new services and resource locations in the consolidated environment.

Chapter 10 examines the role data can play in the decision to merge or consolidate library collections and in improving the quality of the collections-related decisions that these actions necessitate. The authors use as a model the collection mergers at three social science libraries on the Berkeley campus, each involving tens of thousands of items. They show how data was used in deciding which libraries could be consolidated with the least impact on users and, consequently, what materials should be retained on campus, moved to off-site storage, transferred to another on-campus library, or withdrawn. Chapter 11 describes the human logistics involved in implementing the integration of library collections, including the issues that can arise during the cleanup phase and future considerations when dealing with a merged collection. The author draws from the literature and from her experience as a move coordinator for a merger of two large print collections.

In Chapter 12, the authors share what they learned about creating a unified library web presence necessitated by the merger of two Georgia universities. They describe the challenges, and they highlight the opportunities created by this project, including closer relationships with university IT colleagues that led to further collaborations, increased visibility of the libraries' web presence, and the promotion of consensus building between the two libraries. The author of Chapter 13 examines academic library leadership by discussing how leaders differ from managers and how professional education emphasizes management over leadership. She highlights the importance of a leader understanding the organizational culture through a case study of a failed merger between library and information technology services units in a university setting.

The final chapter, Chapter 14, focuses on communication in the context of branch mergers and consolidations, including fostering an understanding of the broader trends in public services and collection management in academic libraries and developing specific messages for key stakeholders and their timing and methods of delivery. The recommendations are based on the author's experiences at the University of British Columbia (UBC) Library related to the consolidation and closure over a two-year period of several branches on the UBC Vancouver campus and at two hospital locations.

We can expect to see more restructuring as academic libraries adapt to the changing educational landscape and the economic realities of providing secondary education in the 21st century. By reading and learning from the experiences described in this collection, those who are charged with leading these efforts will gain valuable insight into methods, processes, and techniques that will help to bring a positive outcome to these difficult decisions.

CHAPTER 1

Merging, Creating, Transforming:

The New Service Model Program at the University of Illinois at Urbana-Champaign

JoAnn Jacoby and Susan E. Searing

THE NEW SERVICE Model (NSM) program at the University of Illinois at Urbana-Champaign is reimagining and reshaping a highly decentralized departmental library system by means of a broadly participatory process that involves library and campus stakeholders at all stages. Since 2007, the library faculty and staff have engaged in a substantive and sustained discussion of "what matters" in a modern research library. From that ongoing discussion, a responsive model for moving forward expeditiously with large-scale restructuring of library services has emerged.

The NSM program has significantly reduced the complexity of the library organization. The monolithic model of departmental subject libraries has been replaced with a variety of service models suited to the needs of different teaching and learning communities. Sixteen departmental libraries were closed, merged, and/or transitioned to virtual libraries, while several critical behind-the-scenes operations were transformed. The University Library now consists of 21 public service locations; five technical services

1

operations; and several administrative, programmatic, or support units. As of May 2014, more than 20 reorganizational projects have been completed or are in final stages of implementation. NSM work is ongoing, though at a calmer pace because much of the original vision has been actualized.

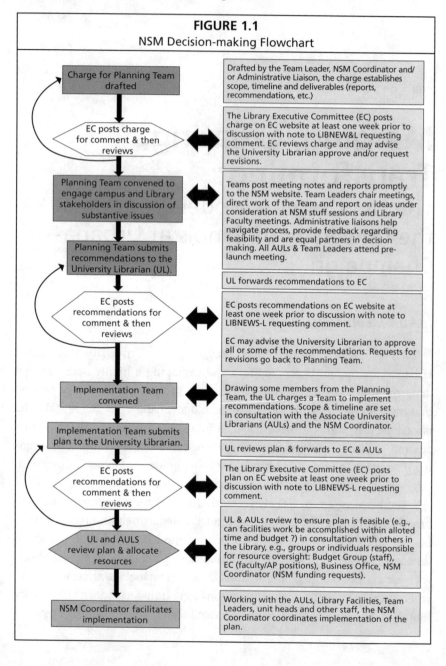

FIGURE 1.1
NSM Decision-making Flowchart

Charge for Planning Team drafted

Drafted by the Team Leader, NSM Coordinator and/or Administrative Liaison, the charge establishes scope, timeline and deliverables (reports, recommendations, etc.)

EC posts charge for comment & then reviews

The Library Executive Committee (EC) posts charge on EC website at least one week prior to discussion with note to LIBNEW&L requesting comment. EC reviews charge and may advise the University Librarian approve and/or request revisions.

Planning Team convened to engage campus and Library stakeholders in discussion of substantive issues

Teams post meeting notes and reports promptly to the NSM website. Team Leaders chair meetings, direct work of the Team and report on ideas under consideration at NSM stuff sessions and Library Faculty meetings. Administrative liaisons help navigate process, provide feedback regarding feasibility and are equal partners in decision making. All AULs & Team Leaders attend pre-launch meeting.

Planning Team submits recommendations to the University Librarian (UL).

UL forwards recommendations to EC

EC posts recommendations for comment & then reviews

EC posts recommendations on EC website at least one week prior to discussion with note to LIBNEWS-L requesting comment.

EC may advise the University Librarian to approve all or some of the recommendations. Requests for revisions go back to Planning Team.

Implementation Team convened

Drawing some members from the Planning Team, the UL charges a Team to implement recommendations. Scope & timeline are set in consultation with the Associate University Librarians (AULs) and the NSM Coordinator.

Implementation Team submits plan to the University Librarian.

UL reviews plan & forwards to EC & AULs

EC posts recommendations for comment & then reviews

The Library Executive Committee (EC) posts plan on EC website at least one week prior to discussion with note to LIBNEWS-L requesting comment.

UL and AULS review plan & allocate resources

UL & AULs review to ensure plan is feasible (e.g., can facilities work be accomplished within alloted time and budget ?) in consultation with others in the Library, e.g., groups or individuals responsible for resource oversight: Budget Group (staff), EC (faculty/AP positions), Business Office, NSM Coordinator (NSM funding requests).

NSM Coordinator facilitates implementation

Working with the AULs, Library Facilities, Team Leaders, unit heads and other staff, the NSM Coordinator coordinates implementation of the plan.

In this chapter, we examine the overall goals, strategies, successes, and challenges in the NSM program. Although the NSM program has produced a successful framework for enacting service-centered changes, including a flowchart for decision making and communication (Figure 1.1), it is not a cookie-cutter solution. Each NSM project has its own trajectory and story. Chapters 2 and 3 in this volume present case studies and deeper reflections on particular NSM projects that transformed library services for international studies, social sciences, and applied health sciences. (For a complete list of NSM projects, see Appendix 1A.)

Although the NSM program has allowed for better use of legacy spaces while reducing the library's overall footprint on campus, neither space issues nor mandated savings drove the process. The focus was squarely on services as described in the "Principles for Decision Making," which guided decisions about which projects to pursue (Appendix 1B).

This chapter describes the process followed at Illinois as its librarians sought to define "new service models that recognize the increasingly interdisciplinary nature of academic inquiry, the critical importance of digital information resources, and the opportunities for collaborative approaches to the provision of library services and collections" (Kaufman, 2008). We outline the factors that were critical to success as well as the major obstacles that were overcome (or still remain) and describe approaches that worked as well as false starts and misfires.

The Changing Nature of Academic Research Libraries

Around the world, academic and research libraries today are changing in response to shifts in the intellectual landscape, new means of scholarly communication, and advances in technologies and theories of teaching. The library service model that served the University of Illinois well for many decades featured a system of departmental libraries aligned with academic disciplines and staffed by subject specialist librarians. This model came into existence a century ago when American colleges transformed themselves into universities on the German model (Ibbotson, 1925). Although the efficacy of departmental libraries was debated (Thompson, 1942; Seal, 1986; Shkolnik, 1991), the model prevailed at large American universities throughout the 20th century (*SPEC Kit 99*, 1983; Croneis & Short, 1999).

Now the departmental library model is coming under increasing pressure. Numerous studies have documented how scholarship is being transformed by digital technologies. For example, the large-scale surveys of higher education faculty in the UK and the US conducted by Ithaka S+R have charted a steady shift in academic work processes—teaching, research, dissemination—toward reliance on online sources and methods and toward increasing openness and interdisciplinarity (Schonfeld & Long, 2014; Schonfeld & Wulfson, 2013). Experts within the field of library and information science (LIS) have looked into the future and identified technological and social trends that will powerfully influence how libraries are perceived and used (Dempsey, 2012; Marchionini & Moran, 2012). Librarians have reacted to current and predicted changes by envisioning a new sort of academic library, one that derives its value from the scope and quality of the services it provides (University of Illinois, 2008a) and focuses on "engagement around services that support the workflow and learning lives of users" (Dempsey, 2012, p. 120). This "service turn," to borrow Scott Walter's phrase, shifts the criteria for excellence from large collections to distinctive services (Walter, 2011). In line with this shift, attention has been focused on the changing roles of subject specialist librarians (Crawford, 2012; Dale, Holland, & Matthews, 2006; Kesselman & Watstein, 2009; Jaguszewski & Williams, 2013; Logue, Ballestro, Imre, & Arendt, 2007; Pinfield, 2001).

However, the transformation of higher education is occurring in a soured economic climate, and new visions for library services are severely limited by fiscal realities and the ongoing costs of entrenched traditional services. The clichéd phrase "doing more with less," unfortunately describes the situation of most academic libraries nowadays; the literature about strategically eliminating services is still scant. Nonetheless, case studies and surveys are beginning to demonstrate how libraries are reducing and reconfiguring legacy services in order to meet new needs (Evangeliste & Furlong, 2011; Vyhnanek & Zlatos, 2011). Faced with hard choices, libraries must "look with cold and hard-headed rationality at our current practices and ask ourselves not what value they offer, but rather what value our patrons believe they offer" (Anderson, 2011, p. 290). The University of Illinois Library has done just that, bringing both qualitative and quantitative data to bear on the design of its service programs.

Overview of New Service Model Program

Librarians at the University of Illinois were confronted by rapidly escalating economic challenges to their traditional model of departmental library service as well as by sea changes in the way that scholarly information is created, disseminated, used, and stewarded for the future. In response, they undertook a broad and inclusive identification of opportunities for strategic investment and engagement with users in far-ranging discussions of and team-based planning for the future of library services.

While the University Library has five primary physical facilities—the Main Library, Undergraduate Library, Grainger Engineering Library Information Center, Funk Library, and Archives Research Center—it supports a much larger number of service points located across campus. The tradition of decentralized subject libraries dates back to the turn of the 20th century and was reinforced by the "holistic librarianship" philosophy of Hugh Atkinson, director of libraries from 1976 to 1986, when Illinois made great strides in networking its catalog (Bregman & Burger, 2002). When the NSM program was launched in 2007, there were nearly 40 separate libraries on campus. Some of these libraries are sizeable, like the Grainger Engineering Library with its own large building. Others were smaller—rooms or suites of rooms within academic buildings, like the Physics Library, the Labor and Industrial Relations Library, and the Chemistry Library. In addition, several self-contained libraries were located within the Main Library building, such as the Slavic Library and the Library and Information Science Library. Each of these libraries offered a focused subject collection of circulating print and other media; non-circulating reference books (often duplicated in other campus libraries); reference and instructional services; course reserves; and, in some cases, special collections of unique uncataloged materials (e.g., files of union contracts in the Labor & Industrial Relations Library). Hours of operation, use policies, and even classification (Dewey Decimal or Library of Congress) varied from library to library. Each library had support staff, student assistants, and at least one professional librarian.

In many ways, the departmental libraries were functional silos. User surveys clearly showed that undergraduate students resented having to travel from library to library to gather the materials they needed. Conversely, faculty and graduate students valued their departmental libraries and the liaison librarians who worked closely with them (University of Illinois, n.d.-b). Yet faculty and graduate students were also forced to use multiple libraries as pre-NSM data visualizations revealed (Figure 1.2).

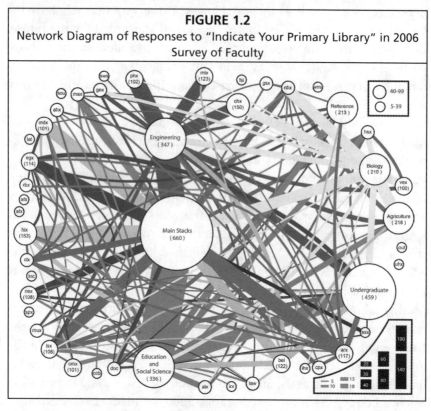

FIGURE 1.2

Network Diagram of Responses to "Indicate Your Primary Library" in 2006 Survey of Faculty

In Figure 1.2, each circle represents one of the campus libraries in 2006. The relative size of the circles shows how many survey respondents identified each library as one of the libraries they used most. Respondents could select multiple "primary" libraries. Lines were drawn when five or more respondents reported using both libraries. Figure 1.3 displays a subset of the data for faculty who identified the Library and Information Science Library as one of their primary libraries (in the lower left corner). Comparing similar analyses for every library designated "primary" by someone revealed that the tendency to use multiple libraries varied among the disciplines. Some information universes are more self-contained than others. These data helped librarians identify libraries sharing a common clientele as potential candidates for mergers. At the outset, the focus was on libraries serving disciplines that have more permeable intellectual boundaries and that encourage more interdisciplinary research—disciplines for which isolated departmental libraries were less functional.

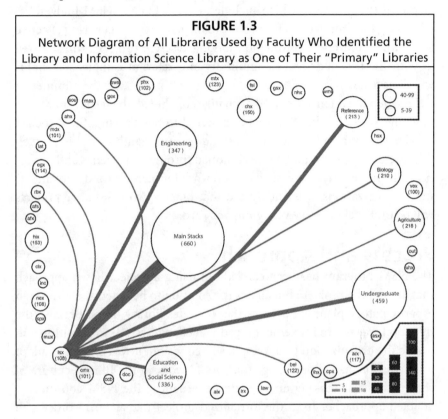

FIGURE 1.3

Network Diagram of All Libraries Used by Faculty Who Identified the Library and Information Science Library as One of Their "Primary" Libraries

The foundational document for the NSM program was an internal report titled *Library Services for the 21st Century at the University of Illinois at Urbana-Champaign* (University of Illinois, 2008b). This report synthesized the library's strategic priorities, ideas from the library faculty and staff, and input from the campus community. It outlined nearly two dozen projects to be pursued over the next few years. The decision process for prioritizing NSM proposals was based on a set of principles that emphasized enhanced digital services for users, stewardship of financial and tangible resources, collaboration, communication, and assessment. Funds were earmarked from the student library-IT fee to cover the anticipated costs of moving collections, enhancing cataloging, reclassifying, and redesigning and furnishing consolidated libraries as well as enriching collections with more electronic resources.

A few months after the report was issued, JoAnn Jacoby, a library faculty member and one of the authors of this chapter, was reassigned to serve as the NSM coordinator. From 2008 to 2012, she provided overall leadership of the program, which included overseeing the NSM budget, establishing the foundations for project management, and ensuring effective communication and coordination among discrete project teams as well as with the broader library community and relevant campus stakeholders. Significant progress occurred during that period. In the summer of 2012, when the intensive period of change concluded, the responsibility for ongoing NSM coordination was transferred to Sue Searing, the associate university librarian for user services and the other author of this chapter. Because the NSM method has been honed through experience and has repeatedly proven to be an effective framework for planning and implementing reorganizations, it is anticipated that one or two NSM-style projects will be undertaken every year going forward.

Process and Approach

The NSM program has been carried out using a project-based approach that defines the problem but allows the solution to be determined through a participatory planning process that includes library users. Because the intention was not to implement top-down change, but to work within and across the organization to develop a shared vision, it was critical to adopt a process for managing change that would work in the Illinois culture of shared decision making and faculty governance. The NSM coordinator adapted approaches from the formalized project management process to provide a framework for defining scope, weighing options, choosing a path, implementing, and evaluating each NSM project (Project Management Institute, 2008).

Most NSM projects proceed in the stages outlined in Figure 1.1. First, the library's Faculty Executive Committee (an advisory group to the dean elected by the library faculty), in conjunction with the library administration, prioritizes NSM projects and forms a planning team composed of library faculty and staff members, as well as faculty from campus programs. Faculty from outside the library who served on these teams were asked to contribute information about trends in their disciplines and serve as a channel for communication between the team and other stakeholders. In addition, the planning teams are charged with gathering input from users and examining existing evidence, as appropriate. For every project, a public webpage links to the team's charge, background documents, minutes of its meetings, and any documentation produced by the team, such as analysis of usage data, summaries of open meeting discussions, and survey results (University of Illinois, n.d.-a).

Planning teams brainstorm, conduct environmental scans and user surveys, and work through contentious issues or diverging viewpoints. Their deliberations lead to a report to the executive committee that outlines findings and recommendations. These reports are posted online, and an invitation to review the report and provide input to the executive committee is sent to the library staff listserv, relevant campus units, and all deans and department heads. Reports are also discussed at library faculty meetings and, during the peak period of NSM activity, at update sessions for library staff. Some reports were also presented at departmental faculty meetings or discussed at specially scheduled open forums for students and faculty. After gathering this input over a period of one to three weeks, the planning team's recommendations are then reviewed and, if necessary, amended by the executive committee. This step provides an important opportunity to reach agreement on the intended outcomes and directions, resulting in a document that then serves as what the project management literature calls a "project charter" (German, 2009). Defining the project scope and outcomes, the planning team's report plays an essential role in the library's distributed decision-making environment. The report is a record of a shared vision that sustains momentum by avoiding the need to revisit decisions that have already been made.

After the planning team's recommendation are vetted, discussed, and endorsed, the executive committee then charges an implementation team to carry the work forward. Knowing that key decisions about direction and scope have been made, the implementation team can focus on realizing the vision. Typically the implementation team has some members who served on the planning team plus others with specific skills and resources needed to move the project forward. When dealing with reconfiguration of departmental libraries, the work of an implementation team includes programmatic planning for new spaces and services, making decisions about weeding and relocating collections, establishing timelines, and developing outcome-based assessment plans. Templates for developing these operational plans (Appendix 1C and 1D) were developed early in the program.

At the height of NSM activity when many teams where working simultaneously, training and information sharing sessions were held to enable team leaders to share best practices, strategies, and moral support.

The structured NSM team approach has not only fostered direct user involvement in library planning but also created unprecedented opportunities for formal and informal engagement around core library service issues with faculty groups, library committees, campus academic leadership, and the campus community at large. Although the process may appear overly deliberative and inefficient, in the Illinois environment it was essential to maintain a transparent and broadly consultative process. By spending time early in the process on brainstorming ideas, intentionally inviting and exploring divergent perspectives, and having a clearly defined path for decision making, the library was able to move forward with speed and certainty once decisions were made.

Projects and Outcomes

Many significant changes have resulted thus far from the NSM program, including the transition of the Labor & Industrial Relations Library, the Library and Information Science Library, and the Business and Economics Library from stand-alone, full-service physical libraries to embedded service models supported by virtual libraries. Other changes include the absorption of the Afro-Americana Library Unit, the City Planning & Landscape Architecture Library, the Physics & Astronomy Library, the Geology Library, and the Biology Library by complementary larger service units. Departmental libraries housed in the Main Library building have also been combined into larger units. For example, the English Library and the Modern Languages & Linguistics Library merged to form the Literatures and Languages Library; the Applied Health Sciences Library joined with the Education & Social Sciences Library to create the Social Sciences, Health, and Education Library; and several smaller units were merged to form a new International and Area Studies Library. Where departmental libraries continue to exist in academic buildings—for example, Chemistry, Communications, and Veterinary Medicine—services and physical footprints have been altered in response to current user needs. Other outcomes include the reorganization of core reference services (on-site and virtual) around three hubs located in the Main Library and Undergraduate Library (social sciences, humanities, area studies, and government information);

the Grainger Engineering Library (physical sciences and engineering); and the Funk Library (life sciences). One of the earliest NSM projects created within the Main Library a Scholarly Commons, where librarians partner with other experts to support digital content creation; numeric, textual, and geographic data analysis; new modes of scholarly communication; and innovative teaching and learning methods. Finally, the NSM program has supported the design and development of forward-looking service programs outlined in the library's strategic plan, including a library-wide approach to health information services.

Although the focus has remained on services to the library's users, workflows have been streamlined in some behind-the-scenes areas as well, including digitization, cataloging, acquisitions, and collection maintenance. An early project studied the digital content lifecycle and implemented more effective ways for the library to manage, preserve, and provide access to library-created digital content. The confluence of improved technical service workflows with the reorganization of departmental libraries has resulted in one of the most important side benefits of the NSM program: enhanced access to library collections through large-scale cataloging of backlogs and previously hidden collections.

It became standard practice under the NSM program to review any service led by a librarian who was retiring. Further, the NSM program provided the impetus and resources for long-desired changes, such as the consolidation of services for international and area studies as well as initiating examination of core services, such as reference, that were overdue for reevaluation. All of the NSM projects were motivated by a desire to transform services, extend the library's reach to users, and design more cost-effective service delivery modes. For example, closing and merging small libraries resulted in longer hours of evening and weekend access to specialized subject collections. Librarians freed from day-to-day management of departmental libraries can now concentrate on assessing user needs, developing new services, reaching out to users (e.g., through an embedded presence in academic units), and enhancing online information.

Change Management

Change on this scale is a challenge for any organization, but Illinois' library faces a number of unique challenges stemming from its unusually flat structure and strong tradition of shared governance. Because of these factors, the only sure path to enduring change is through a consultative, deliberate, and inclusive process. The NSM process was refined over time with the intent to build a foundation of trust that would pave the way for more agile decision making in the future. This necessarily involved laying the groundwork for deeper cultural changes, so although they developed out of a somewhat idiosyncratic environment, the lessons learned are applicable to any library engaged in the process of organizational change.

The literature on organizational leadership and change management provides insight on why large-scale organizational change is so profoundly difficult, including the persistent "imprint" of past periods that can have a surprisingly enduring influence on the structure, culture, and routines across an organization at all levels, from the individual to the collective (Marquis & Tilcsik, 2013). Transformative change is disruptive, and understanding the stress that significant changes have on individuals in order to work through it is essential for the resilience of the organization. Summarizing the key literature on the human dimension of change, Proehl explains,

> [T]here is a universal reaction to change as loss. When change occurs, one thing ends and something begins, and what exists between the two points is unknown. During this period of transition, individuals have to learn to let go of the old and live with the new; move from the familiar to the unknown; and function in the midst of anxiety and uncertainty. (2001, p. 52)

This holds true for most people whether the change is perceived as positive or negative (Scott & Jaffe, 2009). It can be all too easy to misread this process as "resistance to change" (Proehl, 2001), especially for leaders who have had more time than others in the organization to develop a clear vision of what the new model will look like.

Scott and Jaffe (2009) describe five major dimensions of loss that can be experienced when change is introduced. Employees sense a loss of security (feeling out of control and unsure about the future); competence (not knowing what to do when faced with new responsibilities); relationships (missing colleagues, users, and group identity); sense of direction (no longer understanding the organizational mission or the meaning of one's work); and territory (displacement from actual or metaphorical workspaces). The experience of change as loss pertains not just to those working in the library but also to students, faculty, and alumni. In the Illinois NSM experience, feelings of loss were particularly strong among two communities of users: alums of the Graduate School of Library and Information Science, who valued the Library and Information Science (LIS) Library as a locus of the early experience as library professionals in training, and students in the College of Applied Health Science (AHS), who viewed the former AHS Library as an important central location for a geographically distributed college. In both cases, these concerns were openly discussed, and creating a new sense of place, whether virtual (in the case of LIS) or as part of a shared physical facility (in the case of AHS, which became part of the new Social Sciences, Health, and Education Library) became important touchstones in the implementation process.

Grief is the process of working through significant loss, and it is also part of the human response to change. The landmark book *On Death and Dying* by Elisabeth Kübler-Ross (1969) describes the response many people have to a life-changing experience or loss. Kübler-Ross's five-stage model of grief—denial, anger, bargaining, depression, acceptance—has been widely influential in change management. A modified seven-stage model starting with "shock" (characterized by immobilization and paralysis) and adding a "testing and reconstruction" phase before "acceptance" (Ramsay & Happee, 1977) has also been developed and widely used in organizational development literature and change management training programs. Not everyone goes through all these stages and not always in the same order, but these stages provide a useful model for describing what many people experience. The change management literature describes the different types of support that are needed at each stage: communication and information are needed in the first stages, emotional support in the middle, and guidance and direction in the final stages. The NSM process revealed that, while linear theories of change can help leaders and stakeholders make sense of their and others' emotions, the actual process may be more recursive than sequential. When several NSM projects were underway simultaneously, it became (sometimes painfully) evident that every project has a unique emotional trajectory.

Understanding and acknowledging these feelings was essential to our success in leading people in new directions as well as when communicating with students, faculty, and alumni outside the library. For example, some libraries were closed without fanfare, while the staff of other libraries achieved a sense of closure by hosting final-day parties, inviting users, colleagues, and alumni to attend.

Assessment

Ongoing assessment of the NSM is critical. While some of these changes were painful for long-time faculty and staff, for new students (and new faculty), the new model is the only model. Therefore, as the library plans and conducts assessments, the important question is not "Is this better than the old model?" but "How well are things working (or not working) now, and how can we do better?"

All implementation teams are asked to draft an assessment plan (Appendix 1D), but follow-up on completing the assessments has been uneven. A full-time library assessment coordinator, hired just as the NSM program was winding down, is working with individual departmental libraries and service hubs to tailor assessment activities. A year after the LIS Library closed, affected faculty at the library school and the University Library were surveyed (Searing & Greenlee, 2011). This was the first formal, albeit partial, assessment of a new service model. Three years later, LIS students were surveyed; however, unlike the faculty, they knew no other model than the current one (Tracy & Searing, 2014). To date not much quantitative data have been gathered for the specific purpose of evaluating the success of the NSM projects, but more general surveys, including the Ithaka S+R faculty survey administered locally in 2013 and LibQUAL+ Lite in 2014, allow for a degree of analysis at the academic department or major level. In addition, some participants in NSM projects have shared their reflections on the process. Song (2009) examined changes in business information services from the vantage point of the library's value proposition. Jacoby (2011) describes the growing emphasis on new forms of scholarly support services that informed many of the NSM projects and resulted in the creation of the Scholarly Commons. In a talk delivered at the height of the NSM activities, Kaufman (2009) not only told the story of the NSM program and what drove it but also reflected on the outcomes and benefits from the library director's perspective. Conner (2014) chose the NSM program as one of four case studies of future-oriented university libraries, illuminating how an organization that he describes as "the very paradigm of the traditional research library, with a vast collection and a decentralized departmental structure" could transform itself (p. xiii).

Lessons Learned

The NSM program has positioned one of the world's major research libraries to continue sustaining and transforming services in the 21st century. The program provides a blueprint for a process that is open, flexible, and inclusive of librarians, library staff, and library users. At Illinois, librarians fostered large-scale change through a steady series of smaller, focused transformations and, in so doing, solidified a process for planning and implementing change that will continue, even though the intensive period of the program has concluded with most of the original priorities met. Through NSM, the library has cultivated a culture of change among its staff that supports ongoing assessment and assumes dynamic user needs to determine which services ought to adapt. As the NSM program evolved, a number of important lessons were learned.

1. Provide leadership and accountability.

Although the NSM program began without a designated coordinator, it rapidly became clear that someone needed to take charge. Temporarily reassigning a librarian to lead the program was critical to its success. Without such leadership, the pace of change would have been much slower and communication far less consistent. The NSM coordinator not only provided tools, templates, and data to guide the teams but also enforced deadlines and celebrated milestones.

2. Focus on service, not savings.

The state of Illinois was particularly hard hit by the recession, and funding for public higher education suffered. Further, retirement incentives offered by the state resulted in a "brain drain" of library faculty and staff. Because of the NSM program, we could react to the retirements and overall reduction in personnel as opportunities to restructure services. While making the best use of available funds in a time of economic recession was never far from the minds of Illinois librarians and campus administrators, the rhetoric and reality of the NSM program stressed service enhancements, and the program grew organically from the library's own analysis of its deficiencies in the face of present and future needs of scholars and students. Absent a mandate to meet bottom-line savings targets, discussions of service models could be less constrained.

3. Allocate resources to support the process.

A significant amount of money was budgeted to support the NSM program. There were serious costs associated with closing libraries, including the reclassification of books, the physical transfer of materials, and the acquisition of new electronic resources. Remodeling spaces for consolidated services also required funds for new furnishings, electrical upgrades, signage, and other improvements. Illinois was fortunate that a student library-IT fee was being phased in during this period, generating a new source of funds for one-time projects.

4. Involve faculty.

The NSM process has been characterized by deep involvement of campus faculty in the shaping of new services through membership on NSM teams, open town halls, focused discussions at departmental meetings, surveys, and other methods. This commitment to faculty input enabled the NSM program to respond to the varied needs of users in the different disciplines and to gain allies in the affected departments, who could then explain the coming changes to their colleagues, assuage fears, and convey enthusiasm.

5. Value and practice transparency.

Internal communication is seldom easy in a large library, and external communication to users and stakeholders can be even harder. In addition to the NSM website, where all relevant program and team materials were made available, the coordinator issued a periodic online newsletter, set up RSS feeds to provide an option to subscribe to targeted updates on the activities of a particular team, delivered regular updates at meetings of the library faculty and staff, and met frequently with the University Senate's Committee and the library's Student Advisory Committee. Communication with affected campus units was largely coordinated through the subject liaison librarians and the departmental faculty serving on each team, but more formal updates were distributed through emails to all campus deans and department heads. Avenues were also available (including a web comment form) for users to express their ideas and feelings directly to the university librarian, as many did. This transparency is a crucial element of the NSM program, and we believe one reason for its success.

6. Don't expect every idea to flourish.

Of the original 22 proposals, not all have been implemented. A proposal to relocate the Classics Library to a smaller space in the same building was abandoned after vigorous opposition from faculty in the discipline. The timing was simply not right for such a move. A more recent recommendation to create a "humanities neighborhood" on the second floor of the Main Library was vetoed by the incoming dean of libraries, who envisioned a better use for the space to advance an important campus partnership. Other projects evolved in unanticipated directions. For example, the original goal of merging the LIS Library with the Communications Library was examined by a planning team; however, the team recommended instead to disperse the LIS print collection, enhance its website to serve as a virtual library, and embed the subject librarian part-time at the Graduate School of Library and Information Science. Because it is sensitive to user needs as well as library priorities, the NSM process allows for such reroutings.

Conclusion

As an organization, the University of Illinois Library thinks differently and more productively about change as a result of the NSM program. NSM concepts are integrated into decision making and workflows. As the NSM program wraps up the last of the projects identified at the outset of the program, its proponents recognize that the true measure of its success will not be the persistence of the particular new configurations of staff and services, nor whether the university has more or fewer separate libraries in the future, but whether its librarians will continue to respond to new opportunities and challenges with agility and imagination.

References

Anderson, R. (2011). The crisis in research librarianship. *Journal of Academic Librarianship, 37*(4), 289–290.

Bregman, A., & Burger, R. H. (2002). Library automation at the University of Illinois at Urbana-Champaign, 1965–2000: A case study of technological and organizational validity. *IEEE Annals of the History of Computing, 24* (2), 71–85.

Conner, M. (2014). *The new university library: Four case studies.* Chicago, IL: ALA Editions.

Crawford, A. (2012). *New directions for academic liaison librarians.* Oxford, England: Chandos.

Croneis, K. S., & Short, B. H. (1999). *SPEC kit 255: Branch libraries and discrete collections.* Washington, DC: Association of Research Libraries.

Dale, P., Holland, M., & Matthews, M. (Eds.). (2006). *Subject librarians: Engaging with the learning and teaching environment.* Aldershot, England: Ashgate.

Dempsey, L. (2012). Libraries and the informational future: Some notes. In G. Marchionini & B. Moran (Eds.), *Information professionals 2050: Educational possibilities and pathways* (pp.113–125). Chapel Hill, NC: School of Information and Library Science, University of North Carolina at Chapel Hill. Retrieved from http://sils.unc.edu/sites/default/files/publications/Information-Professionals-2050.pdf

Esson, R., Stevenson, A., Gildea, M., & Roberts, S. (2012). Library services for the future: Engaging with our customers to determine wants and needs. *Library Management, 33,* 469–478.

Evangeliste, M., & Furlong, K. (2011). When interdependence becomes codependence: Knowing when and how to let go of legacy services. *Declaration of Interdependence: The Proceedings of the ACRL 2011 Conference.* Retrieved from http://www.ala.org/acrl/sites/ala.org.acrl/files/content/conferences/confsandpreconfs/national/2011/papers/when_interdependence.pdf

German, L. (2009). No one plans to fail, they fail to plan: The importance of structured project planning. *Technicalities, 29*(3), 1–9.

Ibbotson, L. T. (1925). Departmental libraries. *Library Journal, 50,* 853–858.

Jacoby, J. (2011). Moving out from behind the desk and into the flow: Assessing the impact of research support activities. *New Trends in Qualitative and Quantitative Methods in Libraries: Selected Papers Presented at the 2nd Qualitative and Quantitative Methods in Libraries.* Hackensack, NJ: World Scientific.

Jaguszewski, J. M., & Williams, K. (2013). *New roles for new times: Transforming liaison roles in research libraries.* Washington, DC: Association of Research Libraries. Retrieved from http://www.arl.org/storage/documents/publications/NRNT-Liaison-Roles-final.pdf

Kaufman, P. T. (2008, September 2). State of the library, 2008. [Talk delivered at University of Illinois, Urbana-Champaign]. Retrieved from http://www.library.illinois.edu/staff/statetalk/state_of_the_library_2008_2009.pdf

Kaufman, P. T. (2009, September 29). Carpe diem: Seizing opportunities from crisis. [Presentation delivered at the University of Wisconsin-Madison]. Retrieved from http://hdl.handle.net/2142/14287

Kesselman, M. A., & Watstein, S.B. (2009). Creating opportunities: Embedded librarians. *Journal of Library Administration, 49*(4), 383–400.

Kübler-Ross, E. (1969). *On death and dying.* New York, NY: Macmillan.

Logue, S., Ballestro, J., Imre, A., & Arendt, J. (2007). *SPEC kit 301: Liaison services.* Washington, DC: Association of Research Libraries. Retrieved from http://publications.arl.org/Liaison-Services-SPEC-Kit-301

Marchionini, G., & Moran, B. (Eds.). (2012). *Information professionals 2050: Educational possibilities and pathways.* Chapel Hill, NC: School of Information and Library Science, University of North Carolina at Chapel Hill. Retrieved from http://sils.unc.edu/sites/default/files/publications/Information-Professionals-2050.pdf

Marquis, C., & Tilcsik, A. (2013). Imprinting: Toward a multilevel theory. *Academy of Management Annals, 7,* 193–243.

Pinfield, S. (2001). The changing role of subject librarians in academic libraries. *Journal of Librarianship and Information Science, 33,* 32–38.

Proehl, R. A. (2001). *Organizational change in the human services.* Thousand Oaks, CA: Sage.

Project Management Institute. (2008). *A guide to the project management body of knowledge (PMBOK guide)* (4th Ed.). Newtown Square, PA: Project Management Institute.

Ramsay, R. W., & Happee, J. A. (1977). The stress of bereavement: Components and treatment. In C. D. Speilberger & I. G. Sarason (Eds.), *Stress and anxiety* (Vol. 4, pp. 53–67). New York, NY: Wiley.

Schonfeld, R. C., & Long, M. P. (2014). *Ithaka S+R US library survey 2013.* New York, NY: Ithaka. Retrieved from http://www.sr.ithaka.org/research-publications/ithaka-sr-us-library-survey-2013

Schonfeld, R. C., & Wulfson, K. (2013). *Ithaka S+R, Jisc, RLUK: UK survey of academics 2012.* Retrieved from http://www.sr.ithaka.org/research-publications/ithaka-sr-jisc-rluk-uk-survey-academics-2012

Scott, C. D., & Jaffe, D. T. (2009) *Managing personal change: Stay positive and stay in control.* (3rd Ed.). Henrietta, NY: Axzo Press.

Seal, R. A. (1986). Academic branch libraries. In W. Simonton (Ed.), *Advances in librarianship, 14*(1), 175–209. Retrieved from http://ecommons.luc.edu/lib_facpubs/8/

Searing, S. E. (2009, August). *The librarian's library in transition from physical to virtual place.* Paper presented at the Libraries as Space and Place satellite meeting of the IFLA World Library and Information Congress, Turin, Italy. Retrieved from http://hdl.handle.net/2142/13765

Searing, S. E., & Greenlee, A. M. (2011). Faculty responses to library service innovations: A case study. *Journal of Education for Library and Information Science, 52*(4), 279–294.

Searing, S. E., & Offenstein, T. L. (2011). *The LIS virtual library: A case study of library support for an iSchool.* Poster presented at the 2011 iConference, Urbana, IL. Abstract retrieved from http://hdl.handle.net/2142/13765

Shkolnik, L. (1991). The continuing debate over academic branch libraries. *College & Research Libraries, 52*, 343–351.

Song, Y-S. (2009). Designing library services based on user needs: New opportunities to reposition the library. *Proceedings of the 75th IFLA General Conference and Assembly.* Retrieved from http://conference.ifla.org/past/ifla75/202-song-en.pdf

SPEC kit 99: Branch libraries in ARL institutions. (1983). Washington, DC: Association of Research Libraries.

Thompson, L. (1942). The historical background of departmental and collegiate libraries. *Library Quarterly, 12*(1), 49–74.

Tracy, D. G., & Searing, S. E. (2014). LIS graduate students as library users: A survey study. *Journal of Academic Librarianship, 40*(3/4), 367–378.

University of Illinois at Urbana-Champaign, University Library. (n.d.-a). *New service models programs.* Retrieved from http://www.library.illinois.edu/nsm/

University of Illinois at Urbana-Champaign, University Library. (n.d.-b). *UIUC user surveys.* Retrieved from http://www.library.illinois.edu/assessment/libsurv.html

University of Illinois at Urbana-Champaign, University Library. (2008a). *Challenge, change, and the service imperative: The university library in the twenty-first century.* Retrieved from http://www.library.illinois.edu/nsm/background/service_imperatives.pdf

University of Illinois at Urbana-Champaign, University Library. (2008b). *Library services for the 21st century at the University of Illinois at Urbana-Champaign: Final report and recommendations of the Budget Group Plus.* Retrieved from http://www.library.illinois.edu/nsm/background/nsmfinal/nmsreport.pdf

Vyhnanek, K., & Zlatos, C. (2011). *SPEC kit 327: Reconfiguring service delivery.* Washington, DC: Association of Research Libraries.

Walter, S. (2011). "Distinctive signifiers of excellence": Library services and the future of the academic library [Guest editorial]. *College & Research Libraries, 72*(1), 6–8. Retrieved from http://crl.acrl.org/content/72/1/6.full.pdf+html

APPENDIX 1A. New Service Model Projects, 2008–2014

Archives Services

The library's archival collections and service points are geographically dispersed on campus. Although there is insufficient space to house all archival materials together in the Main Library, this project, to be completed in January 2015, will create a combined service point on the first floor of the Main Library. It will also provide better space for staff offices and processing and will consolidate the most heavily used collections for easier access. http://www.library.illinois.edu/nsm/archives/

Biology and Life Sciences

In the summer of 2012, the biology librarian retired, the Biology Library closed, and its active collection was transferred to the Funk Library, thereby completing the multiyear transformation of the agriculture library to a library serving all of the life sciences. Less-used materials were transferred to the high-density storage facility and the Main Library stacks. User services are now provided at the Funk Library and through a set of web portals. The new biosciences librarian holds weekly office hours in a dedicated space within the building that formerly housed the Biology Library. http://www.library.illinois.edu/nsm/biology/index.html

Business Information Services

As a result of this NSM project, the Business and Economics Library (located within the Main Library building) closed in 2012. Its print collection was integrated into other library locations, and two of the three subject librarians assumed additional nonbusiness related responsibilities. One is now affiliated with the Social Sciences, Health, and Education Library and the other with the Scholarly Commons. The former head of the Business and Economics Library remains a full-time business information services librarian. As the Business Information Services Team, the three librarians field reference and consultation requests, maintain a website, offer library instruction, and provide embedded services in several academic buildings.

Going beyond the recommendations of the NSM team, the School of Business remodeled and equipped an office in one of its buildings to serve as a location for library services to doctoral students and faculty, led by the full-time business information services librarian. http://www.library.illinois.edu/nsm/business/

Chemistry Information Services

Occasioned by the retirement of the long-time head of the Chemistry Library, this NSM review involved extensive user input and reached the conclusion that the university continues to need both a librarian and library space dedicated to the chemical sciences. The librarian's role was recast as a chemistry and physical sciences librarian with reference responsibilities in the Grainger Engineering Library as well as in the Chemistry Library; the already streamlined collection was lightly weeded; and additional conference rooms were created within the Chemistry Library. The status of the Chemistry Library will be reexamined in 2018. http://www.library.illinois.edu/cms/nsm/chemistry/

City Planning & Landscape Architecture (CPLA)

Completed just as the formal approach to managing NSM projects was being instituted, the integration of the CPLA Library into the Funk Library in May 2008 brought complementary collections together; provided users of the CPLA resources with access to a better physical facility, including group study space and enhanced technology resources; and allowed the library to meet user needs more consistently owing to a more robust staffing model. The CPLA Library was among our least frequently used departmental libraries, in part because it was located in a building that had long since been vacated by the departments it served. http://www.library.illinois.edu/nsm/cpla/

Communications-LIS Services

On-site usage of the Library and Information Science (LIS) Library was steadily declining, in part because of aggressive provision of e-resources spurred by the Graduate School of Library and Information Science's expanding distance education enrollment. This early NSM project evolved from its original intent—to merge the LIS Library with the Communications Library in the latter's space—to a final plan that involved closing the LIS Library in 2009 and creating a service model based on an enhanced digital presence coupled with embedded services at the Graduate School of Library and Information Science. Subsequently, the LIS Librarian was affiliated with the Social Sciences, Health, and Education Library; embedded services continue. http://www.library.uiuc.edu/nsm/comm_lis

Digital Content Lifecycle Management

During 2008, a task force was charged to determine the most effective way to create, organize, manage, deliver, and sustain access to digital content created within the library. The Google Books project, digitization for the Open Content Alliance, and special projects focused on Illinois newspapers, special collections, and audiovisual media had put in place a variety of workflows and management structures. The proposed model recommended a larger investment of resources to support digitization and more coordination centrally. In 2010, another group revisited the NSM recommendations, which had been incompletely implemented. In light of changes in this fast-evolving area of librarianship, the library continues to tweak its approach to managing the digital content lifecycle. http://www.library.illinois.edu/nsm/digcon/

Geology

In the fall of 2009, discussions that were already underway between the library and the School of Earth, Society, and the Environment were formalized as an NSM project. A team was appointed to plan and carry out the relocation of Geology Library collections and services from their longtime home in the Natural History Building to the Grainger Engineering Library. This team's work focused strongly on accessibility of print and electronic journals, monographs, and maps. The implementation took on increased urgency after structural flaws were discovered in the Natural History Building. Materials were relocated on an accelerated schedule and the Geology Library closed permanently in August 2010. http://www.library.illinois.edu/nsm/geology/index.html

Government Information Services

The University of Illinois Library is a depository for Illinois, US, Canadian, and UN documents. This NSM project dismantled the separate Government Documents Library in 2009, integrated its acquisitions and cataloging functions into central technical services units, and integrated its reference functions into the Main Library's reference department. The former head of the Government Documents Library became the coordinator of Government Information Services, Access and Collections, with campus-wide responsibilities to train other public service providers, coordinate collections, and reach out to users. http://www.library.illinois.edu/nsm/govinfo/index.html

Health Information Services

In spring of 2010, an NSM planning team was charged with articulating the expanding, cross-disciplinary need for health information on the Urbana campus and assessing the growing overlap and gaps in health information services across the library's various units. The team recommended alternative scenarios for expanding health information services by building on the strong tradition of service established at the existing Applied Health Sciences Library. Guided by the in-depth information gathered by this planning team, an implementation team created the Social Science, Health, and Education Library (see below). http://www.library.illinois.edu/nsm/health/index.html

Humanities Hub

This NSM project was driven by the expectation that cataloging operations in the Main Library would be relocated, freeing up prime space that could be better used for user-facing services. The team proposed to move the Classics Library (located elsewhere in the building) into the vacated space and thereby create a "humanities neighborhood" on the second floor, where the Literatures and Languages Library and the History, Philosophy, and Newspaper Library are already located. The central Reference Reading Room would have become more humanities-focused as well. However, after the new dean of libraries arrived in Fall 2013, the plan was set aside. At this writing, a different plan is being developed for the space. http://www.library.illinois.edu/nsm/humanities/index.html

Illinois History and Lincoln Collections

This ongoing project examined the management and operation of Illinois History and Lincoln Collections (IHLC) comprising printed and manuscript sources documenting every period and aspect of the history of Illinois and the life and times of Abraham Lincoln. The team proposed a new operational framework, including creating an archivist position, intended to sustain the IHLC; providing more dynamic access to its collections; eliminating a backlog of unprocessed primary sources; and developing relationships that will result in effective outreach and increased funding. http://www.library.illinois.edu/nsm/ihx/

International and Area Studies

One of the most challenging, but ultimately among the most successful, NSM projects resulted in the formation of a new unit, the International and Area Studies (IAS) Library. Opened in Fall 2011, the IAS Library brought together the former Asian, Africana, and Slavic & East European libraries as well as the staff and services supporting Latin American & Caribbean Studies, Global Studies, European Union Studies, and related areas. The IAS Library is the gateway to information and scholarship related to area, international, and global studies, connecting students and scholars to the knowledge crucial to developing global competencies through the study of distinct nations and regions as well as transnational issues and global concerns. This project is discussed more fully in Chapter 2 in this volume. http://www.library.illinois.edu/nsm/intstudies/index.html

Labor & Industrial Relations

One of the earliest NSM projects resulted in the closure of the Labor & Industrial Relations (LIR) Library in September 2007 following discussions with the School of Labor & Employment Relations (SLER) regarding the school's need for space and the declining on-site use of the LIR Library. In collaboration with SLER faculty and administration, the library subject specialist for Labor & Employment Relations designed a new service model that focused on (1) the relocation of the subject specialist to an office within the school as an "embedded librarian;" (2) the development of a comprehensive web portal; and (3) the processing of backlogs of uncataloged materials, including a unique collection of vertical files now under the curatorial control of the University Archives. The LER subject special-ist now maintains an office in the school as well as a presence in the Social Science, Health, and Education Library. (No URL—the project predates the practice of creating a team page.)

Library Organization Working Group

This team was charged to "begin the process of transforming the University Library's decision making, divisional, and overall organizational structure in order to develop more streamlined processes that respect our history of shared governance while enabling the University Library to more nimbly meet the functional requirements necessary to operate effectively in the 21st Century." The team met only once before being disbanded by the uni-versity librarian due to controversies surrounding its inception and scope. http://www.library.illinois.edu/nsm/liborg/index.html

Literatures and Languages

Following recommendations from a highly engaged team of librarians and faculty from campus departments, this project resulted in the Spring 2011 closure of the English Library and the Modern Languages and Linguis-tics Library and the launch of the new Literatures and Languages Library, supporting the study of English and Western European literatures and lan-guages, comparative literature, cinema studies, linguistics, and translation studies. The team considered, but did not move forward with, a broader commingling of humanities disciplines, including classics. http://www.li-brary.illinois.edu/nsm/lit/index.html

Reference Services

This project resulted in the implementation of the following recommen-dations in July 2011. First, the development of a Reference Services Com-mittee charged with coordinating policy, assessment, and planning for ref-erences services across the library. Second, reenvisioning of the physical reference desks inside and outside of the Main Library into three hubs: a central hub consisting of the Main Library, the Undergraduate Library, and the virtual reference desk; a physical sciences hub at Grainger Engi-neering Library; and a life sciences hub at the Funk Library. Third, the creation of a new Reference, Research and Scholarly Services unit (RRSS) bringing together the Scholarly Commons, central reference services, and the Office of Web Technologies and Content Coordination. The latter was subsequently reintegrated into Library IT. http://www.library.illinois.edu/nsm/reference/index.html

Retrospective Reference Collection

One of the first projects completed after the launch of the formal NSM program, the establishment of the Main Stacks Reference Collection helped move other projects forward by creating a separate place within the Main Stacks for less frequently used reference materials with continuing relevance. This collection houses older reference works that continue to have research value and would be difficult to utilize if relegated to off-site shelving, including large sets and indexes not available online. http://www.library.illinois.edu/nsm/retroref/

Scholarly Commons

This project resulted in the creation of a new suite of interrelated services supporting scholarly work, supported both by experts in the library and campus partners with expertise in areas such as survey research. The Scholarly Commons currently provides faculty, researchers, and students with walk-in and appointment-based access to experts and specialized software for digital content creation and analysis; scholarly communication; and geospatial, textual, and numeric data analysis. It also hosts the recently launched research data services program and library-based publishing platforms. http://www.library.illinois.edu/nsm/scholcom/index.html

Social Science, Health, and Education

This project was the result of extensive deliberation and discussion among constituents of the applied health and social sciences, resulting in the merger of the Applied Health Sciences Library and the Education and Social Science Library. The new Social Science, Health, and Education Library opened in Fall 2012 with a service focus on enhancing opportunities for collaboration across these interrelated disciplines. This project is discussed more fully in Chapter 3 in this volume. http://www.library.illinois.edu/nsm/social/

Stacks Service

A series of interrelated projects designed to improve the user experience and the stewardship of collections in the Main Stacks were completed shortly after the launch of the NSM program. These included recommendations on handling currently received print serials, identifying special collections, improving the handling and shelving of folios and minis, and reconfiguring the circulation desk and entrance to the Main Stacks. http://www.library.illinois.edu/nsm/stacks/

Technical Services Coordination & Consolidation

The project resulted in an extensive review and realignment of technical services infrastructure across the library with the goal of improving processes for the cataloging of materials in all formats and languages as well as eliminating all backlogs. Among other changes, cataloging of special items such as music and books in non-Roman languages was transferred from departmental libraries to the central Content Access Management unit. http://www.library.illinois.edu/nsm/techserv/index.html

Veterinary Medicine Library Service and Space

Working in conjunction with faculty and administrators in the College of Veterinary Medicine, this project outlined the services and spaces required to support the college as part of a planned renovation of the building housing the college and the library. After a hiatus due to leadership changes at the college, planning is back on track. The Veterinary Medicine Library will remain open, but its physical footprint will be reduced by half and its print collection has been deeply weeded. http://www.library.illinois.edu/nsm/vetmed/index.html

APPENDIX 1B. Planning for Library New Service Models: Principles for Decision-Making

New service models will enhance user services and provide opportunities for financial benefit, including reallocation of human or capital resources to other strategic priorities.

New service models will facilitate regular communication and collaboration among faculty, students, librarians, library staff, and members of the public.

Responsible stewardship of content in all forms must incorporate a life-cycle approach to all programs and services. This includes thoughtful selection and acquisition, provision of access, preservation, and active curation, particularly in the case of special collections.

New service model outcomes must be both measurable and predictable (to the extent that they accomplish the intended program goals). All programs and services must demonstrate adherence to a schedule of milestones, outcomes, and completion dates, and progress must be measured using rigorous assessment programs.

Recognizing the increasingly interdisciplinary nature of academic inquiry, new service models will focus primarily on the creation of "hubs" that provide coordination and access to human expertise and content across disciplinary clusters, including both print and digital resources from the library system. While physical space may play some role in these changes, digital information resources and new service delivery models will play a primary role in the development of these models.

APPENDIX 1C. Project Recommendations, Cost, and Timeline Template

Recommendation	Specific Recommendations	Start Date	Completion Date	Cost
Briefly summarize recommendation. Use numbers if the report is lengthy or the recommendations numerous.	*Provide specifics, may want to use sub-points.*			*Specify if funds are recurring, a relocation from unit budgets, to be/ already requested from NSM, etc.*
Example Recommendation #8: Pursue additional funding to work with East Asian, Slavic, Indian, and Middle Eastern resources.	**Recommends** the library pursue an excellent hire of an individual who can work with non-Roman character-based languages such as Chinese, Japanese, Korean, Hebrew, Russian or other Slavic languages, Malay, Tamil, or Indo-Aryan languages.	January 2009	N/A	No cost to the library; comes from the provost
	Recommends the library create a budget of graduate/academic hourly funds to pull in individuals from the campus or community to help transliterate and create basic metadata records.	January 2009	May 2010	$20,000/yr. recurring
	Recommends setting up a process with contract cataloging services to send materials (or scans of title pages) when needed.	June 2009	August 2009	$12–40 per title

APPENDIX 1D. Sample Assessment Plan

This assessment plan includes formal and informal data collections and self-reflection.

In addition to the specific areas identified below, feedback should be solicited from all user groups on an ongoing basis, using both formal and informal methods. The results of these assessments will help inform the continuation and/or revision of existing services and the creation of new services.

Desired Outcome	Criteria or Indicator	Assessment or Data Source
XXX library patrons utilize the office hours and workshops, including relevant Savvy Researcher sessions.	Number of patrons participating in office hours. The variety of workshops and patron participation in them increases.	Desk Tracker notes field or new custom field (baseline will start after unit opens). Savvy Research evaluations. Voluntary assessment of service completed via patron form.
XXX librarians collaborate in the provision of reference services in XXX Reference Services Hub.	More reference interactions involving multiple experts, inside and outside the unit.	Desk Tracker statistics from XXX Hub. Follow-up questionnaire or self-reporting by subject specialists.
Subject and IT specialists from within the library and other campus programs provide support for patron consultations.	Number and variety of collaborative consultations for patrons increases.	Follow-up questionnaire or self-reporting by subject specialists. Voluntary assessment of service completed via patron form.
A robust XXX web portal.	Usage of online resources for XXX patrons increases.	Bean Counter, Google Analytics for webpage, and LibGuides statistics.

Desired Outcome	Criteria or Indicator	Assessment or Data Source
Increased library instruction integrated into XXX courses.	More classes taught to larger numbers of students. Greater awareness of XXX resources on the part of students. All undergrads in XXX receive some library instruction or contact from the XXX subject librarian.	Instruction statistics database. Pre- and post-assessments of students.

CHAPTER 2

Shifting Borders:
Changes in the Scholarly Landscape and Integration of Area Studies Libraries to Accomplish New Service Goals in an Academic Library

Steve Witt, Joe Lenkart, and Lynne M. Rudasill

IN 2012, THE University of Illinois at Urbana-Champaign Library formed the International and Area Studies (IAS) Library as a part of the library-wide New Service Model (NSM) program's approach to librarianship (as described by Jacoby & Searing in Chapter 1) that emphasizes a deepened commitment to research services that aim to better coordinate and collaborate on patron-focused services. The NSM shift created, for the first time at Illinois, one library that combined the librarians, services, and collecting responsibilities representing African Studies; East Asian Studies; European Union Studies; Global Studies; Latin American and Caribbean Studies; Middle East and North African Studies; Slavic, East European, and Eurasian Studies; and South Asian Studies. Through the NSM merger, semiautonomous libraries, reading rooms, and units formed a singular IAS Library. One of the principle challenges of the consolidations was to ensure that the close working relationship among area studies faculty and the library could be maintained, if not enhanced, through a new model of service.

As this chapter describes, the creation of the IAS Library was perceived in various ways by librarians, teaching faculty, students, and staff. For some, it was an economical means to integrate important collections and expertise into the library and campus. For others, it represented a sudden erosion of autonomy and retreat from area studies' strengths developed over decades in partnership with US Department of Education Title VI-funded area studies centers and faculty leaders. As the history of area studies librarianship and contemporary views on the new library reveal, these changes form a distinct pattern of evolution through which a focus on acquiring and building vast area studies collections has transitioned toward a greater emphasis on service and access. This transition over the past half-century shows the library instituting, on a continuing basis, new models of practice ranging from the current NSM to holistic librarianship in an effort to bring expertise to patrons and better facilitate research and teaching. Within this period, area studies has undergone consistent consolidation, change, and reformation as both librarianship and area studies have evolved and changed, responding to Cold War and post-Cold War research imperatives, creating increasingly broad networks of operation, and adjusting to changes in technology and practice that make area studies both more ubiquitous and further refined.

Evolution of Area Studies Librarianship at Illinois

Area Studies Collections Emerge

Although the library had been collecting foreign language materials for decades, the Cold War fueled an increasing emphasis and need for knowledge from across the globe. Programs such as PL 480, the Farmington Plan, and Title VI provided both funding and legitimacy to building collections in non-Western languages (Lenkart, Teper, Thacker, & Witt, 2014). By the mid-1960s, the rate of collecting foreign language materials began to impact the library, and in 1965 the Special Languages Department emerged to solve "problems arising from the Library's accelerated activity in the development of non-western language collections" (Miller, 1965). At the time, non-Western languages were a function of technical services and had little to no outward facing service structure. Reports on the special languages focused on cataloging output, purchases, and growing backlogs of uncataloged materials.

As the special language collections continued to grow, so did the need for services and space for users. Initially, the Special Languages Department included Slavic, Africana, and Asian collections and later split apart to form a distinct Slavic Library and a South and West Asian Library. By 1973, the need for enhanced and specialized services and space began to gain leverage within the library and campus administration. Ironically, it is also at this time that funding for area studies collections diminished with the end of the Farmington Plan and decreased federal funding (University of Illinois, 1973). At this time, the Slavic Summer Research Laboratory began to attract scholars from across the nation to use the collection and work with librarians, becoming a "major national resource" that developed into the Slavic Reference Service (University of Illinois, 1976).

The need for space, services, and scholars drove further change within the Special Languages Department. By the late 1970s the creation of an East Asian Library became one of the library's priorities. As the university librarian, Robert Downs, noted in his annual letter to the university president, "the Asian Libraries, in effect two libraries, one for South Asia and one for East Asia, really have no adequate library. Most of their research collections are housed either in storage in the main stacks or in the Law Library basement and many have to be retrieved by messenger, a very poor way of providing library service" (University of Illinois, 1977, p. 1). By 1979, the East Asian Library was open, and the Area and Special Studies Bibliographers Council formed to "promote coordination among area studies" (Gorman to H. Atkinson, October 11, 1979). The council included African, Asian, Latin American, and Slavic plus Afro-American and Women's Studies. The initial charge focused upon the essential need to have public service representation for area studies based upon the fact that the subjects had a well-defined clientele and public service activities that overlapped with departmental libraries (Gorman to H. Atkinson, October 11, 1979). After two years, the council reorganized again to include "all assistant directors in Public Services" in order to increase communications from other administrative bodies in the library (University of Illinois, 1981).

Holistic Librarianship

In early 1984, the university librarian, Hugh Atkinson, instituted a new model for librarianship that aimed to bring the subject expertise of catalogers and acquisitions specialists into public service areas. Known as holistic librarianship, this change sought to break down barriers to service and expertise presented by divides between public and technical services (Ognar, 2003). Instituted as a top-down administrative initiative, holistic librarianship moved technical service librarians and functions into departmental libraries. Within the library, this was a controversial move. In a memo to the university librarian, the director of general services complained bitterly about the changes and the manner by which they were implemented without consultation or notice to librarians and unit administrators (Gorman to H. Atkinson, January 30, 1984).

The move to holistic librarianship impacted the area studies units variously. For some, such as the Slavic Library, the change had little impact since technical and public service staff had been integrated and in collaboration since the beginning of the Special Languages Department. The Africana bibliographer, however, was moved from a technical services unit to Central Reference. Other librarians, who operated in small service oriented units, added technical services to their professional profiles. In both cases, the organizational shifts were viewed as disruptive. As a member of a one-person area studies unit noted in an appeal for space and resources for cataloging, "Now that I am a holistic librarian, I am expected to do original cataloging" (Stafford to D. Montanelli, April 3, 1984).

Although the implementation of holistic librarianship was controversial, the practice continued a trend toward emphasizing services and access to collections that impacted the University Library as it moved toward the new service model of the 21st century.

Role of Faculty and Centers

During this period of rapid area studies development, faculty and area studies centers played an important role in supporting and encouraging the creation of area studies collections. Beginning with a federally funded center focused on Russian studies, faculty leaders from across campus served as outside advocates and partners in developing what would become nationally prominent collections in a short period of time. This close partnership between centers and the library created a symbiotic relationship through which the library's strength helped to secure outside funding to support area studies on campus. The area centers then leveraged grant support to lobby for additional library funding to strengthen and staff the area studies libraries. This relationship is exemplified in a memo from the director of the Latin American and Caribbean Studies Center to the university librarian in 1987:

> As you know, the Latin American Library is one of the main assets of the Center, and its continued growth and expansion are very important to us… We sincerely hope that in the near future further funding for staff and acquisitions will be made available from library sources, and as in the past, the Center will continue to seek support for acquisitions to maintain our efforts to enhance the Latin American Library. (Mayer to H. Atkinson, August 28, 1985)

Twenty years later, this reciprocal relationship between the area studies centers and "their" libraries continued. As a result of this strong relationship, the library needed to consider the perceptions of area studies faculty as much as the evolving research needs of the campus as it attempted to strengthen services and collections.

International and Area Studies New Service Model

On April 21, 2008, the University Library published a final report of the Budget Group Plus, a committee that advised the university librarian on priorities, directions for new service models, and final recommendations on funding. This committee was comprised of senior library administrators and included the university librarian. The series of official documents and directives attached to this final report provided the administrative rationale for the transformative program known as the "New Service Model."

Among the 25 proposals listed in this final report, one focused on area studies services and collections at the University Library, calling for the consolidation of area studies public service programs into a single unit. The rationale behind this proposal, according to the Budget Group Plus, was

> the model of narrowly-defined Library units was economically unsustainable, and the result was a fragmented

program of Library service and support. There were also ongoing concerns about the need for coordinated and long-term approaches to issues related to the acquisition and timely processing of materials meant to support academic programs in the area studies. (University of Illinois, 2008b, p. 21)

Moreover, the University Library administration issued a supplemental statement to this report, *Challenge, Change, and the Service Imperative*, which highlighted the changes taking place within higher education and the environment in which academic libraries functioned:

Whether the measure is the number of degree programs offered, the changes internal to one or more disciplines, or the movement toward increasingly interdisciplinary and multidisciplinary approaches to the scholarly, it is clear that the departmental library service model is not sustainable in its current form. Each discipline cannot have its own physical library, and the handpicked collections housed in physical libraries cannot keep pace with changes to individual disciplines. (University of Illinois, 2008a, p. 3)

These changes in academia, particularly for the area studies, demanded another reexamination of service points, management of collections, and more importantly, how these service points were meeting the needs of diverse (multilingual) interdisciplinary academic communities in a global context. To address these systemic changes in area studies collections and services, the University Library administration initiated the NSM for area studies.

International and Area Studies New Service Model Team

The International and Area Studies New Service Model (IAS NSM) Team consisted of seven library faculty members, two teaching faculty members from the area studies centers, one administrative liaison in the form of the associate university librarian for services, one employee from the civil service staff, and one academic professional. According to the team's final report, *Recommendations: International and Area Studies New Service Model Team Report*, the IAS NSM Team conducted from December 2008–March 2009 "wide-ranging discussions from many perspectives and an intensive series of meetings," which involved affiliated area studies centers, university administrators, teaching faculty, and library staff from the Area Studies Division (University of Illinois, 2009, p. 15). These deliberations produced multiple documents, which focused on reference and technical services, proposed locations and space allocation and, importantly, analyzed library usage. Although these usage analyses of libraries did not collect student preferences, the data collected from the library usage survey, gate counts, and reference statistics allowed the IAS NSM Team to compile a list, titled "New Service Models Assumptions," for area studies collections and services, which included the following:

- Library service points must be consolidated.
- There will be no new resources for staff or collections in the future.
- We must make the best use of library financial and staff resources.
- Library must think broadly about the entire campus and its international needs. (University of Illinois, 2008c)

Because the planning stage involved staff, library space, and entrenched departmental identities, the IAS NSM Team encountered internal and external challenges. One of the team members interviewed for this chapter recalled the difficulty of forging a consensus around the proposed set of assumptions for the IAS-wide NSM. According to this team member, the consensus building process aimed to reassure affiliated area studies faculty that the service portfolio and identity of subject specialists, technical service staff, and collection strengths would continue. Moreover, this team member noted that the team looked at the organization and administration of area studies at 16 other academic libraries. With the contributions of two teaching (non-library) faculty members, the IAS NSM Team concluded in its final report that the unit have a single unit head and each of the affiliated international and area studies programs and centers at the University of Illinois have a designated service liaison (University of Illinois, 2009).

International and Area Studies Implementation Team

To address the next stage in the NSM process, the University Library administration formed the implementation team for the proposed new unit, the IAS Library. According to the *International and Area Studies Implementation Team Final Report*, the team consisted of eight teaching faculty from affiliated centers and departments, six library faculty members, one administrative liaison (associate university librarian for collections), and one staff member from library civil service (University of Illinois, 2010, p. 15). Since the team was tasked with forming a new library, we interviewed the following individuals to gain their insights into the process: the team leader, the administrative liaison, and the NSM coordinator. The three members interviewed reflected on the changes sweeping higher education and library services in North America. At Illinois, they highlighted the differing levels of service associated with each section within area studies.

To deliberate the service structure of the proposed unit, the team leader with the help of the eight teaching faculty, formed three working groups for assessing collections and space, services, and staff. In addition, the team leader was also tasked with forming a consensus with various stakeholders and academic communities. All three interviewees, when reflecting on the needs of area studies centers and teaching faculty, recalled the symbiotic roles of area studies centers and the University Library. In their view, this relationship is an essential component of research and innovation at the University of Illinois.

Impact and Trajectory for Area Studies and the NSM

In August of 2012, the newly formed IAS Library opened, and by December of 2012, a new permanent unit head joined the faculty to continue the NSM implementation. The consolidation of the various area studies libraries into a single entity brought about numerous changes.

One of the most important shifts occurred in the area of personnel. In this consolidation, the number of professional staff increased despite a number of retirements. The consolidation and NSM recommendations included the need for more full-time library faculty members to support areas studies and develop a baseline level of service across regional specialties. This included the end of several multi-institutional partnerships and part-time assignments. The former Asian Library experienced a deconstruction, with the major countries in the region receiving dedicated library faculty (Chinese, Korean, and Japanese studies, although the latter two are not full-time appointments for the areas). The Latin American and Caribbean Studies position moved from part-time interim to full-time tenure track. The contract work that had been occurring between Illinois and Indiana University in Middle Eastern Studies resulted in the development of a full-time Middle East and North African Studies tenure track position while the former African Studies position was rearticulated to better coordinate regional overlap. In addition the South Asian Studies librarian position that had remained unfilled for several years because of a retirement was filled as a full-time position. Finally, the Global Studies librarian, who also oversees the European Union collections and services, became a member of the new library unit. Although this position is fully embedded in the Center for Global Studies, the change resulted in a closer working relationship that emphasizes collaboration within the unit.

Discussions with a wide range of individuals involved in the planning and implementation of the new unit provided an understanding of some shared aspects of the changes that have occurred. In addition to an increase in staff, changes in the areas of communication, services, and collections occurred.

Communication

When interviewed, individuals of the current library and teaching faculty, both inside and outside of the IAS Library, indicated a good deal of satisfaction related to improved communication between area studies specialists, library faculty, and liaison departments on the whole. Prior to consolidation, the various units met formally on a monthly basis as part of the Area Studies Division. The unit now meets twice each month in staff meetings plus one monthly division meeting, allowing for discussions and joint work on both the operational and professional issues. Moreover, under the leadership of the unit head, IAS Library has formed internal workings groups for assessing services and library-wide engagement initiatives. The result is not only more interaction with other librarians in related areas but also shared input and expertise. These meetings have been articulated as particularly helpful by those individuals who are new to the unit (personal communication, June 10, 2014). Attendance is augmented, especially at division meetings, by members of other international and traditional subject-based units in the Main Library. This provides everyone with a broader understanding of the changes in the library and the profession and enables attendees to look beyond any narrow interests they hold in their specific regions. The IAS Library has begun to address the concept of "silos" through collaborative collection development projects that span regions, a digital archiving project that focuses on environmental NGOs around the world, and shared exhibits that focus on trans-regional themes. Despite these initiatives, more substantial work remains to be done between regions and disciplines.

Interviewees also noted the greater proximity to other area studies faculty provides for the easy sharing of information, projects, and interchange of ideas (personal communication, June 10, 2014). All librarians are not in the unit at all times with one position split between libraries and one faculty member embedded in one of the campus's Title VI National Resource Centers, but ample opportunities for casual conversation encourage collegiality and informal information sharing. These conversations have resulted in collaboration on several exhibits and events as well as research projects.

Services

The rapid growth of vernacular and area studies research resources in the form of indexing/full-text databases, microfilm/microfiche/digital collections, and an increase in use of vernacular language materials via interlibrary loan services required a new service realignment. Building on the Slavic Reference Service (SRS) model, the IAS NSM Team envisioned a service that incorporated these emerging resources with innovative research services for students, faculty, and staff. The SRS is an internationally known resource for scholars in the field of Slavic, East European, and Eurasian studies. Prior to the initiation of the NSM processes, other area studies libraries had been approached to work on expanding the services of this sub-unit to other language areas. Although this move was resisted at first, leveraging resources from one of the Title VI centers enabled the expansion of the SRS model to include bibliographic tools to support access to materials in Turkish, Persian, and Arabic. The NSM work provided the basis for the development of a full-time international reference librarian position to support and expand these services into other regions and languages.

One of the surprising results of the original survey that was presented to the Title VI Area Centers was the realization that the teaching faculty really did not know about the services that were available to them, including a variety of instruction resources such as webpages developed specifically for their classes. It is difficult to compare statistics between the current and previous models, but it is clear that instructional services have greatly increased with related area studies courses under the NSM. In addition, a new consolidated website for the IAS Library provides access to information regarding reference, instructional services, and related services within the unit. The site, which was first pulled together based upon the old models of service delivery, is currently being revised employing user-focused development tools that include teaching faculty and students in the process.

In addition to services for local scholars and students, the architects of the IAS Library wanted a reliable platform to support interlibrary loan requests for vernacular language materials and a growing number of visiting scholars. Discussions with library faculty who are not members of the IAS Library revealed some unexpected opinions on what might be considered to be the core of area studies libraries. Interviewees from the classroom faculty expressed a change in attitude regarding the most important aspects of librarianship in this area. The concept of service was articulated as outweighing the depth of collections in respective area studies. Scholars displayed a growing interest in what the librarians can do for them regarding instruction, liaison activities, and support for new digitization projects (personal communication, June 13, 2014). This may, in fact, not be related to area studies but reflective of a more broad-based concept of what the University Library can provide. With the adoption of new digital technologies, scholars engage physical collections much differently than even a few years ago. No longer working primarily within the library, classroom faculty reported being less exposed to the materials in their physically organized form. This is evident in faculty attitudes regarding the consolidation of area studies libraries. A large concern of the consolidation was impact to access that would be posed by the integration of many non-Western language materials into the Main Stacks. For at least one interviewee, this original concern about closing the "Asian Stacks" was just about forgotten with new enthusiasm for accessing the library's increasing digital collections (personal communication, June 13, 2014). These changes are reflections of the way in which electronic delivery of services has changed both area studies and the profession as a whole.

Collections

The divergent positions of the individuals interviewed provide a variety of perceptions related to the collections and how they may change or are changing in the new environment. One individual spent some time talking about "legacy" collections and the importance of maintaining and enriching these (personal communication, June 13, 2014). The University Library has long recognized that it is impossible to collect everything in any given field. As a result, the strategy is to support collections that are important for scholars at Illinois, particularly unique, or those that are assessed as nationally outstanding. The latter is true of the Slavic, East European, and Eurasian collection as well as the Latin American and Caribbean collection, which both compare extremely well against other holdings in the US. There is little doubt that the University Library will continue to provide strong budgetary support for these areas in the future as long as it is financially possible.

One teaching faculty member had originally felt lack of support for collections in his area; after the changes, particularly with the addition of a full-time library faculty member, he now describes IAS Library work as being on the "vanguard of digitization," providing quick access to many important works. Primarily, his visits to the physical collection occur only when he is showing them to his students or a visiting scholar. He added that he regularly introduces scholars to the librarian for his area when they are on such tours (personal communication, June 13, 2014).

Another library faculty interviewee, who is new to the IAS unit, remarked about concerns related to the concept of unique collections and posed questions about what makes an item or a collection unique and how to best leverage scarce funds to continue developing the collection. Working within a wider unit, however, this librarian expressed appreciation for additional resources, strategies, and colleagues to draw upon to develop strong and unique collections (personal communication, June 10, 2014).

The NSM process also provided additional funds to the unit for strategic purchases. These funds, which supplement many of the losses of federal support received through Title VI Centers, have allowed area studies libraries to collaborate in new ways. For example, a centralized budget pool enables smaller collecting areas to develop new strengths as has been the case for a growing South Asian comic book collection. Further, subject specialists are able to use these strategic funds to partner in developing collections focused on groups and populations missed in regional collections. One example is the collaboration between Middle East, Central Asian, and South Asian subject specialists to jointly develop collections focused on stateless minorities.

Currently, the biggest change to collection development for most of the former units is the requirement for purchases to be coordinated with the acquisitions department, a further retreat from the holistic librarianship model of the 1980s. This change to the purchase of materials is difficult for individuals who had traditionally done ordering independent of the main acquisitions unit, but it is having positive impacts on the control of expenditures while providing newer members of the unit with a clear procedure for acquiring new materials. In addition, the approach helps to expose systemic technical service needs to support non-Roman languages that were previously perceived as isolated within small units.

Conclusion

As the NSM program continues to be implemented, it is clear that the changes instituted by the library to bring the area studies units together are historically significant and have already begun to impact the manner by which these collections are developed, organized, and used. The unique aspects of area studies—multidisciplinarity and language focus—had set them apart from other specializations in the library and in the classroom. This in many ways disengaged these units from the broader view of the university and its library. Internationalization initiatives on campus and the engagement of faculty and students in understanding global and transnational phenomena require a more interdisciplinary approach. Universities, policy makers, and individuals everywhere are beginning to recognize that answers to global problems based upon singular approaches will not find success. The NSM for area studies attempts to provide a unifying approach of making library expertise available from various regions to students and faculty across campus. The shared space, collections, and actions of the new IAS Library are just a beginning. As noted by both librarians and faculty, the new unit opens avenues for collaboration while promoting the means to access knowledge critical for research and understanding amidst global patterns in problem solving. These research problems require information from and about the world in both granular and broad form. The opportunities provided through the new unit move the provision of services to the fore. One member of the library faculty who is not part of the unit indicated that with the new, welcoming space; integrated approach; and simplified management, new energy was being brought to the space that will provide new opportunities to attract people with innovative projects and ideas (personal communication, June 18, 2014).

In addition, the NSM implementation demonstrates a new model for affecting organizational change within the University Library. Compared to the ad hoc development of discrete and often opposed area studies units based upon trends in federal funding and outside support from faculty, the NSM places each of the area studies within a unifying organizational context that strives to focus resources and expertise on developing services and new modes of access to collections that have traditionally been difficult to use and access.

Compared to the implementation of holistic librarianship, which was top-down, the NSM program at Illinois exemplifies new models of shared governance through which multiple stake holders from within the library and the academic community work together to articulate a new vision for service across the library and within a new unit. Although not all parties agreed that change was necessary or even a positive step, librarians, faculty, and staff with various stakes in the outcomes participated actively in all aspects of the process.

Overall, the NSM for area studies has succeeded in expanding the relevance of regional and linguistic expertise while nurturing the important symbiotic relationship shared by the area centers and the library. As the NSM progresses and continues to include many stakeholders and perspectives, the library expects to see growth in the use of these specialized services and collections. Further, the area studies centers see potential to foster new cross-campus and interinstitutional partnerships that revolve around this new shared space and concept of area studies. Perhaps the resultant change due to the NSM progress was best articulated by one library faculty member who indicated, "I cannot believe we have done anything but gain from it" (personal communication, June 18, 2014).

References

Gorman, M. (1979, October 11). [Letter to Hugh Atkinson]. University Library Collection (University Librarian's Office, Library Committee File, 1944, 1974, Box 1, Area Studies and Special Bibliographers Council 1979–1983). University of Illinois Archives, Urbana, IL.

Gorman, M. (1984, January 30). [Letter to Hugh Atkinson]. University Library Collection (Technical Services Subject File 35/2/2 Box 10, Principal Cataloguer's Office—General, 1983-91). University of Illinois Archives, Urbana, IL.

Jacoby, J. (2008a). *Network analysis of libraries used by faculty, staff, and APs: Arranged alphabetically.* Retrieved from http://www.library.illinois.edu/nsm/planningdata/NetworkAnalysisAlphabetical.pdf

Jacoby, J. (2008b). *Network analysis of libraries used by faculty, staff, and APs: Arranged by division.* Retrieved from http://www.library.illinois.edu/nsm/planningdata/NetworkAnalysisByDivision.pdf

Lenkart, J., Teper, T. H., Thacker, M., & Witt, S. W. (in press). Measuring and sustaining the impact of less commonly taught language collections in a research library. *College & Research Libraries.*

Mayer, E. (1985, August 28). [Letter to Hugh Atkinson]. University Library Collection (Technical Services 35/2/2 Box 10, Latin American, 1982-1990). University of Illinois Archives, Urbana, IL.

Miller, L. (1965). *Annual report of the Special Languages Department for the year ending June 30, 1965.* University Library Collection (Technical Services 35/2/2 Box 5, Special Languages Department). University of Illinois Archives, Urbana, IL.

Ognar, S. (2003). Holistic librarianship. *The Serials Librarian, 43*(4), 37–50.

Stafford, B. (1984, April 3). [Letter to Dale Montanelli]. University Library Collection (Technical Services 35/2/2 Box 8, Asian Library 1986–89 Folder). University of Illinois Archives, Urbana, IL.

University of Illinois at Urbana-Champaign, University Library. (1973). *Annual report.* University Library Collection, University of Illinois Archives, Urbana, IL. Retrieved from http://archives.library.illinois.edu/erec/University%20Archives/3501801/ReportsToPresident/1973.pdf

University of Illinois at Urbana-Champaign, University Library. (1976). *Annual report.* University Library Collection. University of Illinois Archives, Urbana, IL. Retrieved from http://archives.library.illinois.edu/erec/University%20Archives/3501801/ReportsToPresident/1976.pdf

University of Illinois at Urbana-Champaign, University Library. (1977). *Annual report.* University Library Collection. University of Illinois Archives,

Urbana, IL. Retrieved from http://archives.library.illinois.edu/erec/University%20Archives/3501801/ReportsToPresident/1977.pdf

University of Illinois Library, Area Studies and Special Bibliographers Council. (1981). [Memo]. University Library Collection (University Librarian's Office, Library Committee File, 1944, 1974–, Box 1, Area Studies and Special Bibliographers Council 1979–1983). University of Illinois Archives, Urbana, IL.

University of Illinois at Urbana-Champaign, University Library. (2008a). *Challenge, change, and the service imperative: The University Library in the twenty-first century*. Retrieved from http://www.library.illinois.edu/nsm/background/service_imperatives.pdf

University of Illinois at Urbana-Champaign, University Library. (2008b). *Library services for the 21st century at the University of Illinois at Urbana-Champaign: Final report and recommendations of the Budget Group Plus*. Retrieved from http://www.library.illinois.edu/nsm/background/nsmfinal/nmsreport.pdf

University of Illinois at Urbana-Champaign, University Library. (2008c). International and Area Studies Team: New service models assumptions. Retrieved from http://www.library.illinois.edu/nsm/intstudies/planningteam/assumptions.html

University of Illinois at Urbana-Champaign, University Library. (2009). *Recommendations: International and Area Studies New Service Model Team*. Retrieved from http://www.library.illinois.edu/nsm/intstudies/planningteam/IntStudiesReport03132009.pdf

University of Illinois at Urbana-Champaign, University Library. (2010). *Library International and Area Studies Implementation Team final report*. Retrieved from http://www.library.illinois.edu/nsm/intstudies/IAS_Final_Report_3.30.10.pdf

CHAPTER 3

Merging the Social and Health Sciences Step by Step

Nancy P. O'Brien, Mary Beth Allen, Peg Burnette, Cindy Ingold, Kelly A. McCusker, and Beth Sheehan

THE NEW SERVICE Model (NSM) program that began at the University of Illinois at Urbana-Champaign Library in 2007 included a proposal to merge the Applied Health Sciences (AHS) Library, the Education and Social Science Library (ESSL), and other dispersed social science library services. The successful implementation of this merger into the Social Sciences, Health, and Education Library (SSHEL) took three full years to plan, organize, and implement. Along the way, a number of additional subject areas were folded into the proposal and lessons were learned about the importance of effective ways to include all the stakeholders in the process. This chapter focuses on the steps taken to achieve this merger, particularly the aspects of the merger that we were closely involved with. These include the steps leading up to implementation, including personnel and facilities issues, the extensive training required for a successful service program both during and after the implementation as well as public service challenges, the nuances of preparing collections for merging, and the importance of creating a robust web presence. Finally, celebrating the successful merger proved to be a powerful way to unite stakeholders and bring closure to the process.

In keeping with the NSM program (as described by Jacoby & Searing in Chapter 1), a planning team was appointed to discuss user needs, best practices, and desired outcomes. The team included faculty from affiliated teaching programs and library personnel. Wide-ranging discussions focused on the varying needs of students from different disciplines, the importance of creating a welcoming space for a diverse group of users, and making the newly consolidated library a "third home" for users after residences and classrooms. Of major concern to all stakeholders was creating a name for the new library that would reflect the more than a dozen disciplines included. The name needed to indicate the breadth of the disciplines, from anthropology to speech and hearing science, as well as the fact that this was an entirely new service point. Incorporating aspects of the former libraries' names was deemed acceptable as long as the name was comprehensive. After extended discussion, a name that included health, social sciences, and education was agreed upon. Social sciences and health encompass a number of different disciplines in the new library, and education was retained because that library had been in existence since 1901 and was well known. An acronym that was memorable was desirable, so SSHEL (pronounced "shell") became both the abbreviated title of the new library as well as an option for the adoption of a seashell graphic image for marketing and promotion.

After much discussion, the planning team prepared a final report that addressed personnel needs, space needs, and service goals (University of Illinois, 2011). Once the work of the planning team was completed, the library's Faculty Executive Committee appointed a SSHEL Implementation Team comprised solely of library personnel to address issues related to realizing the vision for this newly consolidated library. The implementation team kept the project on track, making intermediate adjustments as needed, such as the incorporation of geography material, into the consolidation planning. Once the implementation team's final report (University of Illinois, 2012) was accepted by library administration, the newly appointed head of the merged library began weekly meetings with facilities personnel as well as regular meetings with faculty (librarians) and staff (clerical and paraprofessional) who would be relocating to SSHEL. These meetings covered topics such as furniture and equipment placement for public and staff spaces, artwork for the new space (still to be decided), and arrangement of collections. The new library space would have two wings, SSHEL North

(Figure 3.1) and SSHEL South (Figure 3.2), separated by a large gallery on the first floor of the Main Library building. SSHEL South was renovated first and then SSHEL North. This necessitated multiple relocations of services and collections.

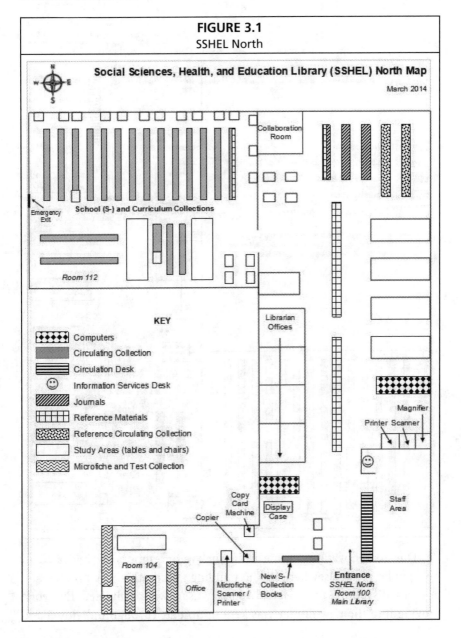

FIGURE 3.1
SSHEL North

FIGURE 3.2
SSHEL South

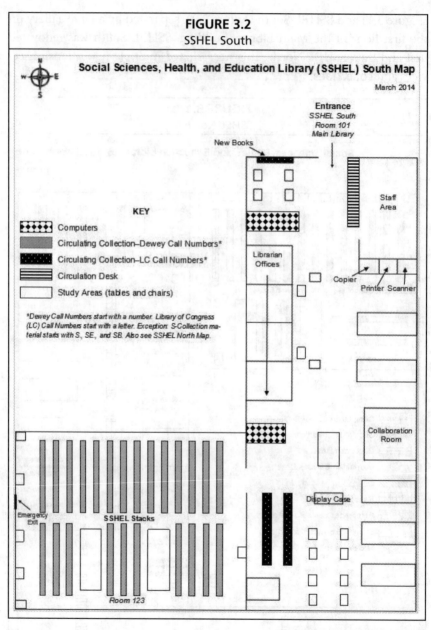

Due to renovations, some personnel were temporarily relocated to non-public areas elsewhere in the building. While this was problematic at times, disruption to services for library users was minimized. Everyone moving into the new library was kept up to date through individual and group meetings as well as email, and suggestions were highly encouraged, which fostered team building and commitment to the new library. The new library benefited from the inclusion of personnel not only from the merging libraries but also from other libraries that were closed as part of the NSM program. Staff assigned to the newly merged library brought with them significant experience and expertise that resulted in recommendations for new procedures, fewer redundancies, and service enhancements. One of the critical aspects of the merger's success was the ownership that all levels of library personnel in SSHEL took in the process of creating a welcoming, pleasant space, filled with relevant resources, subject specialists, and expert staff, and everyone's willingness to consider new approaches and embrace change.

Merging Public Services: Planning, Training, and Adjusting

The SSHEL Public Services Working Group, a sub-group of the SSHEL Implementation Team, developed a list of anticipated public services and respective roles and responsibilities for each level of personnel, including both patron-facing services, such as circulation, point-of-need reference, library instruction, and web presence, as well as other library operations processes such as office management, training, course reserves, special collections, acquisitions, and serials maintenance. As part of its report, the group was also charged with recommending locations and functions of public service points (i.e., circulation, reference-information desks) within the new library and determining the necessary staffing and training requirements. Members of the implementation team assigned to this group included the librarian who managed reference services in ESSL, a staff member who provided reference services and circulation support in the AHS Library, and two other librarians who managed reference services in other library units on campus.

The Public Services Working Group anticipated the need for extensive cross-training to ensure all public service personnel were familiar with subject areas and resources that would be new to them and with new procedures and processes. Discussions regarding SSHEL public service points and staffing decisions revealed that the merging library units had different procedures in place for reference services and differing expectations for the public service roles of librarians, staff, graduate assistants, and undergraduate student assistants. To address the disparities, the group developed a unified public service model with clear expectations and procedures for each level of personnel. This model was used to identify training needs for each SSHEL employee, develop new (or adapt existing) training practices, and coordinate the delivery of this training.

Training decisions related to SSHEL patron-facing circulation and reference services were complicated due to the differing preexisting practices in the merging units. In ESSL, the reference desk was staffed by subject specialist librarians and graduate assistants (GAs) from the Graduate School of Library and Information Science. The circulation desk was staffed by undergraduate student assistants who were trained to refer all questions related to library services or research to the reference desk. Library staff in this unit primarily performed technical services functions and supervised and supported circulation services as needed. In the AHS Library, the primary public service point was the circulation-information desk. Undergraduate student assistants and staff answered library policy and service questions and some basic research questions, referring more complex research questions to the subject specialist librarian for research consultations either immediately or by appointment. In addition to ESSL and AHS personnel, several additional employees would join SSHEL from other library units, each with differing levels of service experience provided at point of need.

While these models had worked well for each individual unit in the past, the merged library would require a completely new configuration of service points and staffing to accommodate the considerable expansion in the number of patrons served, size and scope of the collections, and physical space. The team considered the prior models of service, examined recent reference statistics from the merging units, and tried to predict the pattern of patron use and expected services in SSHEL. Ultimately, they determined that SSHEL would maintain two circulation desks (one on each side of SSHEL) staffed by undergraduate student assistants and an information desk in SSHEL North staffed by librarians, graduate assistants, and staff who volunteered for public service work. The librarian (hereafter referred to as "training coordinator") who had previously been coordinating ESSL reference services was identified as the most appropriate person to take the lead in organizing SSHEL reference services and implementing training.

To define the expected roles and knowledge required for each category of SSHEL public service personnel who would directly interact with patrons, the training coordinator decided to adapt the Reference Effort Assessment Data (READ) scale (Gerlich & Berard, 2007), using it to describe and illustrate each tier of service. Several library units at Illinois (including ESSL) had recently implemented use of the READ scale, and reference desk personnel were already familiar with these definitions. Since the scale provided predefined categories and levels, it provided a convenient way to map patron information needs to the level of knowledge and skill required and map the level of knowledge and skill required for each category of public service employees. (Appendix 3A contains a quick reference chart used to illustrate the READ scale levels and example question types assigned to each public service personnel level in SSHEL.) Public service personnel in each tier required training to ensure that they were prepared to answer all levels of questions assigned to their classification, with the understanding that if they encountered a patron needing assistance beyond their expected tier of service, they would refer the patron to an available employee from a higher tier. The overall goal was to ensure that no matter which service point the patron approached in SSHEL, at minimum, he or she would get answers to the most common basic questions and that the SSHEL reference desk would be staffed by individuals who could assist with more complex questions.

To reach this goal, it was necessary to determine exactly which skills, knowledge, policies, and procedures would be needed and to compare these requirements to the preexisting skills and knowledge of each individual to determine gaps and training needs. The training coordinator created a master list of all subjects and special collections in SSHEL and all procedures and policy topics that would require training. These subjects and training topics were derived from existing subject and procedural training schedules used in ESSL when training new GAs, with the addition of all other merging subjects and any new policies and procedures that were being developed or altered due to the logistics of the new unit. The training coordinator used the master training list to identify topics, services, and resources that each level of personnel would need to know, compared this to each individual's existing knowledge, and distributed personalized schedules of required training sessions.

The first round of training was implemented in the summer of 2012 for librarians, staff (both public service and technical), and GAs. SSHEL subject specialist librarians led the sessions introducing important resources in their subject areas of expertise, and staff and librarians in charge of developing or implementing specific policies and procedures led sessions on those topics. Session leaders took attendance and were responsible for following up with absentees to schedule makeup sessions. With the use of this system, all librarians, staff, and GAs received the training necessary to serve the new patrons of SSHEL.

Training for undergraduate student assistants occurred early in the fall of 2012. Some student assistants had previously worked in either the ESSL or AHS libraries and brought varying levels of knowledge and experience, while others were new hires with limited knowledge of library information services or circulation desk procedures. To ensure that all student assistants, regardless of their prior experience, were trained consistently and understood their new role in contributing to information services in SSHEL, the training coordinator developed a new training program. The program specifically addressed customer service standards and expectations, introduced tips and tools for locating library policies and services, and demonstrated the use of the library catalog to search for and locate known items. The training also provided an overview of the tiered service model, ensuring that even though student assistants did not receive extensive READ scale training, they would understand the types of questions they should be answering and be able to recognize when and to whom a patron question should be referred. Every SSHEL student assistant was required to attend this 90-minute training session at the start of the Fall 2012 semester in addition to the circulation services training delivered by the office manager and circulation supervisor. This training was repeated in subsequent semesters for all newly hired student assistants. This resulted in a consistent standard and level of patron service at the circulation desk and tiered service and management of patron needs in cooperation with the reference desk. The training coordinator also implemented a new documentation procedure to ensure that data on patron reference questions answered at the circulation desk would be recorded and added to the reference statistics recorded by the reference desk personnel. This provides a more accurate record of patron services provided by all levels of public service personnel in SSHEL, which will be crucial to the future assessment of SSHEL's public services.

There were several challenges that affected the coordination and implementation of public services and training during and after the merger.

Although SSHEL was officially "open" as a merged unit as of the Fall 2012 semester, it took nearly one additional year for SSHEL's spaces to be fully renovated and functional, with all public service points installed and operational and all collections in their final locations. Thus, some procedures and policies were not completely established at the time of training. New training was integrated into existing SSHEL librarian, staff, and GA meetings or scheduled separately throughout the year whenever new policies were implemented. It was also not possible to anticipate and assess patron usage patterns and reference services needs until all areas of SSHEL were open. For example, it became apparent that more evening supervision was needed in SSHEL South, the side without the reference desk, to support circulation desk student assistants, monitor their activities, answer higher level patron reference questions, and aid in closing SSHEL South at night. An additional graduate hourly evening position was added in 2013 to provide this support and supervision.

At the time of this publication, SSHEL has been open just long enough to begin analyzing patron reference statistics to determine whether the existing public service and staffing model is efficiently and adequately meeting the needs of patrons. Throughout the implementation process, it became clear that any new service model is by definition experimental and must be flexible enough to allow for adjustment to meet evolving needs or adapt to unexpected outcomes. Evaluation of public service is just one of many facets of assessment that will be expected from SSHEL in the next few years.

Preparing Collections for a Merger

Prior to merging collections into an integrated, multidisciplinary service unit, a number of critical questions were discussed. First, how much space (both square feet and linear feet of shelving) would be available for collections in the newly merged library? How many volumes could and should be housed in the new unit? What criteria would be used to retain print material? How much space would be needed for future growth? Comparing the available new space with the existing collection spaces helped to visualize an initial plan. The SSHEL merger occurred with several goals, one of which was to create newly refurbished spaces for user-centered activities. Because of this, the space that had previously been allocated for collections required significant reduction. The need to reduce collection space, coupled with the consolidation of several large collections, necessitated the development of clear criteria for weeding and retention of print collections and for the acquisition of additional electronic content. What followed was the development of a logical, cooperative plan involving collection maintenance staff and others to weed the collection and move items to storage, update holdings, move retained items to newly integrated spaces, and communicate with the library's users about where materials were located in the new configuration.

Other NSM projects radically downsized or eliminated circulating collections within subject-specific library units; therefore, library administration encouraged the SSHEL Implementation Team to consider following that model. Furthermore, with the Main Stacks nearby and speedy delivery services from other campus libraries, users increasingly chose to request delivery of materials through the catalog rather than browse the shelves in person. Although the newly merged library would contain a vast amount of space (19,838.65 square feet), the intent of the merger was to leave the majority of space for user-centered activities and restrict collections to a clearly defined amount of space. The team eventually adjusted its selection criteria to reduce overall collections in SSHEL by an additional 25%, from the original estimate of 121,470 volumes to just 91,100 volumes, with the future goal of continuing to reduce physical holdings during the first five years of SSHEL's operation.

After a lengthy and complex process of examining the total number of volumes, their sizes, and the linear shelf space used in each source collection and comparing that to the desired use of space in the new unit, the decision was made to retain only the last five years of circulating or published material in the general SSHEL collection. Initially, this meant inclusion of items with either a publication date of 2007 or later or evidence of circulation from 2007 or later. The amount of shelf space in SSHEL was limited to accommodate only a small amount of growth, necessitating a continual process of transferring older and lesser-used material with ongoing evaluation of collection use. The reason for this was to maintain SSHEL's collection size at the same level into the future and not fill the space with collections. In addition, selectors are encouraged to purchase more electronic versions of books and e-book collections, and the University Library is purchasing additional e-book packages as part of centralized efforts, so the need for physical shelf space should diminish somewhat in the future.

The issue of providing enough space for each of the disciplines represented in the proposed library was debated at length. Some stakeholders expressed interest in carving out shelving areas for specific disciplines, essentially creating alcoves that would hold books on a single topic. Over time, it was agreed that the collections should be interfiled, thereby creating connections between subject-focused materials that might otherwise have been overlooked. Setting aside sufficient space for some special collections, such as the School Collection (children's and young adult literature) and the Curriculum Collection (K–12 teaching material), became contentious due to misconceptions about the importance of the material for research and scholarship. Usage data confirmed that this material was indeed high-use and supported core programs in teacher education and library and information science. Ultimately, the decision was made to retain the last 10 years of published or circulated material from the School and Curriculum Collections within SSHEL. All SSHEL personnel participated in reviewing collections for retention or transfer elsewhere as well as physically moving items in coordination with Collection Management Services, the unit responsible for large scale transfers of material within the library.

Of the 91,100 volumes identified for the new unit, approximately 62,000 were moved from the general collections, while approximately 29,000 were moved from the School and Curriculum Collections. In general, older material or material that circulated less frequently was transferred to either the Main Stacks (in the same building as SSHEL) or to the off-site, high-density storage facility, from which requests are retrieved and delivered daily.

To enable the University Library's gradual transition to the Library of Congress (LC) classification system, a plan was coordinated with cataloging staff to begin exclusive use of LC classification in January 2013. A separate section of shelving was identified for housing LC classified material for both the general collection and the reference collection, while existing Dewey Decimal materials would remain as a distinct collection. Thus, the unit is currently supporting dual-classification systems, which has presented some confusion for both SSHEL personnel and users. However, it is anticipated that over time, as materials are weeded due to age or low circulation, the remaining SSHEL collection will be primarily classified in LC, negating the need to reclassify the entire collection. The School and Curriculum Collections, which are housed in a separate area, will continue to be cataloged in Dewey as they are in school and public libraries.

In general, current (unbound) print periodicals and five years of bound journal volumes were retained in the integrated collection. However, concurrent with weeding the low-use books from the collection, drastic reductions were made in the number of print journals. Every selector undertook a process of flipping subscriptions to electronic-only whenever possible. When titles were flipped, the print archive was moved to storage. The library provided modest funding over several years to purchase journal back file packages to support this effort. As a result, very few print journals remain in the new unit.

Because several library mergers had already occurred at Illinois, there was clear precedent for the technical services work involved with weeding and updating the holdings in the catalog, and a dedicated staff team was used expressly for this purpose. Staff were able to generate lists of all items that had not circulated or were published earlier than the target date in the various units, then retrieve those items for transfer to Main Stacks or storage. Holdings records were updated and items that remained were eventually moved and integrated together in the new space.

New signage for the integrated unit indicated locations for all discrete parts of the collection: Dewey and LC circulating collections, Dewey and LC non-circulating reference collections, periodicals, School and Curriculum Collections, media, microforms, and tests. However, staff still spend a fair amount of time directing users to the many and varied parts of the collections, some of which are not visible from the entrances.

There had been significant variation in the source collections' loan periods and circulation patterns, so as much as possible, procedures in SSHEL were adapted to accommodate the varying loan periods and circulation restrictions to allow for maximum use of the collection in a relatively consistent manner. Ultimately, even with all the special situations and exceptions, the result is an integrated collection that effectively serves the needs of a very large, interdisciplinary user group.

Website Development

A major concern with the planning for SSHEL was creating a website that reflected a cohesive new library but also addressed the diverse needs of SSHEL patrons. Each of the former libraries had unique, separate websites (Figure 3.3 and Figure 3.4), which were customized to serve the research needs of faculty, staff, and students in their affiliated departments. Although the consolidation and renovations of the merged library unit would not be fully complete until 2013, the website needed to be ready by fall of 2012, when the former libraries officially closed and SSHEL was open for service.

Another consideration in creating the website was that it would be the default homepage on the public computer terminals in the branch, and patrons from all areas of the university and community would be navigating through it while in SSHEL. Additionally, SSHEL librarians and staff use the SSHEL website to demonstrate access to library resources during instruction sessions and research consultations. Therefore, it was important that the website could accommodate many different needs.

FIGURE 3.3
Former ESSL Website

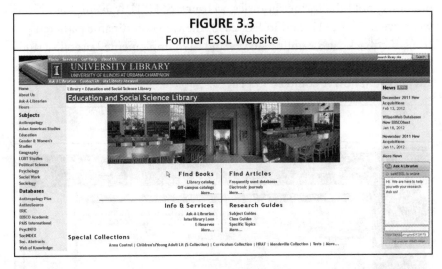

FIGURE 3.4
Former AHS Library Website

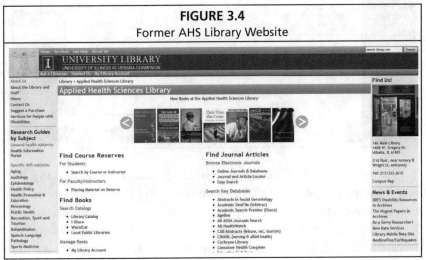

A review of the literature revealed many articles about usability studies and website design but no major literature about redesigning a website when libraries merge. The web coordinator used tried and true methods for website redesign, such as surveys and usability studies, but also studied other University Library websites as well as those of peer institutions to compare different methods of presenting similar information. These comparisons provided a strong base for the design of the new website. Additionally, SSHEL patrons were informally surveyed in 2012 to determine the type of material they would like to see on the new website and gather their opinions about the former libraries' websites. SSHEL's website (Figure 3.5) went live in Fall 2012, and in Fall 2013, the web coordinator gathered patrons' feedback via an online survey and then implemented usability studies the following spring to determine if the website's content and layout was effective and how it could be improved.

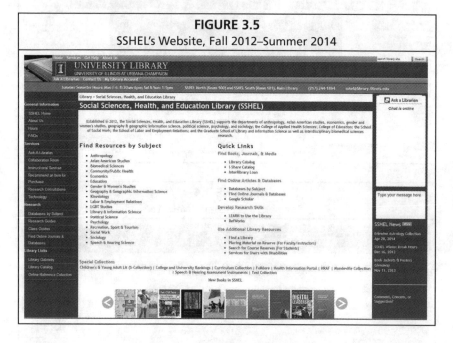

FIGURE 3.5
SSHEL's Website, Fall 2012–Summer 2014

Incorporating feedback from SSHEL graduate assistants, the web coordinator created the Fall 2013 survey using the University of Illinois Webtools software, which seamlessly creates anonymous results. In September 2013, the web coordinator invited all members of the departments the library serves, including faculty, students, and staff both on and off campus to participate in the survey. A link was added to the SSHEL homepage and fliers were placed around the public computer terminals and on tables within SSHEL encouraging users to participate in the survey. The web coordinator also invited student workers in SS-HEL, who may not necessarily be affiliated with a department SSHEL serves, to participate in the survey. Respondents were asked to rate the overall quality of the website; indicate the types of resources they were typically seeking; and add their compliments, complaints, wishes, and frustrations regarding the website. In addition, the survey collected demographic information, such as department affiliation and university status.

Twenty-six people completed the online survey. Though survey participation was low, the results and comments indicated that overall, the webpage was useful, but there were areas that needed improvement. Of those 26 (14 of whom were graduate students), 13 indicated they used the SSHEL website at least six times a week, and 88% of the respondents said the website was of high or very high quality (Figure 3.6). Ninety-six percent of respondents indicated they were usually or always able to find the services, databases, and resources they were looking for.

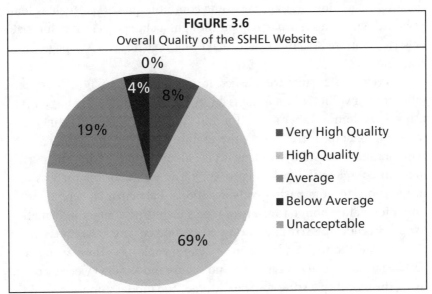

FIGURE 3.6
Overall Quality of the SSHEL Website

Sixty-two percent of the participants indicated the main reason for going to the SSHEL website was to access online databases, while 54% indicated they wanted to access online journals. Respondents also chose library catalog, library hours, and research guide or tutorial about a specific topic. Class guides, library news and events, and library policies were not chosen by any respondents.

Interestingly, multiple participants commented that the homepage was too cluttered or busy; however, there were also multiple comments that the homepage was useful because of the number of options available. Participants particularly liked the links to subject resources and found these subject pages provided many options about one subject, made it easier to find information, and were very thorough. Other compliments included "easy to navigate," "easy to understand," "headings and subheadings clearly organized," and "left-hand navigation made it easy to navigate the website." Complaints revolved around the amount of text and lack of pictures, which, according to one respondent, made "the pages seem boring and hard to read." One suggested addition, which the web coordinator had been considering for a while, was a search box on the homepage. Though the survey was only intended to test the usability of the homepage, respondents commented about other SSHEL pages as well, particularly the FAQs page. One commented that the FAQ page "does not answer some common questions, such as loan periods," while another participant thought a change in font color, size, or style or more spacing would make the text-heavy FAQ page more readable.

Survey participants were asked to include their email if they were interested in volunteering for a usability study. Volunteers were selected using a random number generator and received a $20 gift certificate to the campus bookstore. During the usability study, a moderator (a SSHEL graduate assistant) read each task aloud before asking the participant to complete the task (Figure 3.7). The web coordinator was also in the room to note participants' reactions. Participants were asked to find information about a variety of topics including contact information for a librarian in SSHEL; printing costs; books, journals, and articles about a specific topic; and business school rankings. The participants' verbalizations, facial expressions, and mouse movements were recorded using the usability testing software Morae. The moderator also asked the participants what helped them navigate the website the most and what needed improvement.

FIGURE 3.7 SSHEL's Website Usability Study Tasks				
Assessment: Rubric				
Completed? Task	Successful	Minimal Amount of Struggle	Struggled	Unsuccessful
1. Contact				
2. Printing				
3. Books				
4. Journal				
5. Database				
6. Guide				
7. Special Collection				
8. Helpful				
9. Improvement				

At the time of writing, the web coordinator had recruited two survey participants, both graduate students, for usability studies. Both participants easily found the contact information for the anthropology librarian by clicking on the About Us link. One participant found the printing cost, but the other struggled and in the end, explained she would most likely search the website to find the information. Both participants used the library catalog to find two books on sport psychology, one via the sports subject guide. For the subsequent questions about particular subject resources—finding a geography journal, social work databases, and education statistics—both participants used the subject guides. Additionally, when asked what helped the participants navigate the website the most, both answered the subject links. Both participants struggled with determining if the library had a subscription to the *Journal of Economic Geography*—one went to the geography page while the other went to the economics page. They both were eventually able to complete the task but became frustrated during the process.

The participants were unsuccessful at using special collections to find a ranking of business schools and did not use topical research guides to find a source of education statistics. Instead, both participants went to the education subject guide when asked to find education statistics even though SSHEL has a full guide on statistical sources. One participant became frustrated and said she would probably use Google. As for suggestions for improvement, in both the survey and usability studies, participants commented that the Ask-a-Librarian page, which includes information for contacting SSHEL via email, IM/chat, phone, or in person, should include actual librarian contact information. One participant admitted that she ignored or did not notice the left-hand navigation to begin with but will use it in the future.

Due to the web coordinator's impending departure from Illinois, additional usability studies were not completed. However, during the summer of 2014, the web coordinator updated the content and layout of the SSHEL homepage (Figure 3.8). She took into account comments from both the survey and usability studies. Some of the complaints and wishes were fixed quickly—for example, a map of the School Collection was easily uploaded to the website. Other issues, such as the SSHEL website not matching the layout of the University Library's homepage, could not be fixed as the University Library's homepage will be redone in the coming year.

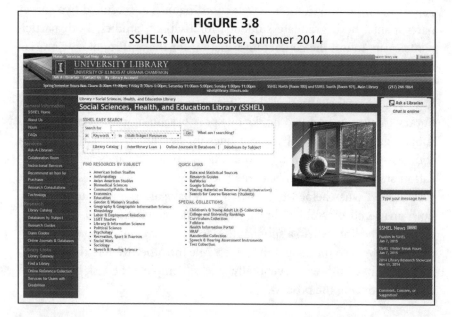

FIGURE 3.8
SSHEL's New Website, Summer 2014

As access to online databases or journals was the biggest reason for using the library website, making the task of easily finding a database, journal, or article was the top priority. Therefore, a search box, which simultaneously searches multiple databases as well as the library catalog, allowing users to search for information about a specific subject was added to the homepage. Additional suggestions that were incorporated include enlarging and emphasizing headers at the tops of pages, adding librarian contact information to the Ask-a-Librarian page, emphasizing important library links such as the library catalog, and adding more images—including an image representing SSHEL on the homepage. A final idea, to be added in the future, is to have a rotating set of images promoting specific areas of SSHEL such as special collections, including the School Collection, or specific services or resources, including collaboration rooms, public computers, and quiet study spaces.

Planning the Celebration Process

The creation of SSHEL represented major physical renovations and reorganizations that included the incorporation of new disciplines and the addition of subject specialists. During this time, as collections and services seemed to be continually on the move, library users endured countless changes and disruptions. Thus, when SSHEL was finally complete, an open house event was planned to celebrate the completion of the project and orient users to the new spaces and services. Planning an event to mark the successful completion of a merger project can serve as a clear line of demarcation from the "old" environment to the new. Beyond signifying a new beginning, the celebratory event for SSHEL provided an opportunity for newly merged staff and faculty to collaboratively interact. The event also provided the impetus for users to acquaint (or reacquaint) themselves to the new spaces and was an effective marketing tool for library services and resources.

Planning began approximately eight months before the renovations were completed with the naming of a planning committee of two librarians and two staff members who collectively represented all merged units. This mix of faculty and staff helped to foster a sense of shared ownership and camaraderie throughout the process and beyond. A brainstorming session during the first planning meeting helped to inform key decisions such as the type of event to be held, the level of formality, and possible themes. Subsequent meetings focused on decisions regarding the budget, an appropriate venue, food and catering options, décor and signage, program considerations, and publicity. A preliminary guest list was developed and included patrons/users, potential new users, library personnel, facilities personnel, information technology personnel, and other campus partners. Key individuals or administrative personnel who supported or were involved in the project received personalized invitations as did former employees and people from units served by SSHEL with whom there was an established relationship. Publicity included university listservs and electronic display boards scattered throughout the Main Library building. In addition, a brief announcement was prepared and distributed to SSHEL subject librarians to forward to academic departments and units.

While there was no formal program, the celebratory open house included brief remarks from the head of SSHEL and the dean of libraries. SSHEL space renovations were well documented through photography throughout the months of renovation. These images were compiled with facts and historical context into a PowerPoint slideshow that was looped continuously on two TV monitors, one in SSHEL North and one in SSHEL South. The slideshow was an effective way to engage visitors and guests while providing them with important or interesting information; it also will serve as a permanent record of the project. Two posters displayed on easels in each wing highlighted the respective collections, disciplines, and subject specialists in each SSHEL location. After the event, these posters became permanent directory signage. Using a predefined script, librarians and graduate assistants provided tours on the quarter hour. This was another effective way of orienting users to the new space, particularly when so many parts of the collection had been relocated.

Hosting a celebratory event after the closure and reconfiguration of library spaces can be an important opportunity to create camaraderie among library personnel and effectively market and promote new spaces and services to library users. The experience of planning a celebratory event was a useful capstone for the merging of library spaces, collections, and personnel. Many personnel from the University Library and the departments that SSHEL serves attended the event and patrons who were wandering through the Main Library building stopped to ask questions and learn about the new space. Given all of the positive and congratulatory comments and feedback, the SSHEL open house was a resounding success and, based on hourly room counts, was a precursor to the subsequent ongoing enthusiastic use of SSHEL.

Conclusion

In the merger of libraries, important aspects to consider are collections, services, facilities, and people. By including library faculty, staff, and students in the process, a commitment to the new library was created. Equitable distribution of tasks and participation in decision making was emphasized by the head of SSHEL in order to encourage library faculty and staff to take ownership of the new library. This focus on the human resources within SSHEL fostered a relatively smooth transition in all areas. Similarly, the inclusion of faculty from the allied teaching departments during the planning stages aided in the acceptance of the closure of branch libraries and their consolidation into a new merged library.

Lessons learned during the transition to SSHEL include the constant need to modify procedures and policies, the ongoing importance of soliciting user and library personnel feedback, and assessing what works. Flexibility in being able to revise decisions and adjust for the unexpected while keeping patron needs as a priority are essential components of a successful new service model. The ongoing success of SSHEL is due to the strong commitment to patron service in a welcoming environment on-site and through a robust web presence, all made possible with support from a well-trained team of librarians, staff, and students. This success has been confirmed by annual statistics that document increases in services provided, circulation of material, and on-site use. The lessons learned through this experience will continue to be heeded as SSHEL moves forward.

References

Gerlich, B. K., & Berard, G. L. (2007). Introducing the READ Scale: Qualitative statistics for academic reference services. *Georgia Library Quarterly, 43*(4), 7–13.

University of Illinois at Urbana-Champaign, Social and Applied Health Sciences Planning Team. (2011, January 10). *Report of the Social and Applied Health Sciences Planning Team*. Retrieved from http://www.library.illinois.edu/nsm/social/sahs_planning/SAHS_NSM_Final_Report.pdf

University of Illinois at Urbana-Champaign, Social Sciences, Health, and Education Library New Service Models Implementation Team. (2012, March 1). *Final report*. Retrieved from http://www.library.illinois.edu/nsm/social/SSHEL_Final_report.pdf

APPENDIX 3A. SSHEL Information Services—Tiered Service Model Quick Reference

Created by Beth Sheehan and Kelly A. Mccusker

READ Level	Examples	Student Assistants	Public Service Staff	Graduate Assistants	Librarians
Read Level 1	Directional inquiries	X	X	X	X
	Library or service hours	X	X	X	X
	Library/information service point locations	X	X	X	X
	Basic technology assistance (locating/using copies, how to print or supplying paper)	X	X	X	X
Read Level 2	Call number inquiries	X	X	X	X
	Item location	X	X	X	X
	Minor machine and computer equipment assistance	X	X	X	X
	General library or policy information	X	X	X	X
	More complex technology assistance (how to save to a disk or email records, launching programs)	X	X	X	X
Read Level 3	Answers that require specific reference resources		X	X	X
	Basic instruction on searching the online catalog, creating VuFind account		X	X	X
	Direction to relevant subject databases		X	X	X
	Introduction to web searching for a certain item		X	X	X

Read Level 3	Complex technical problems and troubleshooting (assistance with remote use, reporting hardware or e-access problems)	X	X	X
Read Level 4	Instructing users how to utilize complex search techniques for the online catalog databases and the web		X	X
	How to cross-reference resources and track related support materials		X	X
	Basic use of citation management tools		X	X
	Services outside of reference become utilized (ILL, tech services, etc.)		X	X
	Assisting users in focusing or broadening searches		X	X
Read Level 5	Interdisciplinary consultation/research			X
	Question evolution			X
	Expanding searches/resources beyond those locally available			X
	Graduate research			X
	Difficult outreach problems			X
Read Level 6	Creating bibliographies and bibliographic education		X	X
	In-depth faculty and PhD student research		X	X
	Relaying specific answers and supplying supporting materials for publication, exhibits, etc; working with outside vendors		X	X
	Collaboration and on-going research			X

CHAPTER 4

Regaining Equilibrium on a Tilting Planet within the Higher Education Universe:
A Scholarly Personal Narrative

Rebecca Rose

WITHIN THE LAST two years, two academic libraries were transformed by separate organizational crisis events that resulted in swift and comprehensive changes to both workplace environments. Additionally, the employees within those organizations were profoundly affected, experiencing added stress within the already dynamic and rapidly evolving milieu of academic libraries. This chapter will attempt to make sense of those specific events and put them into a framework of understanding. The intent is to describe and discuss the effects of the crisis events on the professional librarian staff and connect the overall impact of leadership styles to subsequent voluntary turnover rates of professional library staff.

The first crisis was triggered by the discovery of a $16 million budget shortfall within a state two-year college, resulting in a massive layoff of 9% of the workforce. The second crisis was precipitated by the decision to consolidate two state schools, each with its own historical backdrop, identity, and traditions. One was a successful broad access college; the other was a university with competitive enrollment requirements and graduate programs. The schools were mandated to combine into a unified university within one year.

Much of the material written in this narrative is taken from my personal observations; I was employed in the libraries of these institutions during their periods of transformation. Context for these observations will be given through empirical evidence found in the library and information sciences, social science, and business organization literature. Despite an increase in publications on the topics of library related change and/or disaster management research in recent years, research specifically on the direct effects of crises on voluntary turnover rates in libraries is relatively absent in the library and information science literature.

After reviewing the literature, the chapter provides background descriptions of the downsizing and consolidating institutions that highlight management practices specific to each organization during its crises. Additionally, the results of a survey of academic library managers from across the state about voluntary turnover in their libraries are included for comparison. This data provides a contextual framework across institutions during the time when the crises occurred.

Literature Review

Organizations experiencing either a downsizing or a consolidation are undergoing crisis events. An organizational crisis is defined as an event that (1) threatens the organization's high-level priorities or values; (2) requires a response or action by the organization within a short time span; and (3) occurs unexpectedly (i.e., does not happen as a result of a planned change) (Hermann, 1963). Academic libraries should be considered as suborganizations within a larger academic organization and are, therefore, directly impacted by a crisis that affects the overall institution.

By their definition, organizational crises cause rapid changes in the workplace. Organizational literature recommends collaborative and transformational models of leadership in times of crisis and change. John Kotter (1996, pp. 17–32) makes the important distinction that leaders can influence change outcomes during these times of crisis in organizations. Furthermore, leaders who can successfully establish a shared vision within their organization empower their employees to take actions that facilitate positive changes during times of change (Kotter, 1996, pp. 17–32). Library leaders who cultivate a "trust-based organizational culture" are better suited to managing comprehensive changes than those with a hierarchical style of leadership (Düren, 2012). Also, the ability to develop innovative solutions in response to rapid changes is directly impacted by the leadership style and institutional culture present in the library prior to the crisis (Parker, 2012).

Employees experiencing a downsizing event are dealing with termination of their coworkers, with whom relationship bonds may have been formed. Brockner, Grover, Reed, Dewitte, and O'Malley (1987) found that negative attitudes towards leadership decisions pervaded when employees perceived that those laid off were unfairly chosen, the survivors shared close relationships with the laid off staff, and the threat of future layoffs remained high. The term "layoff survivor sickness" was coined to describe the angry, depressed, and anxious survivors left behind to carry on the mission of the institution after witnessing coworkers terminated through workforce reductions (Noer, 1993).

While studies on the effects of downsizing on academic librarians are few, one study found that dismayed reactions to losing coworkers due to layoffs added to the overall stress of the workplace (Leckie & Rogers, 1995). Many librarians develop friendly relationships with coworkers both inside the library and with those in other departments. Hearing the bad news experienced by so many coworkers darkens the overall workplace atmosphere, even for those not directly affected by the layoffs.

Trevor and Nyberg's (2008) model of voluntary turnover describes a shock occurring in the workplace, such as an organizational crisis, which leads to employee reexamination of loyalties and career options within the organization. This is followed by an exploration, then consideration of external job opportunities and offers, which results in a decision to either leave for another position or remain. Trevor and Nyberg (2008) also assert that voluntary turnover rates increase by 19% after a downsizing event and that high performance workers are the most likely to leave in these conditions. This second wave of departures leaves the remaining employees dealing with keeping the organization running with even fewer workers. With high performers being the most likely to leave, those remaining may face expectations for department performance to remain at previous levels, while the dynamics of the workplace have degraded.

Downsizing because of financial mismanagement in an organization can be referred to as a stigmatizing event because it damages the entire organization's reputation. Other examples of stigmatizing events are organizational corruption, misconduct by executives or employees, and lawsuits (Anders, 2004; Elmore, 2003; Hamori, 2007). Enron, Arthur Andersen, Bear Stearns, Lehman Brothers, and AIG are examples of companies that experienced stigmatizing events where massive layoffs or shutdowns occurred. In some circumstances, working for a stigmatized organization can negatively affect the reputation of the employees as the failings of the organization can be linked to the competencies of the individual (Hamori, 2007). Career experts recommend employees working for a stigmatized organization quickly find another job. Demonstration of the ability to leap to another organization proves the employees' flexibility in gaining employment elsewhere, which helps them to disassociate themselves from the stigmatizing event (Anders, 2004; Elmore, 2003). Employees working for organizations with damaged reputations have good cause to be highly motivated to move to companies possessing positive name recognition. As a result, higher voluntary turnover should be expected in institutions where a stigmatizing event has occurred.

While the consolidation of two colleges into a single entity is not considered a stigmatizing event, it is still considered a crisis event as it is associated with the employees' loss of institutional identity and autonomy (Eastman & Lang, 2001). Challenges that come with consolidating include the possibility of changed services, populations, and programs; job realignments or status; and revamped workflows. In addition, consolidations alter the workplace by melding together workplace cultures that have evolved within their unique historical and organizational contexts.

Leadership practices contribute to the overall morale of employees during these organizational upheavals. In fact, collaborative leadership has shown to have a positive impact during downsizing events, especially when employees participated in decisions related to the downsizing and frequent communication occurred between management and staff (Taylor, 2001). Being consulted on decisions provides a sense of control or empowerment in an environment with disappearing jobs and factors in employees feeling valued by the organization. Achieving positive cultural change is facilitated by presenting opportunities for all levels of staff to be involved in the change process, especially when suggestions are encouraged and the ideas that develop and improve the workplace are implemented (Evans & Ward, 2007, pp. 107–122). Involvement with the planning process by those actualizing the changes gives employees a stake in the new organization's outcome (Armstrong, 2011, Chapter 11; Smith, 2006). Ongoing communication from leadership with frequent updates is identified as being essential during periods of change (Düren, 2012; Rozum & Brassaw, 2013). Effecting change and having it accepted throughout the library is more likely to succeed when all levels of the library staff feel informed and have a voice in changes to be implemented. Demonstrations of flexibility by management while working through the changes can ease an otherwise stressful situation.

Downsizing Narrative

Less than two years ago at this writing, I worked at an open access two-year college comprised of five separate campuses, possessing a long tradition of concentrating on student success. The institution was still struggling to recover from the economic challenges of the Great Recession, operating with reduced funding because of government cutbacks to higher education budgets throughout the state (Biemiller, 2011; Jones, 2009).

In this state of belt tightening and economic downturn, in May 2012 the school president announced that the two-year college was in a budget shortfall of $19 million. Soon after the announcement, the president was removed from the college and then resigned. The interim president declared that the school would have to borrow an additional $6 million in order to finish out the year, causing the shortfall to total $25 million (Sheinin & Salzer, 2012). In the days that followed employees were terminated using a reduction in force (RIF) clause. The impact of the RIF was considerable, affecting 282 individuals across four campuses (*Collegian*, 2012).

Those 282 were terminated within a four-day period, which was devastating for those who lost their jobs as well as for the survivors. Employees who witnessed their colleagues cleaning out their desks and being escorted off the premises declared feelings of guilt, anger, and disbelief about what was happening to their workplace. These reactions fit in with descriptions of a layoff survivor effect (Brockner et al., 1987; Noer, 1993). The suggestion of fiscal mismanagement followed by a downsizing was highly publicized in the local news outlets, so therefore fits the description of a stigmatizing event.

The college's libraries also suffered terminations, with two campus libraries hit hard. One campus lost three of its four full-time librarians, including its director, leaving one full-time librarian, a full-time paraprofessional, and scant part-time paraprofessional staff. Another campus downsized its two full-time librarians to one library director. Throughout the five campus libraries, four full-time librarians and several paraprofessional positions were eliminated (*Collegian*, 2012).

As mentioned previously, fallout from a downsizing event often generates a rise in voluntary employee turnover rates (Trevor & Nyberg, 2008). The "survivors" begin to reevaluate their own job and work situation, with the layoff negatively impacting their commitment to the organization (Brockner et al., 1987; Knudsen, Johnson, Martin, & Roman, 2003). Likewise, simply announcing an impending RIF quickly affected the library with an almost immediate retirement of the executive library director and other librarians leaving voluntarily afterwards with varied reasons given. Of the 20 remaining full-time librarians, nine left (45%) in less than two years after the announcement of the budget crisis: three retired, four left to work at other library jobs, and two left with no job prospects stated.

A myriad of factors could explain the large number of voluntary turnovers from the library after the layoffs. The institution's continued strained budget shortfall generated a climate of uncertainty and instability. Strict belt-tightening measures were enacted to repair the budget through the next year, which eliminated upward job mobility or growth. At the same time, the subsequent departure of survivors exacerbated shortages caused by the RIF. Vacancies left many departments on a given campus with insufficient staff to function, requiring employees to cover multiple campuses without compensation.

Reorganization necessitated by the RIF affected all five campus libraries. The Technical Services Department permanently reassigned two of their full-time library staff, transferring them to another short-staffed campus library with new duties as a desk reference librarian and circulation clerk. When voicing concerns about the transition, one of them was told she should be grateful to have a job. These jobs not only required skills outside of the positions they were hired for but added considerable mileage to their daily commutes. Reorganization tactics also affected the library management, with one library director told to manage two campus libraries 40 miles apart. Duties of part-time paraprofessional and clerical staff, whose positions were also cut back or eliminated, were heaped onto professional staff.

Many of these reassignments were unsustainable, resulting in additional readjustments and transfers. Fears of being moved to another campus added to the atmosphere of instability, which turned out to be well founded. For example, I was told that I would be required to transfer 40 miles away, necessitating a commute into a large metro area, with added responsibilities, no reimbursement, nor promotion. Under the terms of the RIF, promotions or pay raises were not allowed to compensate workers for the extra responsibilities and inconvenience as a result of layoffs. My job reassignment order, although later rescinded, was the pivotal incentive for me to leave.

Adding to the workplace instability, fears of additional terminations persisted, fueled by emails from the interim president urging the importance of upcoming fall semester enrollment targets. Failing to reach target enrollment numbers could result in additional budget cuts and, perhaps, the re-implementation of furloughs (Diamond, 2012). Although additional jobs cuts were not threatened by the administration, the recent RIF caused this fear to be pervasive and discussed as a possibility among employees.

The leadership of the campus libraries was directly impacted, with one library director terminated in the RIF and two library directors retiring within two months of the layoffs. The executive library director was the first to retire, leaving days before the RIF. The new interim president immediately appointed the recently displaced personal assistant of the fired college president to fill the executive library director position as interim. While formerly a campus library director at the college, the new executive director was perceived to have had little involvement with the two-year college library since his administrative promotion four years earlier.

The interim executive library director was tasked with conducting the RIF business, which included firing four librarians, suspending part-time hours for the summer, and then reorganizing the campus libraries, which necessitated shuffling library staff to fill gaps in personnel. Much of this was implemented with little or no collaboration or input from the librarians, and as these decisions rolled out, their impact generated much speculation and anxiety.

One task handled collaboratively involved reducing online database subscriptions by one-third to accommodate a budget cut, with the final decision needed within a matter of days. The interim executive library director asked the Reference Committee to recommend the cuts. The committee, comprised of all of the college's reference librarians, traditionally evaluated subscription databases each year. This effort established a healthy partnership and a relationship of trust, essential for successful collaboration during times of crisis (Parker, 2012).

The committee's most recent recommendation given in April was still fresh in their collective memories, and thus they were prepared for rapid, yet informed decision making in revising the recommendation.

Almost every librarian was able to participate in the emergency budget meetings, which were held online. Those in attendance offered suggestions and opinions about alternative budget options. A final recommendation was created, then agreed upon via a follow-up vote with all of the librarians participating. The revised recommendation was submitted to the interim executive library director within days of the request. While no one was happy that the database budget had been cut, efforts to collaborate and build consensus to meet the challenge were successfully implemented. Because of the established workplace atmosphere under collaborative leadership, they were able to act quickly and decisively in a time of crisis.

This is a single example of a positive approach to a crisis situation at the two-year college. Other leadership decisions during this time had a negative effect on morale, evidenced by the subsequent high voluntary turnover rate. Many top-level decisions generated additional issues for the library that were poorly suited for collaboration or consensus style problem solving. For example, the employees selected for termination created uneven staffing across campuses, which caused the remaining employees further disruption. Some employees were involuntarily moved to other campuses and reassigned to roles they had not been hired for. Due to the atmosphere of job instability and low morale, many librarians began to reevaluate their job situations, and then chose to seek alternative employment options. I was among those who chose to leave the two-year college after the budget shortfall.

Consolidation Narrative

In January 2012, a state university and a state college were listed among four pairings of higher education institutions (HEIs) mandated for consolidating across the state. Seen as a cost-cutting initiative by the state's HEI governance, the consolidation process was to be ready for approval one year later in January 2013 (Board of Regents of the University System of Georgia, 2013). HEI consolidations are becoming more common in the current era of economic hardships. Martin and Samuels (1989) see them as a way to achieve desirable outcomes such as academic excellence, financial stability, administrative efficiency, and enrollment stability. For example, bringing together institutions with differing academic programs offers more classroom options for their students. Additionally, colleges with larger enrollments will experience increased revenues, which can be used towards improvements that attract and retain higher quality students and faculty. Administrative overlap can also be eliminated, resulting in a leaner organization. For example, a single president, provost, dean, or department head can now preside over the combined institutions, instead of two sets of administrators leading two smaller organizations.

The terms *merger* and *consolidation* appear to be used interchangeably within the scholarly literature. For clarity and for the purposes of this chapter, the term *merger* is defined as the occurrence of one organization overtaking the other organization, with one set of policies and culture dominating or completely replacing the policies and culture of the other. *Consolidation*, on the other hand, is defined as creating a new institution out of the old, while retaining, at least in part, the values and identities preexisting within each of the campuses.

In the case described here, it was the stated goal that the new consolidated university would identify and retain the best practices from both institutions without sacrificing the original missions and unique campus cultures. For example, the former state college's campus would remain a broad access institution, focusing on two-year and selected four-year degrees, and the former state university's campus would continue to be more competitive in their enrollments, offer only baccalaureate and graduate programs, and retain a historic military college. So that no school would have their culture dominate, the consolidated university would be given a new name and a new mascot selected via student votes.

As with most large organizations, each campus department, including the library, had its own organizational subculture within the wider campus culture. Additionally, the libraries at each college had developed their own unique established policies and workflows, which evolved over time, with adjustments arising organically to fit the needs of their respective organizations.

Prior to consolidation, the state college already consisted of two campuses, having added a small satellite campus in 2001, with neither possessing student housing. By contrast, the university had been a single residential campus for over 100 years, adding another campus just four months prior to consolidation. The transition to a multicampus institution from a solitary or two-campus organization required new approaches to address the issues of a four-campus institution. Multicampus academic library settings often face the challenge of physical distances erecting barriers to communication and collaboration. The separation of facilities and staff across campuses can create feelings of isolation (Crockett, 2000). More specifically, the distance between campuses affects daily operations such as moving library materials and documents between facilities and logistics for chat reference and meetings.

In response to the announcement of consolidation, both institutions were thrown into a state of intense pre-planning and reorganizing in preparation for unification. Adjustments in the organizational structure had to be implemented due to the presence of redundant positions within converging departments, and the library was no exception. The consolidation of two different library policies and cultures necessitated the scrutiny and rebuilding of almost every single aspect of the library's organizational structure and workflow dynamics. A preliminary libraries consolidation working group made up of library faculty and staff from all campus locations began laying the groundwork for consolidation as early as the spring of 2012. The group met every other week and tackled approaches to topics such as the library mission statement, collection development policy, organizational structures, instruction catalog, assessment options, and library webpage. This working group met through August of 2012 when the library was reorganized with the selection of the dean for the consolidating libraries. A director position was transitioned to an assistant dean of libraries at one campus, and each of the other campus libraries added a head librarian position, all reporting to the dean of libraries. A Library Leadership Team (LLT) was formed, comprised of the head librarians and dean, with biweekly meetings to collaborate on the establishment of policies and workflows for the newly consolidated multicampus library environment.

One of the areas that needed attention in the pre-consolidation process was the drafting of new promotion and tenure guidelines for each department. Arguably the biggest decision for the librarians involved their eligibility for tenure as the librarians at the state college were tenure track and the university librarians were not. Some of the librarians at the state college were already tenured. All non-tenure track librarians were given the choice to convert their individual position to tenure track. The promotion and tenure guidelines were written entirely by the library faculty, with the final document taken directly to the dean who presented it to the provost's council for approval. Library faculty concerns and suggestions were discussed and given serious consideration as the document was developed.

This collaborative model of leadership was extended to other areas within the library reorganization. An Access Services Committee with representation from all four campuses was formed to establish common circulation policies and write the access services handbook. An Integrated Library System (ILS) Consolidation Committee with representation from each campus facilitated the combining of policies from two separate configurations into one ILS, with help from the state and the ILS provider on the actual execution. The policies decided on by the Access Services Committee steered the actions of the ILS Consolidation Committee. The library webpage was given over to a two-person committee, one librarian from each of the two larger campuses; they worked with the Information Technology and University Relations Departments to adhere to the new university's branding requirements.

Restructuring also extended to the models used for library instruction and collection development, which at the university library was the work of subject specialist liaisons. There the librarians were responsible for both library instruction and collection development for specific subject and departmental areas. Given the new consolidated library arrangement, this model needed to be revamped, especially for collection development responsibilities. Librarians at multiple campuses were involved throughout the decision making process and asked for input on how to formulate an even distribution of responsibilities. The restructured collection development model splits away from the old liaison model, with subject areas assigned to all librarians across the four campuses. The library instruction responsibilities at the university campus are still organized along the former liaison roles but allow for more flexibility for entry-level classes with heavier demands for instruction. Because of the significant distances between the four campuses, the decision was made for the librarians on each campus to continue library instruction as before the consolidation.

Workflows for acquisitions and cataloging needed to be centralized for efficiency rather than continuing to operate those functions separately. The decision to move all technical services operations to the existing state university campus was facilitated by the presence of a technical services librarian and staff with ample space to accommodate processing materials for the entire university at that campus library. Establishing the selection process for the online database subscriptions also needed consideration. Recommendations for database subscriptions from librarians and other faculty are now directed to the head librarians, who discuss them with the dean of libraries either in LLT meetings or via email, with the dean making the final decision based on these recommendations.

Logistical details for meetings needed to be ironed out, as face-to-face meetings would be difficult and costly due to the distance between campuses (as much as 60 miles). Recognizing this expense, the administration allocated travel funds for inter-campus meetings. When meeting in person was not feasible, online meetings using video conferencing technology enabled the participation by the librarians from each campus.

Before the implementation of each major part of the library reorganization, the librarians met either face to face or via video conference and were given a chance to provide input and feedback. Throughout these decision-making meetings, the dean of libraries was reassuring, stating often that if later it became apparent that these decisions needed revision then they could be reviewed and changed.

The collaborative management style experienced by the libraries must be taken within the larger context of the whole institution undergoing massive changes. Outside of the library, the consolidation process was unfolding within each department throughout the university during this transitional period. Some areas experienced difficulties and upheaval that often affected the university as a whole. For example, complex systems such as student registration and financial aid had delays in their implementation, which caused additional stress to faculty, staff, and students. While staffing in the libraries remained stable throughout the consolidation, this was likely not the case across all departments.

Turnover Statistics Methods, Results, and Discussion

To gain a perspective for the higher education library job landscape within that time period, I polled the 31 academic libraries governed by the same state authority to measure voluntary turnover rates during the time period of the consolidation and downsizing as described in the present narrative. The queried libraries experienced similar regional variables, such as economic factors and employment opportunity alternatives as well as comparable job benefits, such as vacation and insurance.

A survey link was distributed through the state library association's listserv and direct emails were sent to library leaders (i.e., deans, directors, and managers). Fifteen library leaders self-reported data for their libraries (out of 31 possible institutions) including the two institutions discussed in this paper. The data needed to originate from library leaders as they are in the unique position of knowing the reason an employee left. Turnover data is potentially sensitive because information could be matched to specific individuals. For this reason, specific libraries' survey results remain anonymous.

To determine turnover rates, the survey asked for the largest number of full-time professional librarian positions held at their library from January 2012 through April 2014. The decision to ask for data about the full-time professional librarian positions was made due to the permanence of these positions as compared to those of part-time professional librarians or even full-time paraprofessional positions, which often are transitional jobs.

Respondents were asked to state the number of full-time professional librarians who left voluntarily for the same time period. Voluntary turnover included only those who chose to retire or leave to pursue other jobs or activities. Not counted as voluntary are those who left because they were fired, laid off, or deceased. Also, for the downsized library, only the jobs that remained after the layoffs factored in calculating turnover rates. The positions eliminated due to the layoffs were not counted in the calculations. Respondents were also asked if their library experienced a crisis event. Crisis events were described as one of the following: downsizing, consolidation, natural disaster, or other (offered as an open-ended answer option).

The number of full-time professional librarian positions in the responding libraries averaged 9.7, with a range from 20 to two positions.

Those leaving voluntarily averaged less than two (1.8), ranging from nine to zero during those months. The survey revealed an overall voluntary turnover rate of 19% (SD=10%) for the 15 responding libraries during this time period. Five of the 15 libraries self-reported that their library experienced a crisis event: three consolidations, one downsizing, and one move. The voluntary turnover rate for libraries that experienced a crisis event was 35% (SD=21%). By contrast, the crisis-free libraries experienced an 8% (SD=9%) voluntary turnover rate. A further breakdown of the results for libraries experiencing crisis events revealed turnover in nine out of 26 positions, or 33%, in libraries that consolidated; two out of 11 positions, or 18%, in a library that moved; and nine out of 20 positions, or 45%, in the downsized library.

Table 4.1			
Voluntary Turnover at Academic Libraries during January 2012–April 2014			
Surveyed Libraries	**Total Number of Positions**	**Number of Voluntary Exits**	**% of Voluntary Turnover**
All (N=15)	146	28	19
Crisis, None (N=10)	89	8	8
Crisis, All (N=5)	57	20	35
Crisis, Moved (N=1)	11	2	18
Crisis, Consolidated (N=3)	26	9	33
Crisis, Downsized (N=1)	20	9	45

The numbers provided by this data establishes a baseline for the average voluntary turnover rates for libraries in the state comparable to the libraries discussed in the present narrative. The large difference in rates strongly suggests crisis events did affect voluntary turnover rates in the polled libraries, with libraries free of crisis having a rate of 8% compared to 35% for libraries experiencing a crisis. While other factors can certainly influence voluntary turnover rates, the significantly higher reported rates for libraries undergoing a crisis warrant further scrutiny.

While the selection of the libraries for the sample attempted to poll libraries in a similar region within a shared governing body, there are still differences between those libraries such as their FTE, budgets within their institutions, salaries, work cultures, and other differences. Further research that includes a wider sample would provide a broader examination of turnover rates in academic or all types of libraries. Tracking these same libraries over an extended period of time could provide useful information for indicating the time required for turnover rates to level out after experiencing a crisis event.

Analysis

My experience with these episodes of downsizing and consolidation within a short time frame gives rise to comparisons of the two events. I left the downsizing library after working there for over five years, necessitating the sale of my house and separation from coworkers who had become close friends. Coming to the consolidating library only a month before the official unification, I did not have a stake in the history or memories of either consolidating institution. Furthermore, I was hired to head the library at a new campus location that opened its doors only three months prior to my arrival. My expectations were prepped for renewal and rebirth as I had made the decision to work at this institution being fully aware of the upcoming consolidation. The new campus location was at least a half an hour away from the other campuses within the new university. Staffing at this campus was minimal, meaning that everyone was busy filling multiple roles, with the purpose of establishing a fully functional, vibrant new campus. Therefore, exposure to the possible rumblings and grumblings of disgruntled or discontented coworkers was minimized as the consolidation moved forward.

I witnessed in both situations the pain of coworkers mourning the loss of their previous institutional culture, which became a smaller part of something new and different. The intensity of the grief expressed repeatedly in conversations with faculty and staff across all campuses was remarkably similar in both organizations. Mourning for days past, hearkening back to the glory days that are forever lost was a familiar theme in these conversations. The idealization of the way things used to be, accompanied by a pessimistic outlook for the future was also commonly heard. However, in the consolidation experience, some did express optimism and excitement about the school's future, especially at my campus. Very few expressions of optimism have been mentioned by former coworkers at the downsized two-year college, with the prevailing sentiment being worry about continued decisions rolling out and their impact on the entire school and library. The process of hiring replacements for those who left voluntarily has been slow and arduous, with my position taking eight months to fill.

After both of these crisis events occurred, a state of confusion arose among faculty and staff about norms and rules that guide the procedures and operations of the changed organization (Danns, 2014). This was caused in part because all of the schools involved continued to conduct business as usual while their crises unfolded. The crises required rapid decision making and implementation of those decisions. Yet significant time is required to adequately reexamine an organization's processes and policies, and then to reevaluate their functionality and effectiveness within the revised organizational structure. Even if policy changes are decided quickly, communicating those decisions and understanding implications of the changes require time to ensure that employees internally absorb and incorporate them into their daily operations.

In a merger, as described earlier, the preestablished policies and norms of one of the institutions predominate while those of the absorbed institution are replaced. Merging in this sense can minimize time needed and reduce confusion as the processes are new or modified to only one group instead of the entire institution. The organization whose policies predominate would possess working historical knowledge and experience of them and could serve as a source of clarity on the established procedures and workflows to the group new to those policies. Yet, handling a merger in this way would erase the opportunity to scrutinize and sift through policies and practices, keeping the best practices and improving upon, or eliminating the others. It would also hinder efforts for each school to retain its institutional mission and individual campus culture. The logistics of adding together campuses and departments demand revisions at some level from established policies if they are to successfully accommodate new intra-campus operations. Library examples include the need to reevaluate continued support of independent technical services departments for each campus and existing collection development practices that focus on pre-merger campus arrangements.

Academic librarians typically embrace intersecting common core values that should facilitate the creation of a collective vision in a consolidation situation. Along those lines, HEI libraries intrinsically possess a mission of service to their students and faculty. This should also serve as a binding agent, cutting across the procedural or organizational differences that could be divisive. In addition to collaborating with their librarians while deciding on policies and procedures, leaders guiding libraries through crisis situations can appeal to these common values of achieving student success and delivering quality library services, thus ensuring broader acceptance of change.

A crucial difference between the two crisis experiences is that, unlike in the downsizing, during the consolidation great effort was made on behalf of the administration to retain jobs, even though duplications of positions were present. Furthermore, very few employees were asked or required to change campuses in order to retain their jobs; the option to move to another campus was usually offered as a choice to be made by the employee. In the library no campus reassignments were forced on librarians. The presence of job stability in the consolidating library, along with the collaborative atmosphere of committee involvement in decision making, limited voluntary turnovers, avoiding a situation similar to the one experienced by the two-year college library after the budget shortfall.

The survey data reveals that since the announcement of the consolidation in January 2012 to April 2014, only 17%, or three out of 17 librarians, chose to leave voluntarily. This number contrasts sharply with 45%, or nine out of 20 librarians, voluntarily choosing to leave the downsizing college during the same time frame. Additionally, the survey reveals that the consolidating library enjoyed a lower rate of voluntary turnover in comparison with librarians choosing to leave consolidating libraries overall (33%). The difference in the rate of voluntary turnover is similar when compared with libraries undergoing all types of organizational crisis events with 35% of librarians choosing to leave. The only downsizing organization in the survey was the one described in this chapter, so a direct comparison with another downsizing library is lacking. Still, the 45% voluntary turnover is considerably higher when compared with the overall rate of 35% voluntary turnover for all institutions undergoing a crisis event. It is reasonable to ascertain that the conditions experienced at the downsized library are connected to the higher voluntary turnover rate.

At the college being downsized, the librarians' ability to collaborate in recommending cuts to subscription databases to accommodate the reduced budget in a short amount of time was a positive experience. However, overall decisions unilaterally handed down from leadership hurt professional library staff retention. Little to no room for collaboration or negotiation with professional library staff was possible with two libraries left stripped of staff. Had the RIF been applied in such a way as to eliminate reassignments of campus locations, the aftermath would not have included the stress of possible mandated relocation. The instability factor was so great at the downsized library that in comparison, I considered the changes present at the consolidating library a much more tolerable experience.

Conclusion

Many academic libraries are undertaking dramatic changes considered as crisis events, downsizing and consolidating being two types of crises. Establishing a library management team structure that encouraged communication, collaboration, and team building was a major stabilizing factor for the consolidating library. This type of management positions the library staff to better weather crisis situations when they arise. I found opportunities that gave professional librarians and library staff a voice in the decision making during both institutional transformations of downsizing and consolidating were found to be empowering and positive experiences. Participating in the creation of policies and procedures for a new library organizational structure, while a stressful venture, is also exciting as it presents opportunities to tailor library services to fit the situation. In particular, major decisions made with consideration of input from the librarian staff will facilitate the creation of a revised common vision and shared history for the reorganized or transformed library.

References

Anders, G. (2004, Jul 27). Moving on after Enron means being humble and minimizing role. *The Wall Street Journal*. Retrieved from http://www.wsj.com/articles/SB109087957464674267

Armstrong, M. (2011). *How to manage people*. London, England: Kogan Page.

Biemiller, L. (2011, October 23). Atlanta colleges strive to outrun the recession: Region's 11-percent unemployment means layoffs and scholarship cuts. *The Chronicle of Higher Education*. Retrieved from http://chronicle.com/article/article-content/129487/

Board of Regents of the University System of Georgia. (2013, November 26). *Campus consolidations*. Retrieved from http://www.usg.edu/consolidation

Brockner, J., Grover, S., Reed, T., Dewitte, R., & O'Malley, M. (1987). Survivors' reactions to layoffs: We get by with a little help from our friends. *Administrative Science Quarterly, 3*, 526–541. doi:10.2307/2392882

Collegian. (2012, June 22). GPC employee lay-off list. *The Collegian.* Retrieved from http://www.collegiannews.com/2012/06/gpc-employee-lay-off-list/

Crockett, C. (2000). Reconfiguring the branch library for a more virtual future. *Library Administration & Management, 14*(4), 191–196.

Danns, G. (2014). *The dialectics of consolidation: Utopia, dystopia and creativity at the University of North Georgia.* Manuscript submitted for publication.

Diamond, L. (2012, July 20). Georgia Perimeter prepares for fall semester, but concerns over budget shortfall remain. *The Atlanta Journal-Constitution.* Retrieved from http://www.ajc.com/news/news/local/georgia-perimeter-prepares-for-fall-semester-but-c/nQXNc/

Düren, P. (2012) Leadership in libraries in times of change. *International Federation of Library Associations and Institutions, 39*(2), 134–139. doi:10.1177/0340035212473541

Eastman, J., & Lang, D. W. (2001) *Mergers in higher education: Lessons from theory and experience.* Toronto, ON: University of Toronto Press.

Elmore, B. (2003). Life after Andersen. *Baylor Business Review, 20*(1), 2.

Evans, G. E., & Ward, P. L. (2007). *Management basics for information professionals.* New York, NY: Neal-Schuman.

Hamori, M. (2007). Career success after stigmatizing organizational events. *Human Resource Management, 46*(4), 493–511. doi:10.1002/hrm.20179

Hermann, C. F. (1963). Some consequences of crisis which limit the viability of organizations. *Administrative Science Quarterly, 8*(1), 61–82. doi:10.2307/2390887

Jones, W. C. (2009, August 23). Georgia's public colleges brace for cutbacks. *Florida Times-Union (Jacksonville).* Retrieved from http://jacksonville.com/news/georgia/2009-08-23/story/georgias_public_colleges_brace_for_cutbacks

Knudsen, H. K., Johnson, J. A., Martin, J. K., & Roman, P. M. (2003). Downsizing survival: The experience of work and organizational commitment. *Sociological Inquiry, 73*(2), 265–283. doi:10.1111/1475-682X.00056

Kotter, J. (1996). *Leading change.* Boston, MA: Harvard Business School Press.

Leckie, G. J., & Rogers, B. (1995). Reactions of academic libraries to job loss through downsizing: An exploratory study. *College & Research Libraries, 56*(2), 144–156.

Martin, J., & Samuels, J. E. (1989). College mergers have become creative, effective means of achieving excellence and articulating new missions. *The Chronicle of Higher Education.* Retrieved from http://chronicle.com/article/College-Mergers-Have-Become/70433/

Noer, D. (1993). *Healing the wounds.* San Francisco, CA: Jossey-Bass.

Parker, S. E. (2012). Innovation and change: Influences of pre-disaster library leadership in a post-disaster environment. *Advances in Library Administration & Organization, 31*, 121–171. doi:10.1108/S0732-0671(2012)0000031006

Rozum, B., & Brassaw, L. (2013). Merging two academic libraries: Finding unity from diversity while maintaining institutional identities. In A. Woodsworth & W. D. Penniman (Series Eds.), *Advances in librarianship series: Vol. 37. Mergers and alliances: The operational view and cases* (pp. 201–221).

Sheinin, A. G., & Salzer, J. (2012, September 20). Audit: Ga. Perimeter College leaders ignored signs of severe financial trouble. *The Atlanta Journal Constitution.* Retrieved from http://www.ajc.com/news/news/state-audit-finds-no-fraud-in-georgia-perimeter-co/nSGgw/

Smith, I. (2006). Continuing professional development and workplace learning—15: Achieving successful organisational change—do's and don'ts of change management. *Library Management, 27*(4/5), 300–306. doi: 10.1108/01435120610668232

Taylor, S. (2001). *The impact of downsizing strategies and processes on Ontario academic research* (Doctoral dissertation). Retrieved from ProQuest Dissertations and Theses database. (UMI No. NQ63634)

Trevor, C. O., & Nyberg, A. J. (2008). Keeping your headcount when all about you are losing theirs: Downsizing, voluntary turnover rates, and the moderating role of HR practices. *Academy of Management Journal, 51*(2), 259–276. doi: 10.5465/AMJ.2008.31767250

CHAPTER 5

The Very Model of a Modern Major Library*

Nancy Roderer, Blair Anton, Will Bryant, Robert Gresehover, Stella Seal, Claire Twose, and Sue Woodson

ON THE SURFACE, the saga of the Welch Medical Library is about a library building and a collection of books within it, but it's also a story about the dramatic evolution of library services and expectations in the context of changing technology. While these threads are tightly interwoven, and both are important, it seems likely that it is the latter that will have the most lasting impact on users of the library and the work that they do.

Our story begins with the opening of the Welch Library building in 1929. The library was to function as a central library for the medical campus of Johns Hopkins University, and it also accommodated the Institute of the History of Medicine (IHOM) and its collection. As the campus grew, so did the library's staff, collection, services, and locations, but the building continued to serve its central function reasonably well for over 50 years. Of particular importance to the Hopkins community was the grand West Reading Room (Figure 5.1), which houses the painting of the *The Four Doctors*, commemorating the founding of the Johns Hopkins Hospital and School of Medicine in 1889 and 1893 respectively.

---

*With apologies to Gilbert and Sullivan.

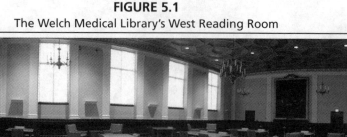

FIGURE 5.1
The Welch Medical Library's West Reading Room

The Welch Library staff aggressively pursued the application of evolving technology to library services and collections, and as elsewhere, library materials and services increasingly began to be used from outside the library building. By 2000, both the problems with the existing building and the direction of electronic services seemed to call for a new vision, both for library services and the building. Through consultation with library users and with the assistance of an architectural team, it was envisioned that by 2013 library services and collections would be predominantly electronic, provided to users "wherever you are" (Johns Hopkins University, 2010b).

The period of 2000–2012 saw rapid increases in electronic collections and evolution of embedded services to library users, both guided by a series of action plans. All branches of the central library were closed, and plans were developed to reuse the central library portion of the Welch Library building (Figure 5.2) in support of graduate student education. The library staff moved out of the Welch building, maintaining a small service desk on-site.

While library efforts over these years accomplished much, there is still much to be done. The remainder of this chapter reviews the current status of the library's services, collection, and facilities, revealing both what has been accomplished and questions that remain to be addressed. Additional sections describe the staffing and financial issues that undergirded the library's evolution, and the chapter ends with a brief description of the current library plan.

FIGURE 5.2
The Welch Medical Library Building

Environment

The Welch Library serves the John Hopkins University's Schools of Medicine, Nursing, and Public Health and the Johns Hopkins Hospital and Health System. These entities are concentrated on the East Baltimore medical campus of Johns Hopkins but also include health care centers and affiliate hospitals in Maryland; Washington, DC; and Florida. Collectively the whole is referred to as the Johns Hopkins Medical Institutions (JHMI). Individually and collectively, the organizations have a long and distinguished history. From the beginning, the university was committed to advancing human knowledge through research and scholarship, and it has seen these as intertwined activities. The result is a very research-focused institution—one that is ranked very highly in terms of education, research, and clinical practice.

The East Baltimore campus has expanded substantially over its long history, most recently with the construction of the Anne and Mike Armstrong Medical Education Building and two major hospital buildings, the Sheikh Zayed Tower and the Charlotte R. Bloomberg Children's Center. The Welch Library building was built to house a central medical library for the campus and the IHOM and its separate library. The building also houses the John Singer Sargent painting of *The Four Doctors* commemorating

Drs. Welch, Halsted, Kelly, and Osler, lead teaching physicians during the formative years of the Hopkins School of Medicine (Koehler, Roderer, & Ruggere, 2004). The Welch Library building was central to the East Baltimore campus when it was built but now lies near the northeast corner of a considerably larger campus.

The total user constituency of the Welch Library is over 50,000 individuals, including faculty of the three schools, students, and clinical and other staff. This includes about 4,000 students and over 5,000 faculty. Needs for library services are driven by the tripartite mission of research, education, and clinical practice in the context of excellence and discovery. The emphasis on research fuels both the work of the library users and the work of the library itself, which has continually strived to develop and adopt new approaches to library systems and services.

Given the complex nature of the Hopkins organization and the clear need to make decisions about future directions of the library, several planning activities were undertaken beginning in 2001. The first was the engaging of Hillier Architecture and consultant Shirley Dugdale of DEGW to provide what was called an architectural plan. This effort included consultation with representative user groups and resulted in a report outlining changes in both library programs and facilities (Hillier Architecture & DEGW, 2002). Following the architectural plan, the library staff worked with consultant Alice Haddix to develop ongoing action plans to monitor progress against the specified goals (Johns Hopkins University, 2006; 2010a). This series of planning tools reflected an evolving vision of an ever more user-centered library supported by the "three-legged stool" of an all electronic collection, excellent interfaces, and human help aiding users wherever they were.

The Collection

In 2000, based on in-depth investigation of user needs and with an infusion of funds, Welch Library began aggressively increasing the number of its journals subscriptions in electronic format. Three years later, cancellation of the print versions of those journals began. Today, Welch's essentially all-online collection represents a radical transformation of its traditional print-based collection of 14 years ago. Fewer than a dozen print subscriptions remain, and the collection includes over 7,000 electronic journals titles, more than 400 databases, 11,000 plus e-books, and roughly 2,200 streaming videos. The collection includes online backfiles for many titles including all those from the three most represented publishers. For those older journals that the library has only in print, articles are scanned and delivered to the reader electronically. The Welch collection really is available wherever you are.

As part of the transition to a primarily online library and in an effort to make the best use of its building, the collections staff began planning to reduce the size of its print holdings. To that end, a major weeding project began in the summer of 2010. The first phase involved closing down the Lilienfeld Library in the School of Public Health, Welch's last satellite library. While this move was somewhat controversial, the support of School of Public Health management and the conversion of the space into study space eased the transition. The next phase addressed the collection in the Welch building. Weeding the remote storage facility will allow Welch materials to be moved there.

At the beginning of this effort, criteria were developed for determining candidate titles/volumes for weeding. These included online access to the title with dates of online coverage that matched Welch holdings and print holdings in a trusted, third-party, non-commercial repository. All proposed discards were to be reviewed by the curator of the IHOM collection and assessed for potential donation to the following programs: (1) MedPrint, the National Library of Medicine's web-based cooperative print retention program; (2) the catalog of the Regional Library for the National Network of Libraries of Medicine at the University of Maryland, Baltimore; and (3) Better World Books (BWB). None of the organizations were able to use the journals, but BWB accepted a selection of the books. The remaining volumes were recycled.

Thus far, 80,000 volumes have been removed including many of the titles from major publishers (e.g., Elsevier, Springer, and Wiley). Roughly 200,000 volumes of Welch's legacy print collection are still housed in the main Welch building with approximately 145,000 more held in remote storage. More than three-quarters of the monograph titles are 15 years old or older, and most have not circulated within the last five years. Further weeding is certainly possible. While there is no urgency to empty the building, at some point it seems almost certain that the legacy print collection currently housed in the Welch building will be further reduced given the cost of space and campus priorities for its use. Medical libraries around the country are being asked to give back large portions of their space (Haynes, 2010; Persily & Butter, 2010; Thibodeau, 2010; Tobia & Feldman, 2010). Welch's proactive approach has been to begin weeding and develop a list of titles for potential withdrawal and procedures for removal.

Library Users and Use

In 2000, the Welch Library electronic collection was a modest 2,100 journals, 130 databases, and 159 books. Today, the collection has more than three times as many e-journals and databases as it did in 2000, and the e-books collection is 70 times larger. The number of downloads of electronic journals alone in 2010 was over 7 million or on average one download per person on campus per day. Visits to the library's website were over 1,600,000 in 2010, on average about 5 visits a month per person.

Use of the building and services located within declined significantly from 2000 to 2010. In 2000 the gate count was over 128,000 with over 30,000 loans, and 17,900 questions answered. By 2010, loans had fallen to just over 19,000, and 38,000 people (or one visit per person per year) came through the doors asking 14,900 questions. Clearly, while there was a dedicated core of users who wanted to be in the building, most users preferred having library resources available to them at their fingertips.

Proposals to reduce the accessibility of the physical space were handled in stages, so as to gradually accustom users to the changes. In 2010, based on falling physical usage statistics previously discussed, a recommendation to reduce the library's opening hours from 77.5 to 51 was presented to the library's advisory committee. This proposal was approved and the library's new hours began January 1, 2011. There were some complaints about the reduction in service hours, primarily from students with one or two from faculty who were not current users of the building but felt that it should nonetheless be maintained for future generations of clinicians. During this period, two studies were conducted by library staff. An observational study showed that 70% of users came to the library to work on computers, either their own laptops (27%) or library equipment (43%), or to study or read (20%). The exit survey corroborated the observation study with 28% of respondents stating they came to use the computers or printers, 20% to access library resources, 18% to study, and 16% to borrow library materials.

By 2012 library staff were ready to move to the next phase. With the acknowledgment of the advisory committee, it was announced in November that effective January 1, 2013, the building would no longer be accessible to the public. Reaction was swift, vocal, and negative. A town meeting was called in December 2012 for the library to present its case and listen to its users. As a result of this meeting, the building closure and collection recycling plans were suspended and a Committee for the 21st-Century Welch Library was formed. This group was charged with reviewing the library's data and developing recommendations for the direction of the library both physical and virtual.

Today there remains only a small staff presence in the Welch Library building and limited services are provided from within it, primarily circulation, basic reference, document delivery, and maintenance of the stacks. Usage statistics continue to be monitored to inform future decisions.

Library Services

Providing an all-electronic collection allows the library to address a key aspect of library usability: convenience. It has been well established that Zipf's principle of least effort is in play—library use increases as the effort required by the user decreases (Case, 2006). This has been well demonstrated with the increased use of electronic collections made available to users in the office, lab, classroom, etc. Welch's long-term goals included not only the delivery of an all-electronic collection but also creating the best possible online interfaces for use of the library collection and services and moving other library services to the users' locations.

Through a series of websites and supporting software, online access to Welch services has been continuously strengthened. Noteworthy developments were the creation of the individualized My Welch portal to library and other resources (Zhang, Zambrowicz, Zhou, & Roderer, 2004); the creation of a Hopkins-wide repository; and the Hopkins-wide adoption of Blacklight, an open source discovery tool, and Xerxes, open source software that improves access to a library's online resources (Rochkind, 2014). Reference assistance began to be provided online in 2001. Delivery of books to users' offices was initiated in 2004 and expanded to include convenient pickup locations in 2011.

Beyond online access, an important user requirement identified in early planning efforts was the assistance of librarians for in-depth support of users with complex information needs. To meet this requirement, an evolving system of informationist services was developed, beginning in

2000 (Davidoff & Florance, 2000; Grefsheim et al., 2010; Oliver & Roderer, 2006; Rankin, Grefsheim, & Canto, 2008). Informationists are professional librarians and others trained in the information sciences who are embedded in the environments of their patrons. They are knowledgeable and experienced in medical- and health-related subject disciplines and are skilled to provide information expertise within the contexts of research, clinical care, and education.

The first step in this evolution was the implementation of a traditional library liaison program. A professional librarian was assigned to be the first point of contact for users in pre-identified departments in the schools of medicine, nursing, and public health. Liaison librarians assisted with a variety of services, including answering reference questions, bibliographic instruction in the use of databases, and expert literature searches. As user traffic into the Welch building diminished over the next decade, taking advantage of opportunities to build rapport and relationships with library users grew more important. Two of these early partnerships were with the McKusick-Nathans Institute of Genetic Medicine in the School of Medicine and the Hopkins Population Center in the School of Public Health.

By 2003, these in-depth collaborations resulted in the creation of tailored combinations of space, expert services, and online portals geared to a wide array of user groups. Library users gained heightened awareness about the range of support and active roles informationists could play on research and clinical teams. Requests for research consultations with librarians increased, and meeting patrons in their work environments was a logical way to deliver effective services tailored to their needs, whether on a clinical unit or in a research lab. The proactive effort to embed informationists' expertise on research and clinical teams developed over time. Patron requests for informationist participation on in-depth collaborative projects increased, with an estimated 42% of an informationist's time spent on large-scale, evidence-based systematic reviews of the literature and other comprehensive reviews for publication. Informationists' search expertise, knowledge of citation management techniques, and critical appraisal skills also contribute to the work of preparing National Institute of Health (NIH) research proposals and fulfilling the work on funded grants.

By 2013, Welch Library had 11 informationists (six clinical, four public health, and one basic science), delivering customized information services to the faculty, staff, and students of the JHMI. In addition to supporting the grant and publication enterprise at Hopkins, the informationists' skills and expertise were incorporated into departmental research committees and research groups, including the Cochrane Collaboration and the Agency for Healthcare Research and Quality, which funds the Evidence-based Practice Centers, clinical rounds, and case conferences as well as education, ethics, and care practice policy committees. Currently, informationists have either library or user supported spaces where they can meet with patrons in the Johns Hopkins Hospital and in each of the Schools of Medicine, Nursing, and Public Health buildings.

The ongoing development of the informationist program, specifically balancing the depth and breadth of services coverage within the fast-paced, decentralized, research-oriented environment of academic health sciences is perhaps the primary challenge faced by the library leadership. Related to this is the challenge of maintaining a cohesive professional team in a large, diverse, physically dispersed service environment. Informationist presence continues to expand in digital environments to serve the needs of library users working in remote locations and overseas. As data management becomes a higher priority for funding bodies, the role of informationists in that arena remains to be explored.

Library Facilities

As noted earlier, the Welch Library building opened in 1929, adequately housed the entire print collection, and was a comfortable work space for the staff of approximately 10. By 2000, the building infrastructure was rapidly failing; off-site storage was required for the over-crowded stacks; and library staff numbering almost 80 were spread throughout the main building, four branch locations, a warehouse storage annex, and a separate office building. Additionally, the campus view of the library as a destination had changed dramatically. In order to use the library and its services, faculty, staff, and students no longer needed to trek across campus to search the cramped stacks, lounge in the grand reading rooms, or visit the librarians staffing the reference desk. Door counts had decreased, and the physical library building had been replaced by online and informationist services as the major means of using the library.

Over the next decade (2000–2010), all branch locations were closed and the print collections in the branches merged or were deaccessioned. One of the library reading rooms was converted into staff space. A new shared climate control storage facility replaced the annex warehouse in 2002, and by 2007 approximately 145,000 volumes were relocated to this off-site building. Short-term mechanical system "band-aids" were applied to the aging infrastructure. Although the staff size was growing smaller, it was still difficult for the now 55 staff members to effectively function in the library building and one adjacent office building. Use of the building by faculty, students, and staff was minimal, and closing the library building to users was proposed (DEGW North America, 2010). While this proposal was met with resistance and eventually abandoned, it became apparent a solution for staff space was required.

Over the next three years, library leadership and institutional administration agreed on a plan to partially renovate the aging building to promote additional use by students and host events. There was a key interest in providing support to the graduate medical education program located in a nearby building with limited study space. The majority of library staff was relocated to an off-campus location in newly renovated office space. A small service desk to support the remaining print collection still exists in the library building, and the library's team of informationists has on-campus office space near the users they serve. While the new off-site staff location has not been without logistical challenges, it did significantly improve working conditions.

It remains to be seen if use of the building is bolstered by the recent renovations or what the ultimate change in functionality of the building will be. Much is related to the remaining and largely unused print collection housed in the tiered stack levels. The archaic building design is a significant impediment to further change in the building. This institutional and architectural treasure has now been preserved for an alternate use yet to be determined.

Library Staffing

When reviewing changes in a library over time, there is often intense focus on the physical building or implications for the collection. However, no resource is more important than the people who provide service to users. This valuable pool of talent is essentially the brain and circulatory system of the library body, providing direction and sustaining all functions while continuing to grow and adapt to the changing needs of information management.

The staff of the Welch Library has seen significant change over the years, but none more transformative than the decade from 2000–2010. The staff size in early 2000 was approximately 80 FTE consisting of a fairly equal balance of support staff, paraprofessionals, reference librarians, IT staff, and management. This top-down organizational structure was typical for a library of this size and scope. Services were also typical and structured in a reactive environment to respond to user requests and demand as required.

By 2010, the staff size had been strategically reduced to about 55 FTE but was transformed into a very effective workforce with specialties in informationist outreach and advanced technologies. Adopting a matrix management system, Welch Library maintained a departmental structure but also established a flexible system of committees through which key functions could be carried out interdepartmentally. A small contingent of support staff remained, but positions were restructured and new skill sets were added to further enhance employee responsibilities. The most significant change occurred as reference librarians evolved into informationists and became embedded in user groups throughout the campus. The matrix management system provided the majority of staff with opportunity to see and participate in library goal setting and action planning. The transformation was not without challenges. Continued budget pressure required constant staffing adjustments that occurred through attrition and not through reductions in force. The emotional toll on staff was high, as significant change often brings, but restructuring and retraining led to additional opportunities for many staff.

Since 2010, the overall staff size has not changed much in terms of the total number of employees. However, the mix of staff and expertise continues to change dramatically. As the embedded informationist program gains popularity, the requirement for highly skilled, discipline-specific knowledge experts increases. The challenge is to successfully find and recruit individuals with in-depth information skills, relevant subject education and/or experience, and a willingness to be proactive in supporting their constituency. Faculty and other users look for validation of subject knowledge and desire fully functioning partners from the onset of projects. It remains to be seen how many of these specialists will be required. While addressing this question would be aided by gaining a better understanding of the return on investment, to do so in a rigorous way would be challenging.

Future changes in library staffing will be inherently linked to the evolving changes in how libraries function and what services are provided. It is vital to actively recruit and retain staff that can adjust and thrive in an environment that is undergoing change.

Library Finance

Many of the issues in making difficult decisions about merging or closing library facilities are related to financial support. Rising labor, collection, and facilities costs place undue pressure on already constrained funding resources, requiring strategic management of those funds. Not all library needs can be met, and priorities must be evaluated and selections made between competing programs. Many library budgets are now remaining flat or facing downward pressure, leading inevitably to reallocation of expenditures between budget categories as well as to overall cuts.

Historically, the Welch Library budget, like that of many other libraries, was very labor intensive with staffing making up, on average, nearly 50% of the total budget. Collection cost was next with a percentage share of between 20–30%. This was closely followed by facilities costs ranging from 10–15%. Not much of the budget was left after these three major categories. The budget scenarios have rapidly changed as collection costs now either meet or exceed lower staffing budgets and facilities costs for older buildings are significantly more.

The reallocation process is one of the ways that the Welch Library budget was modified in support of the changing library environment. In 2000, the library budget matched approximately the historical mix described above. Over the next decade, the budget was relatively flat with only modest adjustments available for increased costs. This dynamic required significant internal reallocation to balance the rising cost of maintaining a strong collection (Figure 5.3). By 2012, the cost of collections exceeded the total staffing budget for the first time in the library's history.

Changes in the building costs over this period were a significant driver, especially the dramatic increases in utility and maintenance costs from about 2005 to 2010. Overall building costs were about $651,000 in 2000 and $1,100,000 in 2012. With the staff moved out of the Welch building, the library budget no longer includes the cost of the historic facility and the building costs are about $500,000.

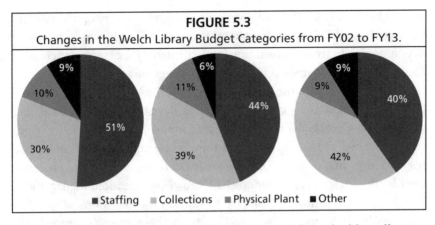

FIGURE 5.3
Changes in the Welch Library Budget Categories from FY02 to FY13.

■ Staffing   ■ Collections   ■ Physical Plant   ■ Other

The downside to the successful retention of the valuable collection was the loss of several library positions through attrition as well as the continuing deterioration of the physical building. All capital projects for the building and deferred maintenance were put on hold. Only emergency building repairs were performed. Recruiting and retaining the higher level of staff with the expertise required for the popular informationist program was equally challenging. Staffing in more traditional areas of library operations such as technical services and collection management required fewer people, allowing the transfer of unused salary budget in support of the informationist program and information technology positions.

Another separate, yet competitive, challenge was the rapidly expanding umbrella of Hopkins, including partner hospitals, affiliate care centers, and international agreements with medical schools and health ministries. Contractual obligations are made at the highest institutional level in these negotiations assuming that the valuable resource that is the Welch Library will be available to all equally. Licensing restrictions and access issues remain a huge and expensive hurdle to providing extended service.

However, the future outlook does show promise. Increasingly, the library is understood to provide value across JHMI in terms of increasing research funding, improving clinical outcomes, and supporting education. This strengthens the case for the return on investment provided by the library and for appropriate funding of it.

Planning for the Future

The architectural and action plans developed for the Welch Library as described here provided the framework for changes in library operations and services through 2014. As this planning period was drawing to a close, a new approach to strategic planning implemented by the Hopkins School of Medicine provided a model for a new planning effort.

In the fall of 2013, the leadership team of the Welch Library revisited the library's missions, goals, and strategies developed a few years earlier to assess how much the academic research and health care delivery environment had changed within that time frame and how the library had responded to that change. The assessment determined that the processes used by the Welch user community in knowledge creation, management, and sharing had sufficiently evolved to warrant the development of a new set of goals, strategies, and actions. The team also recognized the value of articulating the library's leadership role within the institutional mission by redrafting the language of the library's mission statement to better align with the current language used by its parent institution.

The process of developing goals was facilitated by the strong relationships of library leadership with the disparate parts of JHMI and by a recently completed strategic plan within the institution. The Welch leadership team was made up of experienced professionals who had developed close working relationships with disparate academic, research, and clinical units of the multiple institutions. The success of those close working relationships was the result of a service strategy developed some years ago by the library. Each member of the team was able to bring to the strategy creation process a different and important perspective of the user community they represent. The resulting goals and strategies (Table 5.1) represented the melding of these perspectives. The current institutional strategic plan (Johns Hopkins Medicine, n.d.) also provided a framework upon which the goals would fit. Each of the two-year goals was associated with one of six Johns Hopkins Medicine strategy areas: people, biomedical discovery, patient- and family-centered health care, education, integration, and performance. The availability of a current institutional plan also allowed the team to use the terminology adopted by the parent institution, thus eliminating the need to translate library-speak into the nomenclature familiar to the institutional leadership and user community.

The draft mission, goals, and strategies were shared with all library staff and the Welch Library Advisory Committee (WLAC). Both groups were encouraged to identify areas needing clarification and provide opinions regarding any goals that should not be within the purview of the library as well as any goals that appeared to be missing. The draft goals shown in Table 5.1 are the result of multiple drafts by the Welch leadership team and input from library staff and the WLAC. In addition to the goals, the Welch leadership team developed measurable objectives that will be used to quantitatively assess progress towards attaining the goals.

Table 5.1 Welch Goals FY2014–16	
JHM Strategy Area(s)	**Welch Goals (FY2014–2016)**
Biomedical Discovery	Collaborate with the JHMI research community in the arenas of evidence-based practice, data-intensive health sciences, and knowledge management.
Education	Engage in teaching to support the lifelong learning of JHMI faculty, staff, and students.
Health Care	Partner with health care providers and researchers to increase patient safety and quality care.
People	Promote and reward professional development and advance employee engagement in service innovation and enhancement.
Performance	Assess the value of the library's contributions to the JHMI mission and goals through meaningful performance indicators.
Integration	Expand the library's role in enhancing knowledge sharing among JHMI faculty, staff, and students, and with the global health care community.

Strategies developed for achieving the Welch goals include engaging the JHMI community (including partner hospitals) in an ongoing dialogue to identify e-resource and online clinical tool cost-containment ideas and priorities; facilitating the sharing of tacit knowledge about bioinformatics tools and current data management practices among faculty across the JHMI; and ensuring that all library staff members, regardless of their role, are able to see the connection between their work and its value to our user community. The concept of embeddedness or a close working relationship with the user community is evident in every strategy, whether it entails library staff working within the academic and clinical environs or library staff working with users to identify and prioritize resources and service.

Like the library itself, the plan for the future, including the goals identified above and the strategies we use to achieve them, will evolve as the priorities and interests of the Welch user community change. This story of the Welch Library is about identifying and engaging in strategies that integrate information and knowledge services with the goals and priorities of a dynamic academic research environment and a distributed and expanding health care delivery system.

References

Case, D. O. (2006). Principle of least effort. In K. E. Fisher, S. Erdelez, & L. McKechnie (Eds.), *Theories of information behavior* (p. 92). Medford, NJ: Information Today.

Davidoff, F., & Florance, V. (2000). The informationist: A new health profession? *Annals of Internal Medicine, 132*(12), 996–998. doi:10.7326/0003-4819-132-12-200006200-00012

DEGW North America. (2010). *Vision for a graduate center for the Johns Hopkins School of Medicine.* Retrieved from http://welch.jhmi.edu/welch/newlibrary/pdf/Graduate_Center_031312.pdf

Grefsheim, S. F., Whitmore, S. C., Rapp, B. A., Rankin, J. A., Robison, R. R., & Canto, C. (2010). The informationist: Building evidence for an emerging health profession. *Journal of the Medical Library Association, 98*(2), 147–156. doi:10.3163/1536-5050.98.2.007

Haynes, C. (2010). Integrating with users is one thing, but living with them? A case study on loss of space from the Medical Center Library, University of California, San Diego. *Journal of the Medical Library Association, 98*(1), 32–35. doi:10.3163/1536-5050.98.2.007

Hillier Architecture, & DEGW North America. (2002). *William H. Welch Medical Library master plan* [Executive summary]. Retrieved from http://welch.jhmi.edu/welch/newlibrary/pdf/summary.pdf

Johns Hopkins Medicine. (n.d.). *Johns Hopkins Medicine strategic plan.* Retrieved from http://www.hopkinsmedicine.org/strategic_plan/index.html

Johns Hopkins University, William H. Welch Medical Library. (2006). *Welch Medical Library action plan 2006–2011.* Retrieved from http://welch.jhmi.edu/welch/docs/management/30jun2006.doc

Johns Hopkins University, William H. Welch Medical Library. (2010a). *Welch Medical Library action plan 2011–2012.* Retrieved from http://welch.jhmi.edu/welch/docs/management/2011-2012_ActionPlan.doc

Johns Hopkins University, William H. Welch Medical Library. (2010b). *Wherever you are: Annual report 2009–2010*. Retrieved from http://welch.jhmi.edu/welch/docs/management/annual_report_2010.pdf

Koehler, B. M., Roderer, N. K., & Ruggere, C. (2004). A short history of the William H. Welch Medical Library. *Neurosurgery, 54*(2), 465–478.

Oliver, K. B., & Roderer, N. K. (2006). Working towards the informationist. *Health Informatics Journal, 12*(1), 41–48. doi: 10.1177/1460458206061207

Persily, G. L., & Butter, K. A. (2010). Reinvisioning and redesigning "a library for the fifteenth through twenty-first centuries": A case study on loss of space from the Library and Center for Knowledge Management, University of California, San Francisco. *Journal of the Medical Library Association, 98*(1), 44–48. doi:10.3163/1536-5050.98.1.015

Rankin, J. A., Grefsheim, S. F., & Canto, C. C. (2008). The emerging informatics specialty: A systematic review of the literature. *Journal of the Medical Library Association, 96*(3), 194–206. doi:10.3163/1536-5050.96.3.005

Rochkind, J. (2014). Umlaut: Mashing up delivery and access. In N. C. Engard (Ed.), *More library mashups* (pp. 59–76). Medford, NJ: Information Today.

Thibodeau, P. L. (2010). When the library is located in prime real estate: A case study on the loss of space from the Duke University Medical Center Library and Archives. *Journal of the Medical Library Association, 98*(1), 25–28. doi:10.3163/1536-5050.98.1.010

Tobia, R. C., & Feldman, J. D. (2010). Making lemonade from lemons: A case study on loss of space at the Dolph Briscoe, Jr. Library, University of Texas Health Science Center at San Antonio. *Journal of the Medical Library Association, 98*(1), 36–39. doi:10.3163/1536-5050.98.1.013

Zhang, D., Zambrowicz, C., Zhou, H., & Roderer, N. K. (2004). User information-seeking behavior in a medical web portal environment: A preliminary study. *Journal of the American Society for Information Science and Technology, 55*(8), 670–684. doi: 10.1002/asi.20001

CHAPTER 6

Change in the 21st-Century Library:
Fate or Opportunity?

Tomalee Doan, Linda Rose, and Mary McNeil

COLLEGE AND UNIVERSITY campuses and their libraries are adapting to major changes in 21st-century higher education. In 2004, Purdue University Libraries recognized a need for significant changes to the services and organizational structure of the libraries. A new dean of libraries had arrived on campus bringing a new style of leadership, significant experience managing several other academic libraries, and a vision for moving Purdue University Libraries forward. The dean and others he recruited to join the leadership team recognized a need for substantial adjustments to the organizational structure and services to meet the changing learning and research needs of the campus. Charlene Sullivan, associate dean of undergraduate programs in the Krannert School of Management, described the changing needs as follows:

> Just as physical space in today's libraries is too valuable to
> be used for housing print collections and more for a student
> workspace, time in the 21st-century classroom is too valu-
> able to be used lecturing to students or quizzing them about

what they already read. Rather, the time is for real-time testing of ideas, breaking down accepted theories and practices,
and piecing them back together into insight that explains the
future. (Personal communication, June 9, 2014)

This value on educational space and time is something that the Purdue
University Libraries has understood and taken seriously. This chapter will
describe the changes made by the libraries as a result of this shifting academic atmosphere.

It Starts with a Vision and a Plan

The libraries' Strategic Plan 2006–2011 (Purdue University Libraries, 2006)
outlined the vision of achieving preeminence as an innovative and creative
research university library by meeting the challenge of the Information
Age. Along with the move from print to electronic publications for traditional scholarly journals and monographs came the necessity of providing
access to newer forms of collections, such as born-digital materials as well
as digitized special collections.

At the same time, a reconceptualization of Purdue Libraries' spaces
was also beginning with the closure of three departmental libraries—Psychology, Consumer Science, and Biochemistry—which in turn necessitated the consolidation of staff and print collections into other libraries in
the organization. A major renovation of the Management & Economics
Library began in 2009 and has resulted in a 21st-century library learning
space that serves as a model and benchmark for other learning spaces on
campus as well as nationally. The phased renovation of the Hicks Undergraduate Library began in 2013, and planning is underway in 2014 for a
$79,000,000 combined Science and Engineering Library and active learn-
ing classroom facility.

Moving into the 21st century, Purdue University Libraries reorganized
from a decentralized system of 15 specialized libraries and other units to
an organizational structure loosely arranged around four broad areas, or
divisions: Archives and Special Collections (ASC); Humanities, Social Sciences, Education, and Business (HSSEB); Health and Life Sciences (HLS);
and Physical Sciences, Engineering, and Technology (PSET). Thinking di-
visionally has facilitated the sharing of staff and other resources as well
as the repurposing of spaces into areas accommodating contemporary in-

structional models as well as both collaborative and individual study spaces. The HSSEB division includes what were originally the Management & Economics Library (now the Parrish Library of Management & Economics); the Hicks Undergraduate Library; and the Humanities, Social Sciences and Education (HSSE) Library.

The restructuring of Purdue University Libraries has proven to be quite impactful on the overall organization. The new structure provided opportunities to centralize and clarify library services to the campus while also creating a more flexible framework for anticipating programmatic changes and increased interdisciplinary activity on campus. One of the first steps in centralizing and making services more accessible to all campus users was the standardization of circulation and reserve policies across the libraries. The standardized policies were the result of extensive collaboration by a system-wide committee of staff working in these areas.

From a management point of view, the reorganized structure of the libraries made sense in light of the changes happening in higher education in general—and more specifically at Purdue—where interdisciplinary collaborations were becoming more common for researchers and incentivized by administration. The division-based structure also enabled efficiencies around human and financial resources, which, while not the driver of the change, has proven to be very timely as the organization continues to adapt to meet campus needs for library services. A robust planning process now takes place in the Libraries Planning and Operations Council and includes a prioritization process that ranks positions across the Purdue Libraries. This planning process has proven to be beneficial because it focuses the discussion of open positions not simply on whether to replace a position, but instead on a review of overall needs for the unit, department, or the libraries as a whole and hiring strategically in the area of greatest need.

This case study highlights a 10-year period within the Purdue Libraries and primarily focuses on the HSSEB division (a detailed timeline of this 10-year period is included as Appendix 6A). The chapter also addresses the redesign of the business library into the Roland G. Parrish Library of Management & Economics—an innovation that paved the way for the subsequent merger of collections and staffing of the Hicks Undergraduate and HSSE Libraries. The new service models that contributed to as well as emerged from the changes are considered from the perspective of the head of the HSSEB division libraries. The operational challenges, such as collection rightsizing, transfers, and storage, as well as staff reorganization necessary to support transformative education, will be discussed from the perspectives of the division head and the division's operations manager.

Why the Need for Space Redesign?

Alongside the organizational changes in Purdue University Libraries, there has been a reconceptualization of libraries' spaces to fit 21st-century modes of education. The HSSEB division's libraries have undergone significant change and renovation since the division was formed in 2010 in an effort to reflect the transformations in the libraries' strategic plan. The redesigns and renovations within the HSSEB division have four key elements:

1. Student-centered spaces that provide a variety of learning and collaborating areas to fit the "third place" (the places outside of home and work that facilitate interaction and creativity) needs on campus.

2. Innovative space design, focusing on blending formal and informal learning spaces to enhance learning, collaboration, and scholarship.

3. Multifunctional areas to create a dynamic and flexible environment for hosting events, conducting research, accommodating group and individual study, holding informal meetings, practicing presentations, and serving as instructional and lab classrooms.

4. Frequent opportunities to connect with constituents, which allow the libraries to become more integrated with other academic and administrative departments throughout campus.

The first space where these elements were adopted was the then named Management & Economics Library (a diagram of the space is included as Appendix 6B). In a climate where peer institutions were closing business libraries, the goal of creating what would become the Roland G. Parrish Library of Management & Economics was to transform a traditional library into a space that reflects the modern students' expectations, facilitates new pedagogies, and supports a variety of learning styles. Built in 2009, Phase 1 added a dedicated quiet study room with seating for 40 and the Learn Lab (Figure 6.1), a medium-sized instructional classroom that can also be used as a computer lab as each of the 40 seats has a computer. The room has three flat LCD panels positioned so there is no "front of the room." The most low-tech but highly important feature is the easily portable white boards that can be used either at tables or hung on the walls. As can be seen in Figure 6.1, the Learn Lab was designed for multimedia instruction. Staff members at Parrish help instructors become familiar with the full functionality of the room to enhance their teaching experience and their students' learning.

FIGURE 6.1
Roland G. Parrish Management & Economics Library Learn Lab

Implementing the Plan

Implementation required innovative approaches to solve problems and meet goals for the space. Budget difficulties were addressed by developing a three-part phased approach to the project, the first of which was relinquishing library space to generate funding and cultivating relationships with donors. In the second part, resources were made more readily accessible by moving away from print to digital resources, eliminating entrance security, and adding pull-down gates to allow for 24/5 access to the space. Finally, new workflows were created by revising staff job descriptions and training staff to support the learning-centered space, freeing faculty from the public service desk, called the "iDesk" (Figure 6.2).

FIGURE 6.2
Roland G. Parrish Management & Economics Library iDesk

Design of the next two phases of the project accommodated the students' need for 24-hour access to the library space. This, along with other needs, was identified by obtaining feedback from students. In "Solving the Information Workflow Tracking Dilemma," Cullen, Doan, and Pearlstein (2008) describe the necessity of using concrete data in making service decisions, especially statistics at the iDesk. Data from the existing library showed that services were little used after midnight—what users wanted after this time was primarily a place to study and meet with groups—so service hours were adjusted accordingly. To meet the challenge of keeping the space open without staff present, lockable roll-down covers (Figure 6.3) were installed on the general collection and reserve bookshelves.

Large lockable drawers were added at the iDesk to store laptops and other library materials, and pull-down gates were installed in the ceiling to close off designated areas. A 24-hour, unstaffed space also presented a security issue. A unique solution was developed in partnership with campus police, in which members of the student security patrol, trained by campus police, monitor the space after services ended at midnight. These students carry two-way radios to report any issues to the police.

FIGURE 6.3
Lockable Bookshelves in the Roland G. Parrish Management & Economics Library

Furniture styles were chosen in response to student requests and in recognition of the importance and necessity of technology. Plugs for laptops were scattered throughout the space as well as a laptop lockers for storage and recharging. The second phase, built in 2010 and designed for group work, is located adjacent to the Learn Lab. The space (Figure 6.4) includes high stools at tall tables with laptop plug-ins placed near the café area for relaxing, checking email, or having a snack.

FIGURE 6.4
Group Workspace in the Roland G. Parrish Management & Economics Library

Instead of traditional enclosed study rooms, high-backed, u-shaped bench seating was placed around moveable tables to provide a degree of privacy in the open space and facilitate collaborative study. Quick stop, stand-up computer stations were installed near the library's entrance for students wanting to use email or the libraries' catalog. Once the project was underway, further student input was solicited by placing an array of furniture options in the library for them to test and rate. Their responses guided discussions with the furniture manufacturer who was willing to adapt furniture designs based on student feedback.

Staff member job responsibilities and operational roles as well as the changing faculty roles were also considered in the renovation. Rather than enclosed offices, desks were located in an open area to facilitate collaboration. Breakout rooms with large monitors were constructed adjacent to the faculty work area to allow for small group meetings. The staff duties that had been associated with the large print collection were replaced by responsibilities that were appropriate for the transformed library. These included supporting users of the Learn Lab and meeting rooms by scheduling these rooms, assisting with the technologies in the rooms, and cleaning the frequently used space. Following the attrition of some staff, position descriptions were rewritten to better reflect the technology and service skills required for both staff and faculty moving forward with a 21st-century library.

During 2007–09, the increasing availability and demand for digital resources allowed for the downsizing of the print collection. After determining the research and curriculum needs of the Krannert School of Management and the Departments of Agricultural Economics, Hospitality and Tourism Management, and Consumer Science, some of the print collection was deselected and the little-used and quickly dated reference collection was totally eliminated. Based on usage and demand, much of the collection was transferred to a nearby compact storage area in the School of Management, while more highly circulated items remained in the library. To ensure that the needs of users were quickly met, a successful twice daily delivery service was implemented for requested print materials located in compact storage.

In addition to using circulation statistics to help determine where print materials would best be located, data analysis informed other decisions made during the process. Much of this process was overseen by the operations manager, whose role was to translate and support the division goals set by the associate dean and the division head into the daily operations of the physical library. This required transferring and resizing collections, revisualizing the libraries' services, and updating or creating staff position descriptions. The libraries' administration created the operations manager role by upgrading the position of operations supervisor (whose responsibilities mainly included staff supervision, overseeing circulation, and working a set 40-hour schedule) to that of operations manager (OM). The OM position has more flexibility in working hours and expanded responsibilities in selecting and determining staff job descriptions, providing reference assistance, and overseeing the transfer and shifting of collections. Two OMs were designated for the HSSEB division. One OM was given responsibilities across the division as well as managing daily operation of the HSSE Library, which is the largest campus library. The other OM was given responsibilities for the two other divisional libraries, Hicks Undergraduate Library and the newly renamed Parrish Library. The OMs worked closely together to expedite the transitions in the three libraries.

Success through Collaboration

During the Parrish Library transformation, the Purdue University Libraries also focused on collaborations with a provost-driven initiative to support student success across campus. This initiative, Instruction Matters: Purdue Academic Course Transformation (n.d.), or IMPACT, is a program that aims to improve student competency and confidence through the redesign of foundational courses. This is achieved by incorporating research findings in student-centered teaching and learning and assessing the program and courses to support those research findings. With the blending of formal and informal learning spaces along with the support of information literacy and current technologies, the libraries had positioned themselves to become key partners in the IMPACT program. Tomalee Doan (2013), one of this chapter's authors, summarizes the impact that the Parrish Library has had for Purdue University Libraries, stating that "libraries' spaces, designed in collaboration with campus partners, are serving as incubators to pilot new active learning experiences and environments" (p. 5). Doan was later invited to participate in the redesign and development of active learning spaces and currently serves as a member of the campus-wide IMPACT steering committee and management team for course redesign to facilitate student-centered learning in the classroom. Since spring 2012, 120 courses have been redesigned, providing an active learning environment for over 22,000 students. The goal is to reach 100,000 students by 2016. IMPACT's focus on student-centered learning has had a significant positive effect for the libraries. Provost office funding for the IMPACT program has provided the libraries with funds to create three new active learning classroom spaces in the Hicks Undergraduate Library and support one new information literacy instructional designer position. New library learning spaces increased library faculty's ability to share their pedagogical and information literacy expertise within the IMPACT course redesign process.

The Next Step: Merging Two Libraries

The success of the Parrish redesign suggested that other library spaces could better serve the needs of today's students by offering an array of individual and collaborative study areas as well as additional IMPACT classrooms. The Hicks Undergraduate Library, which is centrally located on campus, became the next target of transformation. Because the Hicks Undergraduate Library had historically held a large print collection initially designed to support undergraduate students, this would mean a dramatic downsizing of the existing collection. Because of the proximity of the HSSE Library, transferring most of the Hicks Undergraduate Library collection, including the media collection and viewing equipment, to the HSSE Library made sense. In line with the libraries' strategic goal of making collections accessible to patrons, this consolidation benefitted library users who would no longer have to travel between the two libraries to find all of the resources on a particular subject.

To facilitate the massive transfer of materials, the divisional OM created and communicated detailed procedures to all those who would be involved. Since the two libraries are in the same division, the OMs and staff members were accustomed to working together, making it easier to establish a plan, develop the workflow, and identify appropriate staff to collaborate with to accomplish the transition. Throughout the transfer process, the divisional OM alerted each unit when their assistance was needed and made tweaks in the procedures whenever implementing them revealed inefficiencies. Those from all levels of the organization had a role in the move. The libraries' resource services unit (technical services) assisted the divisional OM in generating circulation statistic reports. Using these usage statistics, libraries' faculty members set criteria to determine which books would be transferred to the HSSE Library, other campus libraries, or light archive repositories where items would be made available for request. Items held in duplicate or with low usage were considered for withdrawal. In some cases, the divisional OM communicated with librarians from other divisions to make decisions about transferring titles that appeared more appropriate to their subject areas. The OM also worked with staff at the HSSE Library to ensure that there would be room for the incoming items. HSSE staff measured shelves, did the necessary shifting, and pulled the titles identified for transfer or withdrawal to accommodate the incoming books and media.

Once the Hicks Undergraduate Library print collection had been relocated, the space was filled with new furniture, décor, and technologies. Figure 6.5 shows photos of the space before and after the renovation.

FIGURE 6.5
Hicks Undergraduate Library Space, Before and After Renovation

In addition, three state-of-the-art collaborative classrooms were created in the space. New questions then had to be addressed. How would libraries' staff best support the transformed space? Circulation services would hardly be needed, and fewer reference questions were likely to be asked as the new space was more conducive to general studying, collaborating, and even socializing. Taking these factors into consideration, how would the service desk be staffed?

Using the renovated Parrish Library as a model, a reference triage system was implemented in Hicks Undergraduate Library. Rather than spending time at the service desk waiting for customers to appear, faculty members could devote more of their time to liaison, research, and teaching responsibilities. The desk would be staffed by administrative professional and clerical staff members with training in reference skills. If a question was too in depth for one of them to easily address at the service desk, the customer would be referred to the appropriate subject librarian. Libraries' faculty and other staff members created LibGuides, easily accessible from the libraries' website, to provide answers for most service desk inquiries.

Traditional tasks, such as circulation and re-shelving, were no longer relevant in the redesigned space of Hicks Undergraduate Library. Student worker duties were revised to include basic space maintenance such as pushing in chairs, cleaning up spills, and seeing that the printers and copiers have paper. In a change from the traditional model of staffing that assigns each position a clearly defined set of responsibilities, a more fluid approach was employed in the new environment. Everyone, from operations manager to the newest student worker, contributed to keeping up the space.

The newly redesigned spaces called for staff members with skill sets quite different from those required in traditional library spaces. Normal staff attrition allowed the hiring of several staff members whose qualifications were appropriate for the transformed spaces. The two OMs created new position descriptions for the job searches. They sought candidates who were technologically savvy to support the array of technologies in the new classrooms, who were flexible to accommodate the 24/7 facility that demanded staffing outside of the traditional 9–5 period and the new divisional thinking that meant they could be expected to work in more than one library, and who demonstrated customer service skills as every staff member would work at the service desk.

Today, the two libraries serve as extensions of each other, with Hicks Undergraduate Library functioning as a learning commons for study and collaboration while the HSSE Library largely serves the needs of those requiring print resources. Once the Hicks Undergraduate Library redesigned space was opened in Fall 2013, traffic was heavy and constant. In addition, the space was available to students 24/7 by card swipe and, like the Parrish Library, was monitored by student security patrol. The Hicks Undergraduate Library has gone on to be one of six spaces recognized in 2014 by *American School & University Magazine* as "Outstanding Designs," and the consistently high usage of the redesigned spaces attests to its popularity with students.

Still there remain some who miss the books and ask, "Is this a library?" For this question, there are several responses. A library is a place where one can access information. Assistance with this access is available at the service desk as is help with the online catalog and library guides that facilitate access to print resources, many of which are conveniently located in the nearby HSSE Library. Information can also be provided by classmates, and Hicks Undergraduate Library provides the space where users can easily collaborate and share with each other.

Conclusion

The successes of the transformations outlined in this chapter have not been devoid of their own unique challenges. Challenging as well was the overarching goal of transitioning the library to fulfill 21st-century educational needs. These challenges include redefining the perception of what a library is supposed to be, communicating the vision of a library transformation, and addressing the value of libraries in higher education. These challenges can, however, be seen as an opportunity to be proactive. Rather than suffer the fate of getting into the game too late, Purdue Libraries has taken this opportunity—10 years in the making—to redefine itself. The HSSEB division, in particular, created a vision, developed and implemented a plan, and promoted Purdue Libraries' values, while being recognized as a key participant in several important teaching and learning campus initiatives.

The April 2012 dedication of the Parrish Library culminated a long but rewarding process that began with a white paper: "Customer Derived Vision for the Management and Economics Library" (Purdue University, 2005). All involved with the transformation and renovation learned a great deal about managing a project as the complexities of conceptualizing the project and bringing that vision to fruition were addressed. The leadership of the HSSEB division in designing the Parrish renovation has been acknowledged throughout the university, and the completed Parrish Library has become a prototype for redesign of library and classroom space across campus. It was awarded the SLA Center of Excellence Award and the Interior Design Excellence Award (IDEA) in 2013. Since 2012, the provost office has provided $1.8 million to create three active learning classrooms and renovate informal student collaborative and individual spaces in the Hicks Undergraduate Library (a diagram of the space is included as Appendix 6C). Associate professor of libraries, Hal Kirkwood (2012) explains that the library "is no longer just a repository of information, but a place where learning, exploration, and knowledge creation takes place" (p. 5). By rightsizing library collections and renovating spaces to support new learning strategies, those who transformed the HSSEB division's libraries have embraced this philosophy.

The Purdue University Libraries' Strategic Plan (2011) states that the libraries envision themselves as "leading in innovative and creative solutions for access to and management and dissemination of scholarly information resources and for the provision of information literacy and the creation of leading edge learning spaces, both physical and virtual" (p. 2). Learning has remained of strategic importance. The renovated spaces and reorganization of the Purdue University Libraries are clear indicators of these innovative and creative solutions to providing scholarly information and information literacy. Attesting to the successes of the two renovated libraries, these innovations in space design, staffing, and collection models are being used as a test bed model for the recently approved Active Learning Center (ALC), which will combine six of the science libraries in a building featuring 20 collaborative classrooms. All of the lessons learned have impacted the design of the ALC and the overall philosophy of how we utilize library space, personnel, and resources in the Purdue University Libraries.

"[H]aving library faculty available to work side by side with departmental faculty to plan for that conversation in a classroom that is supported by real-time access to digitized resources and creating active learning exercises is critical to providing a competitive advantage [to the university]" (personal communication, June 9, 2014). Purdue University Libraries has answered that need, and the Parrish Library of Management & Economics, the Hicks Undergraduate Library, and the future Active Learning Center all serve as a model for 21st-century educational facilities.

References

Cullen, A., Doan, T., & Pearlstein, T. (2008). Solving the information workflow tracking dilemma. *Information Outlook, 12*(11), 40–46.

Doan, T. (2013). Learning spaces with impact. VOLUMe. Retrieved from http://oldsite.lib.purdue.edu/Volume/2013/

Kirkwood, H. (2012). Authors of our success. VOLUMe. Retrieved from https://www.lib.purdue.edu/Volume/2012/

Purdue IMPACT. (n.d.). Instruction matters: Purdue academic course transformation. Retrieved from www.purdue.edu/impact

Purdue University, Management and Economics Library Task Force. (2005). A customer derived vision for the Management and Economics Library. West Lafayette, IN: Author.

Purdue University Libraries. (2006). Strategic plan 2006–2011. Retrieved from https://www.lib.purdue.edu/about/strategic_plans/2006_2011

Purdue University Libraries. (2011). Strategic plan 2011–2016. Retrieved from https://www.lib.purdue.edu/sites/default/files/admin/plan2016.pdf

APPENDIX 6A. Purdue University Libraries HSSEB Division Timeline of Transformation

Transforming the 21st Century Academic Library:
Purdue University Libraries HSSEB Divison Timeline of Transformation

Key:
Strategic Change
Space Change
<u>Collection Change</u>
Staffing Change**

2017
Active Learning Center (20 classrooms and 6 combined Science Libraries) slated for completion ($79,000,000)

2014
Phase II of Hicks construction completed ($325,000)

2013
Phase I of Hicks construction completed ($325,000)
SLA Center of Excellence Award granted to Roland G. Parrish Library
Interior Design Excellence Award (IDEA) granted to Roland G. Parrish Library
Created Hicks Customer Service Coordinator position**

2012
2012-2017 Strategic Plan begins
Operations Managers begin running library units
Phase III of MEL construction ends
Dedication of Parrish Library of Management & Economics ($2,350,000)
Renovation of Hicks 980D & 8853 into IMPACT classrooms ($1,000,000)
Created Parrish Library Reference Coordinator position**

2011
Design for Phase III of MEL construction continues
Phase III of MEL construction begins in May
Renovation of Hicks B848 into IMPACT classroom ($65,000/6 weeks)
<u>Hicks Collection analyzed and moved into HSSE Library</u>

2010
IMPACT Initiative and Steering Committee forms
Phase II of MEL construction begins in May ($850,000)
Acquired donors and major donor for MEL
Phase II Construction ends in September

2009
Libraries become more centralized through divisionary model
Tomalee Doan becomes Head of HSSEB Division**
Phase I of MEL construction begins in May ($1,000,000)
Phase I of MEL construction ends in September
<u>Downsizing of MEL collection finished</u>

2008
Design work begins on Phases I and II of MEL
Tomalee becomes Head of Hicks Undergraduate Library, in addition**

2007
<u>Downsizing the MEL print collection begins</u>
<u>Compact storage built in Rawls Hall</u>
<u>Meetings begin with possible donors for MEL renovation</u>

2006
2006-2011 Strategic Plan Begins
Tomalee Doan joins Purdue Libraries as Head of Management & Economics Library**

2005
Customer derived vision for the Management & Economics Library (MEL) – White Paper

2004
New Libraries Dean arrives on campus**

APPENDIX 6B. Management & Economics Library

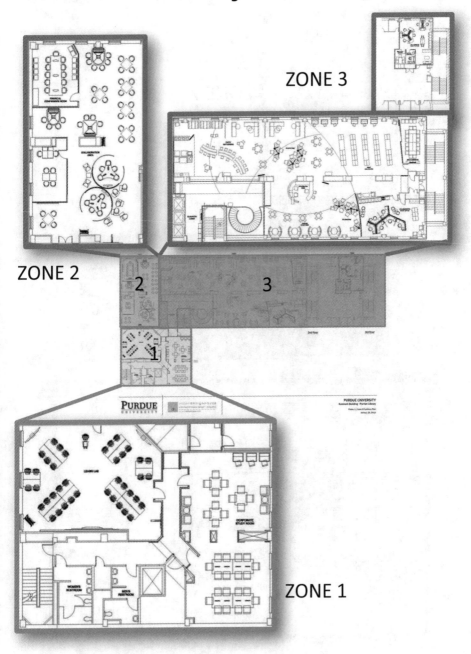

APPENDIX 6C. Hicks Undergraduate Library

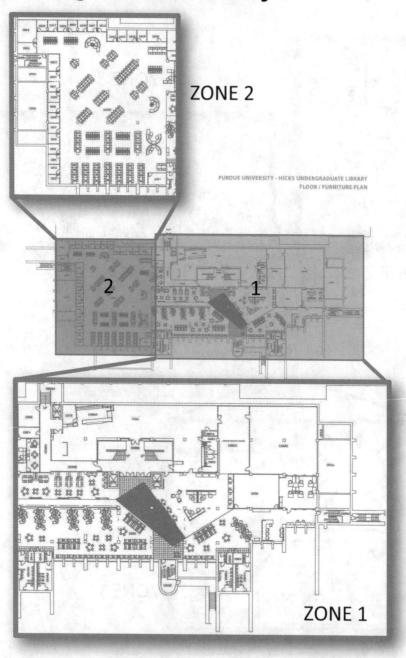

ZONE 2

PURDUE UNIVERSITY - HICKS UNDERGRADUATE LIBRARY
FLOOR / FURNITURE PLAN

ZONE 1

CHAPTER 7

Unanticipated Opportunities from Closed Libraries:
Pivoting for the Future

James T. Crocamo, Jeffrey Lancaster, and Ellie Ransom

FOR MUCH OF the 1990s and 2000s, Columbia University planned to build a consolidated library that would contain collections and staff from seven of its eight science and engineering libraries. During the summer of 2009, four of these science libraries were closed; staff and collections were moved to various locations on campus, although the new library space was not due to open until 2011. On January 18, 2011, Columbia opened the new science library that integrated the collections and staff from the four closed departmental libraries: Biology, Physics & Astronomy, Psychology, and Chemistry. Though the remaining science libraries—Engineering, Mathematics, Geology, and Geosciences—were not part of this initial consolidation process, the Engineering Library was closed in 2014 and planning is underway to close the Geosciences Library in 2015. This chapter focuses not on the process for closing these libraries, but on what has happened so far as a result of the closures.

Staffing, services, and relationships with faculty, researchers, and students have changed as a result of the multiphase closure and merger of these libraries. We, the authors of this chapter, are librarians who all hold positions that did not exist before the libraries merged, and we offer unique perspectives on the migration away from departmental librarianship toward a team-based, service-oriented approach to outreach and research support that has been fostered directly in response to the closures.

This chapter is about making the most of opportunities for inter- and multidisciplinary research support that will be the hallmark of 21st-century research libraries.

Background

Prior to 2009, the Science & Engineering Division Libraries on Columbia University's Morningside Heights campus were structured according to a traditional department-based model. The division was comprised of seven libraries—Biology, Chemistry, Geology, Engineering, Mathematics & Science, Physics & Astronomy, and Psychology—distributed across campus in the buildings that housed their associated departments or schools. The five professional librarian staff lines shown in Figure 7.1 focused on collection, instruction, and outreach according to specific library locations: Biology and Physics & Astronomy, Chemistry, Geology & Geosciences, Engineering, Math & Psychology. For decades, these five subject specialist librarians concentrated on building strong collections of print and electronic resources for their disciplines. Each librarian had excellent relationships with faculty, and each departmental library had its own unique set of services and relationships with its users.

In the early 2000s, two initiatives led to an assessment of the division's structure and a reconsideration of whether subject specialty was the optimal model to address the changing and increasingly inter- and multidisciplinary research needs of Columbia's faculty, researchers, and students. The first initiative began in 2002 when, in conjunction with the New York Public Library and Princeton University, Columbia opened ReCAP (Research Collections and Preservation), a large off-site storage facility in Princeton, New Jersey. To date, Columbia University Libraries have accessioned over 4.2 million items to this facility. Quick and reliable delivery of off-site materials to researchers on the Morningside campus has greatly alleviated major issues around the space required to store library materials on a university campus in the heart of Manhattan where space is all too valuable. The second initiative during this same period was the rapid adoption and growth of electronic resources available via e-book and e-journal packages. The availability of these packages has reduced the time necessary for science and engineering librarians to develop the libraries' collections.

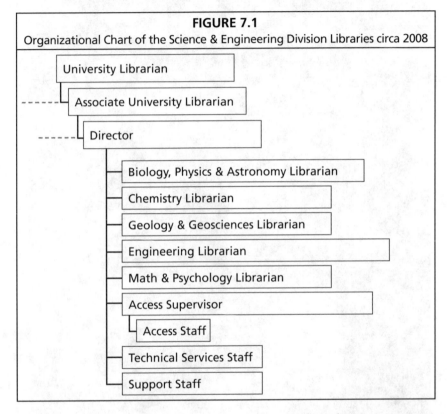

FIGURE 7.1
Organizational Chart of the Science & Engineering Division Libraries circa 2008

In the mid 2000s, planning began for a new interdisciplinary science research building to complete the Morningside campus plan developed in the 1960s (Figure 7.2). An integrated science library was included in the building plans for the Northwest Corner Building and was originally intended to house collections from all seven on-campus science libraries. Plans were scaled down after the refusal of the mathematics department to close the doors of its departmental library. The consolidated collection now available in the integrated library is comprised of high use astronomy, biology, chemistry, physics, and psychology materials. The library space was also designed to house a Digital Science Center with state of the art technology and a selection of high-end software applications to enable scientific analysis and visualization (Figure 7.3).

FIGURE 7.2
The Exterior of the Northwest Corner Building

FIGURE 7.3
The Interior of the Science & Engineering Library

In line with national trends to close libraries after the economic down-turn in 2008 (Guarria & Wang, 2011; Kaser, 2010), the libraries were forced to prematurely close four of the departmental libraries a year and a half prior to the anticipated opening of the new integrated science library. The libraries had recently hired a new division director with experience closing libraries who was able to shepherd the division and collections through the closing process. With only six weeks' notice, science librarians were relo-cated to other library spaces where they worked for the next two years until the integrated science library opened. Once outside of the departmental li-braries, they no longer saw students and faculty on a regular basis, and the impact on staff who were accustomed to face-to-face interactions was con-siderable. Librarians planned for the challenge of working in a new library that would contain few print materials (15,000 print volumes, no print journals, and few reference materials) and very sophisticated electronic equipment and resources. The division was confronted with the need to develop support services for many new technologies and to train librarians so that they would be able to assist students using these resources.

Once the work of closing four departmental libraries was done, the promise of the new consolidated Science & Engineering Library forced the professional staff to take stock of each others' abilities with new technologies, assess patron needs and expectations, and develop new models of service to better address researchers of the 21st century.

Taking Stock of Skills

The Digital Science Center in the new Science & Engineering Library was planned as a hub for emergent research methodologies in the sciences with access to subject experts having the technical skills necessary to consult with modern researchers. From the beginning, the deep information resources at the Digital Science Center included access to the software necessary to undertake science and engineering research in addition to the expected electronic content and databases provided by the libraries. The center was designed as a collaborative environment where students, faculty, and staff could leverage high-end workstations and expensive software to more efficiently carry out their work.

Patrons have an increasingly broad range of software skill levels, research questions, and technical issues, and the staff of the Science & Engineering division has been charged with the tailored support of the software, its technical troubleshooting, and the research support that surrounds the use of the software. To develop these new services, and to identify the levels of support the librarians could collectively expect to provide to patrons, staff members within the division undertook an informal skills assessment survey. Crucially, the survey was not tied to performance evaluations or job security; it was quite simply meant to assess the division's current understanding of and ability to use the various software programs in the Digital Science Center and to involve staff in the process of learning and skill development. New technologies and new library directions require new skills, and this approach engaged staff as active participants and stakeholders in their own professional development and engendered an inclusive, supportive framework for improvement.

The survey consisted of three basic questions about the 60+ software programs offered in the Digital Science Center: Do you know what it is used for? Do you have any expertise using it? Do you want to learn how to use it? Additionally, each staff member was asked to identify how he or she best learns.** A training plan was then generated based on several streams of data:

** Response options included tutorials (lecture plus hands-on); hands-on (e.g., doing); task-based (e.g., open-ended homework); figuring it out on your own; step-by-step instructions; handouts and reference materials; lecture (e.g., show-and-tell); and online videos.

the survey results collected via Google Forms, patron questions collected via Desk Tracker, software use collected via KeyServer, entry data collected via a Lenel entry system, center ownership of support responsibilities, and recommendations from the emerging technologies coordinator. Based on the survey results of how staff best learn, the most effective plan was determined to be a combination of brief presentations, homework assignments, and seminar style problem-solving activities using various software tools. This system continues to form the basis of the division's team-building approach to learning new skills as feedback about the skills assessment from staff encouraged the continued development of internal training opportunities. In addition to professional development related to software, the division has built a series of periodic internal staff trainings related to topics as varied as Google Apps, data and data management, and understanding code.

Staff were becoming more familiar with the resources available in the Digital Science Center, the methodologies of modern research, and the new technologies and workflows to aid in their work. Ultimately, the division settled upon a strategy wherein the base level of support all staff should be able to provide to patrons is built upon an understanding of what each software program is and does. This basic understanding about software has become their knowledgebase to be called upon as part of the general reference interview, alongside an understanding of traditionally available resources such as books, journals, and databases. When a patron requires support beyond a staff member's expertise, they are referred to the library's "software owner," a staff member who is usually an expert user and who is responsible for the configuration and maintenance of the software program in collaboration with IT staff. In rare cases where the software owner is not an expert or is not able to assist, patrons are referred to a partner affiliate—such as an expert professor—who has generously agreed to provide technical support.

Several staff left the division before a follow-up assessment could take place in order to collect longitudinal data, but in many cases, new staff have been hired because they have the skills that existing staff were being trained for. Several of the new professionals have advanced degrees in the disciplines the division works with, and they are able to effectively engage students, faculty, and staff in new ways given their content expertise.

The skills assessment was fundamentally about organizational change. Redeveloping skills enabled the division to address user technological needs, and the new services developed to support users have in turn led to a new openness towards trying new things, such as new software, and pivoting to stay current in support of patrons. Furthermore, the skills assessment enabled the division to identify gaps in the skills currently available to support patrons and craft job descriptions with the goal of hiring staff who already have valuable skills instead of relying solely on developing the skills internally with existing staff.

Filling Staff Vacancies

Between 2009 and 2013, five professional librarian positions were vacated. Staff vacancies were not always filled, and subject librarians often took on additional subject areas for collection development. During those years it became clear that science and engineering librarians at Columbia needed to improve their technical skills, expand their educational backgrounds, and increase their knowledge of the scientific research process. Previously, instruction and outreach programs had been limited to new student orientations and assisting faculty who needed to find articles and other material. To address the evolving roles librarians were being asked to fulfill, the division embarked on a dynamic reorganization that would facilitate providing services to patrons built upon the functional strengths of staff instead of primarily relying upon subject expertise. Library administrators were remarkably supportive of the incremental reconfiguration that involved developing new positions and reconfiguring existing positions.

One critical addition to the division was an emerging technologies coordinator, a staff member with a sophisticated technical background who was hired to plan for the implementation of the Digital Science Center in the new merged library. To create this position, a professional access services position was eliminated because that position's areas of responsibility were considerably reduced after the merger. The emerging technologies coordinator has steered the development of the Digital Science Center and has supported long-term staff in their migration to using more advanced technology. Notably, the emerging technologies coordinator does not have a library degree but does have a PhD in chemistry and teaching experience as well as extensive knowledge of Columbia and the research process. This expertise represented a much-needed expansion of the division's skills.

With the impending closure of the Engineering Library and an engineering librarian vacancy, a second new position evolved as a hybrid between traditional departmental librarianship and a consultative functional role within the division: research services coordinator. In addition to liaison and collections responsibilities to the School of Engineering and Applied Science and the Departments of Mathematics and Statistics, the research services coordinator assesses the services provided by the division, determines what the division can improve, and forecasts how the division can continue to evolve in the future. The coordinator has completed assessments that have analyzed current and future services to remote users, the roles of librarians in MOOCs, and what the libraries can do to better communicate with users. The staff member in this position has a master's degree in math and statistics along with a library degree.

Not all of the changes to the organizational structure of the division have resulted from new hires; existing staff have also been promoted into new functional roles built upon their strengths. By 2012, the geology and geosciences librarian had taken responsibility for the collections and liaison duties in biological sciences and psychology as a result of various professional staff vacancies. That position was subsequently reconfigured as a head of collection development, who now oversees the division's collections budgets; coordinates with selectors to make decisions about renewals, new purchases, and cancellations; and is responsible for assessing the use of collections provided by the division. Soon thereafter, the vacant biological science, physics, and astronomy librarian position was reconfigured to a two-year collections assessment librarian position that reports to the head of collection development. The collections assessment librarian assesses the relationship between the division's print and electronic collections and will guide the continued optimization of collections and resources.

The final staff vacancy, a chemistry librarian, has been repurposed as a digital science librarian. This librarian will provide additional technology support to researchers who are engaging with issues of data, computational methods, and research workflows. At the time of writing, the position has not yet been filled. Table 7.1 represents the net effect of the incremental reorganization from 2008 to 2014, and Figure 7.4 charts the organization of the Science & Engineering division in 2014 resulting from incremental rearrangement.

Table 7.1
Summary Reconfiguration of Staff Lines from 2008–2014

Subject-Based, 2008		Functional, 2014
Biology and Physics & Astronomy Librarian	→	Collection Assessment and Analysis Librarian
Math and Psychology Librarian	→	Operations and Undergraduate Coordinator
Geology & Geoscience Librarian	→	Head of Collection Development
Chemistry Librarian	→	Digital Science Librarian
Engineering Librarian	→	Research Services Coordinator
Head of Access	→	Emerging Technologies Coordinator
Director	→	Director

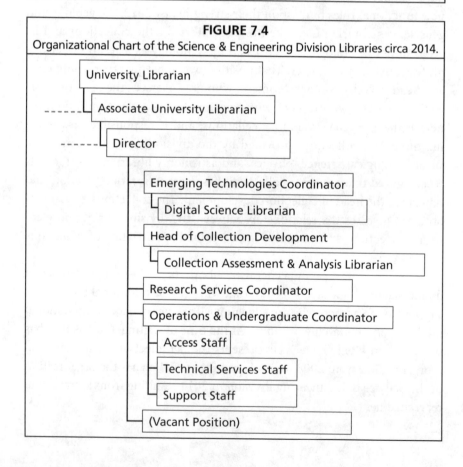

FIGURE 7.4
Organizational Chart of the Science & Engineering Division Libraries circa 2014.

Team Approach

Throughout the transition from discipline-oriented areas of expertise to skills- and strengths-oriented support, the librarians of the Science & Engineering division have consciously developed a team-oriented, service-focused approach to providing patrons with research and curricular support. The skills assessment enabled a culture of action built upon the division's various strengths and has empowered staff to overcome the restrictions of departmental liaison affiliations.

Some librarians are inherently more skilled—or are more interested—than other librarians in certain areas: instruction, reference, web content development, collection development. Traditionally, the librarian responsible for service to a department would also be responsible for each of these areas, regardless of that librarian's ability, in order to best communicate to that constituency. However, by identifying strengths and interests, the division staff members have been able to better collaborate with each other across traditional subject-specific boundaries. Furthermore, having local expertise in particular skills has facilitated the professional development of both the expert and the non-expert staff. By sharing knowledge, strategies, and experience, this team approach is improving the abilities of all staff members.

As research in the sciences becomes increasingly inter- and multidisciplinary, a team approach built upon functional strengths and diverse subject expertise is also improving the level of service the division can provide to patrons. All reference questions related to science and engineering, and even some that are not, are funneled through the head of collection development who acts as a point of triage. The question is either answered or passed on to the relevant member of the professional staff who has the necessary functional or subject expertise to answer the question. All reference staff are copied on responses in order to share knowledge amongst the group. This knowledgebase of answers is especially useful to staff when similar questions are asked in the future. Furthermore, delivering reference services as a team also provides coverage in case of absence.

The team approach has also impacted how the division carries out instruction and collection development. For example, to keep the attention of a large workshop or instruction session, several librarians will divide the presentation content into short segments to provide students with fresh perspectives. Rotating speakers can overcome fatigue on the part of the students and the librarians involved. Similarly, collection development responsibilities are shared among librarians who can best manage complex vendor relationships, and web content development is shared among librarians who have skills with web design, information architecture, and user experience design.

Supporting Undergraduates

As Columbia University is a research institution with very high research activity, library support for scientists and engineers is mostly focused on graduate student researchers, not on undergraduate science and engineering majors. Graduate students tend to have more complex research needs than undergraduates and are enrolled in much higher numbers, while undergraduates spend the majority of their time in lecture and laboratory courses. Additionally, Columbia University has a complex undergraduate landscape comprised of several schools and programs. For the Science & Engineering Libraries, the constituencies most impacted by the closure of the various libraries have been undergraduate students in Columbia College, general studies, continuing education, and the School of Engineering & Applied Sciences.

Undergraduate coursework in Columbia College is based around the core curriculum and includes a requirement for non-science majors to take three non-research based science courses. Students in these courses rarely come in contact with science librarians because of the decentralized undergraduate infrastructure in which students are not firmly associated with the culture of a department. This distance challenged the division because undergraduates predominantly occupy the consolidated library space.

Undergraduates needing research assistance in a particular subject are typically matched with the appropriate subject specialist librarian. Though one other library division includes a staff member dedicated to serving the undergraduate population, there had been no comprehensive undergraduate support plan for students working in the sciences. With the variety of undergraduate students working in the Science & Engineering Library every day, it was easy to recognize that students likely do not know who librarians are, what they do, or how librarians might help them.

The move away from the subject specialist model opened an opportunity to implement new methods of targeting undergraduates in a more active way as opposed to simply waiting for students' consultation requests or faculty members' instruction requests. In line with the move to functional roles within the division, an access supervisor with an MLIS was promoted to a professional librarian role dedicated to serving undergraduates. In addition to overseeing access issues and reserves, this librarian coordinates undergraduate orientations and instruction sessions in collaboration with the rest of the division.

The undergraduate coordinator regularly provides research consultations for undergraduates and teaches in-class library instruction for several sections of the university writing program, a one-semester course that all first-year undergraduates must complete. He also makes contact with incoming freshman at a variety of orientation week events before the start of the fall semester, and he connects with new transfer students at the start of the spring semester. These touch-points take various forms including tours, short introductory sessions about library services, and working the libraries' information table at meet-and-greet events.

An increasingly popular undergraduate major and concentration in sustainable development has built upon the successes of the undergraduate writing program to foster more substantial contact between undergraduates and science librarians. The rising number of undergraduates studying sustainable development has led to more requests for in-class instruction and follow-up consultations from students who regularly use the Science & Engineering Library. The ability to interact with students and build relationships during their first year has been invaluable; it is a marked contrast to hoping they get in touch later in their college experience when they have a research need.

Remaining Relevant without a Physical Space

The high undergraduate population in the Science & Engineering Library and the focus on outreach to graduate students has enabled the Science & Engineering division to think deeply about how to better support researchers who are not—or physically cannot be—present on campus. Planning is underway to develop services that better serve researchers in the field, faculty on sabbatical, and distance-learning students who are engaged in online courses. The division now frequently supports tools that enable researchers to leverage cloud-based resources to access the information they need, independent of their current location.

To provide services despite fewer available library spaces, the librarians in the Science & Engineering division are delivering instruction, materials, and consultative advice in new ways to students, faculty, and staff. The research services coordinator has identified several areas in which the division can better connect with remote users: recordings of workshop presentations, web-based instruction that includes formative assessment, and consultation via web VoIP services such as Skype and Google+. These areas represent iterative developments upon the services already provided to on-campus users, so the startup time and cost for each is remarkably low.

Several workshops throughout the past school year were recorded in collaboration with the Columbia Video Network, the distance education program in the Engineering School, and were made available on YouTube. Topics for these on-campus workshops were identified in conversation with the Engineering School and were chosen via a survey asking students' interests and needs. The workshops were aimed at filling the gaps left by departments in the professional training of engineering graduate students. PowerPoint presentations, handouts, and video recordings from orientations, workshops, and classroom instruction sessions were put online in a chronological list in order to deliver content asynchronously to students who could not attend the on-campus sessions.

The division will next implement some of the same topics in a more robust web-based format. The production team from the Columbia Video Network has agreed to record, edit, and host short web tutorials developed by librarians. An evolving set of meaningful distance instruction sessions will be created that include formative assessment to engage users throughout a series of videos. Interestingly, the best practices adopted for web pedagogy are in turn influencing the in-person sessions delivered by librarians.

In addition to providing remote access to workshops and instruction, the division's librarians will also offer web-based consultations to remote users (Cohen & Burkhardt, 2010; Steiner, 2011). Consultations to remote users can be offered with minimal additional costs using free web VoIP services such as Skype and Google+, and the cost of upgrading to reliable hardware (i.e., inexpensive webcams and microphones) has not been prohibitive. An existing online form was modified slightly to enable users to request consultations via videoconference. Future iterations of this service may include using enterprise screen-sharing tools such as WebEx.

It is especially important to promote web-based tools and resources to re-mote users. To spark interest in new tools, the division hosts contests through-out the semester using marketing grant money to pay for modest prizes. To date, contests have been held to encourage the use of 3D modeling software (http://3dprint.cul.columbia.edu/?page_id=1817), increase the division's so-cial media footprint, and gather images of the research that takes place in the departments served by the division (http://bit.ly/instagramScience). Web-based submission interfaces and social media platforms have enabled librari-ans to more effectively interact with students, faculty, and staff whether or not they are ever able to set foot into one of the division's library spaces.

As new needs arise and as new constraints are placed upon patrons, the Science & Engineering division will continue to evaluate new models of developing services and will iteratively evolve existing services.

Optimism for the Future

With the several libraries already closed and with the Geosciences Library slated to close in 2015, the Columbia University Libraries Science & Engi-neering division has established a framework that enables it to continue to meet the needs of researchers, stay relevant as the technological landscape continues to evolve, and adapt as new user needs arise. Merging four de-partmental libraries and closing others has caused rippled effects in the division's staffing configuration that have enabled the division to devise a functional approach to services layered atop the subject expertise already present in staff. As the skills necessary to support Columbia University stu-dents, faculty, and staff change, the division has recognized where it can train internally and where it may need to hire new staff to inject those skills into its repertoire. To sustain its momentum through pivots and iter-ations, the division candidly reviews its activities. Assessment with the goal of team building ensures continued delivery of relevant services that meet a wide range of patron needs in an ever-changing landscape of minimized library footprints and maximized library expectations.

The Science & Engineering division at Columbia University has main-tained an optimism about the future of library services despite closing five of its eight libraries, opening a new library, and planning for additional closures. Though these strategies apply whether or not libraries are clos-ing, argue that the opportunities presented by a closed library are real, are worthwhile, and should be taken advantage of as fully as possible.

References

Cohen, S. F., & Burkhardt, A. (2010). Even an ocean away: Developing Skype-based reference for students studying abroad. *Reference Services Review, 38*(2), 264–273. doi:10.1108/00907321011045025

Guarria, C. I., & Wang, Z. (2011). The economic crisis and its effect on libraries. *New Library World, 112*(5/6), 199–214. doi:10.1108/03074801111136248

Kaser, D. (2010). Proving your worth. *Information Today, 27*(6), 16.

Steiner, H. (2011). Bridging physical and virtual reference with virtual research consultations. *Reference Services Review, 39*(3), 439–450. doi:10.1108/00907321111161421

CHAPTER 8

A Tale of Three Libraries:
Lessons Learned from Three Branch Mergers at McGill University

Jill T. Boruff, Katherine Hanz, Sara Holder, Maya Kucij, Jessica Lange, and Amber Butler Lannon

MCGILL UNIVERSITY LIBRARY, located in Montreal, Quebec, is the fourth largest research library in Canada and is a member of the Association of Research Libraries. In 2010, it comprised 13 branches, 12 of which were located on its small downtown campus at the base of Mont Royal. That same year, the McGill Library welcomed a new Trenholme Dean of Libraries. Immediately the new dean saw the need for substantial renovations to the library's main branch, the Humanities and Social Sciences Library. This branch had not undergone any significant renovation in many years and was no longer meeting the needs of students. The dean also identified a pressing need for storage as most of the shelves throughout the library system were at capacity. With a flat or declining budget anticipated, some difficult decisions needed to be made.

Within a few weeks of the dean's arrival, a decision was made to merge the Howard Ross Library of Management into the adjacent Humanities and Social Sciences Library. This merger was completed by October 2010. In 2013 the university was faced with a significant budget cut midway through the budget year. Not only were operating funds cut, but also a voluntary retirement incentive program was announced that reduced the number of library staff by almost 30 FTE. In one library branch, three of the four library staff members retired. In order to restructure in the face of so many retirements and operate with the reduced funding, it became apparent that more branch mergers would be necessary. A consultation process was initiated to explore the potential closings of both the Education Library and Life Sciences Library (LSL). In September 2013, the Education Library was merged into the Humanities and Social Sciences Library, and the LSL was merged into the Schulich Library of Science and Engineering. This chapter will examine these three closings with an aim to uncover best practices. Despite taking place within the same system, the mergers unfolded in very different ways and were met with very different user reactions.

Challenges

Merging or closing libraries is a challenging task for librarians. Not only does it require careful organization and coordination, paramount to the process is developing buy-in from key users. Developing this buy-in is very difficult as user groups form an emotional attachment to their physical libraries, which remains even when they no longer use the physical facilities. For the librarians and administration leading these projects, a number of challenges arise: how to conduct proper consultation, how to develop buy-in from key individuals and groups, and how to manage the message throughout. Once all of this work has been done, there is still a need to carefully plan and execute the merger and manage the transitions for users and staff.

Education Library

Prior to the summer of 2013, the Education Library and Curriculum Resources Centre was one of 13 branches of the McGill Library. The library occupied the first floor of the Education Building and provided resources and services primarily to support teaching, learning, and research in the Faculty of Education, with a physical collection numbering over 100,000 volumes. The library's holdings included its main (general) collection as well as a children's and young adult literature collection and a curriculum resources collection. The library facilities included a study area with approximately 60 public computers, two group study rooms, and a smaller room containing the curriculum resources and children's and young adult literature collections. The loan of laptops and audio-visual equipment was also handled by the library, a service that had been previously administered by a unit within the Faculty of Education. The library was staffed by four library staff and three librarians, with one of the librarians serving as branch head.

The Education Library was completely renovated in the summer of 2007. In 2012 some minor refurbishments took place to add compact shelving and more seating. The 2012 renovations were jointly funded by the library and undergraduate and graduate student associations. In early April 2013, potential branch mergers were mentioned by library administration as a source of cost savings in the wake of severe reductions in funding from the provincial government. No specific branches were named at the meeting; however, shortly following the meeting, a communication plan about the merger of the Education Library with the Humanities and Social Sciences Library was drafted.

Unfortunately, this communication plan was derailed by a CBC News report that aired on April 12 (CBC News, 2013). The news report informed the McGill community of the forthcoming closure prior to any official announcement being made to library staff, faculty, and students. A link to the CBC News story was circulated widely amongst the Faculty of Education community, and unsurprisingly, many in the community reacted negatively to the news of the potential closure while also protesting the lack of official communication from the dean of libraries and the dean of education. The following week, the dean of libraries met with the librarians and support staff at the Education Library to officially inform them of the decision to close the branch.

Education undergraduate and graduate students started a Facebook page (Save the McGill Education, 2013) to communicate frustration with the library's decision and to publicize other "Save the Education Library" events and initiatives, including a "Study in Solidarity" event, an online petition, and a student-organized town hall. Students used the page to write about their experiences with the Education Library and to voice their concerns about the closure. Education students created a video that highlighted their perspective on the unique nature of the Education Library and its collections, and a group from the Faculty of Education communicated its displeasure in a letter to the university provost that included a signed petition requesting a stop to the merger. Additionally, two faculty members wrote an opinion piece against the merger (Low & Winer, 2013) that was published in the *Montreal Gazette*.

In May 2013, in reaction to the community's negative response, library administration worked with the dean of education to find a means of communication that would address the community's concerns. A consultation plan was put in place that would include a town hall at the end of the month and consultations carried out in each department. The Education Library Advisory Committee (ELAC), a standing committee established by the Faculty of Education's constitution, was asked to examine the issues, gather feedback from constituents, and communicate recommended changes. ELAC was headed by the dean of education and consisted of representatives from the four education departments—integrated studies in education, kinesiology and physical education, educational and counseling psychology, and information studies (which was at that time, a part of the Faculty of Education); representatives from the undergraduate and graduate student associations; and the head of the Education Library.

Two sub-working groups—Curriculum Working Group and AV & Digital Working Group—were formed within ELAC in early June to address the faculty's specific concerns about the potential removal of curriculum materials and audio-visual equipment from the Education Library.

Following two open-forum discussions and departmental consultations, ELAC drafted a report focusing on three aspects of library resources and services deemed particularly important to the academic activities of the Faculty of Education: (1) physical space and space use, (2) collections and resources, and (3) library and information services. The report made a number of recommendations to the library administration:

1. Physical space and space use: No furniture or equipment should be removed, and any space freed up from the removal of the collection should be made available to the faculty for future teaching and learning and should be accessible throughout the day and evening to benefit students taking classes.

2. Collections and resources: Certain materials should remain accessible in the Education Building, including the teacher preparation curriculum collection and related audio-visual material, the professional book collections, the children's book collection, and course reserve items.

3. Library and information services: Access to academic librarians for research and teaching-related activities should continue to be available in the Education Building and consideration should be given for flexible work time scheduling of staff to better serve the graduate student population.

In July 2013, the dean of libraries and dean of education responded to the ELAC recommendations in a letter to the Faculty of Education. They confirmed the following:

1. Physical space and space use: The majority of the space previously housing the Education Library would fall under the jurisdiction and care of the Faculty of Education, and the library would donate all computers and furniture currently in the public areas.

2. Collections and resources: The curriculum resources collection (including the children's and YA literature collection) and the reserve materials for Faculty of Education courses would remain in their current space in the Education Building (to be renamed the "Curriculum Resources Centre") along with essential volumes associated with particular teaching needs (as per the recommendations of the Curriculum Working Group). The main collection, journals, and theses would to be moved to the second floor of the Humanities and Social Sciences Library.

3. Library and information services: The Curriculum Resources Centre would be staffed by a library assistant Monday through Friday, 9:00 a.m. to 5:00 p.m. The education librarians would be based at the Humanities and Social Sciences Library but would maintain regular office hours in the Education Building and continue to provide the same services, including individual consultations, research, and teaching support.

As requested, it was also confirmed that there would be a reassessment in 12–18 months to determine if the implementation of these changes met the needs of students and faculty.

Several challenges came into play during the time around the merger. The biggest challenge was the library's loss of control over the message about the merger when the CBC report came out. The report influenced how the community reacted and its confidence in the genuineness of the consultation process. Another challenge was the lack of agility and timely response to community concerns. Additionally, the dean of education left

McGill to take a position at another university shortly before the report was released. Her exit from the faculty around the time the report was being drafted slowed the release of the report to the community. The timing of the consultations was another challenge as many students had already departed campus by the time the process was implemented.

On the McGill campus, as on many other campuses, space is at a premium. The space opened up by the departure of the main stacks in the Education Library has provided potential opportunities for the addition of teaching and research labs as well as the continued use of the space for student study. Though planning is still in process for the redesign of the former Education Library space, students gather there daily to study, do group work, use the computers, and access the Curriculum Resources Centre collections and course reserves. Librarians are available for office hours almost daily, and continue to teach course-integrated workshops in all of the Faculty of Education departments.

Life Sciences Library

The McGill LSL was founded in 1823 as the library of the Montreal Medical Institution, which became the McGill medical college in 1829. At the time of its merger, the LSL was located on two floors of the McIntyre Medical Sciences Building, which served as the hub for students and faculty in medicine, dentistry, nursing, occupational and physical therapy, biological sciences, and other health sciences disciplines, all of whom had courses in the same and neighbouring buildings. The team of seven librarians was strongly connected to faculty and students, leading to embedded information literacy workshops, one-on-one research consultations, and involvement in curriculum reform, among other activities. The librarians continued to increase their involvement in a growing number of programs.

In April of 2013, the dean of libraries called a meeting of the LSL librarians and support staff, during which she informed them that the LSL would be merging with the Schulich Library of Science and Engineering due to budgetary concerns. Though questions were asked about how much money it would save, why LSL was chosen from among the branches, and how exactly the merger would take place, no further information was given at the time. All of those present at the meeting were told not to share this information with anyone.

That afternoon the information was leaked anonymously to the students and faculty. A Facebook page (Save the McGill Life Sciences, 2013) was created and quickly gained many followers. Over the course of the next few days, many students and faculty called for a consultation process to discuss the closure and propose other solutions. As a result, a process was created by the library administration in which two representatives, one from medicine and one from the library, were appointed to consult the faculty, students, and library staff and write a report with their recommendations. As part of the process, there were two town hall meetings, one for students and one for faculty. The meetings took place at the end of the semester when much of the campus community had already left for the summer, making it difficult to get the word out to the interested parties, and many students and faculty were surprised to learn about the merger long after the fact.

After the town hall meetings, the two representatives met with the library staff. The librarians and the support staff presented several possible scenarios for the future of the library, the most highly recommended being one in which the monograph collection would be downsized to keep only core and highly used titles, the journal collection moved to storage to free up floor space, the newly vacated space used to create classrooms to be shared by the library and the Faculty of Medicine, and the librarians would keep their current office space.

At the end of May 2013, the representatives' report was presented to the library staff in a meeting called by the dean of libraries. The report recommended that the high use journals and monographs be moved into the Schulich Library and the low use journals and monographs be moved into storage. The librarians' offices would move to the Schulich Library and all but one of the library assistants would also be moved to the Schulich Library. The reserve collection would remain in the LSL space, and one library assistant would staff the reserves desk. The librarians would continue to maintain a reference service in this space. The space would keep the name "LSL" but control of the floor would revert back to the Faculty of Medicine (which controls the rest of the medical sciences building where the library is located). The new configuration would be in place by September 1, 2013.

The library's associate director for planning and resources organized the merger in consultation with the associate director for client services

and the head of the LSL. During the planning stages, the head of LSL re-
signed, leaving no one to manage the day-to-day operations of the move at
LSL. A coordinator was selected from among the librarians to continue in
this role. Even with this position filled, project management was difficult as
there were a complex array of tasks to be completed in a small amount of
time with many different parties involved, but no single person had ownership of the project.

One of the main tasks that the librarians had to undertake was preparing the collection for the move. Journals and monographs had always
been shelved separately at LSL so they were treated as two different entities. Librarians selected a list of print journals that had the highest use for
relocation to the Schulich Library. To make these selections, they used the
following criteria: titles in high use because electronic access was not available or electronic runs were incomplete or unreliable, Canadian titles, core
titles such as *JAMA* or *Nature*, and titles that library was still receiving in
print. Journals titles that did not meet the criteria for relocation to Schulich
were sent to on-site storage.

Monograph titles that had not circulated in 10 years were chosen for
removal to on-site storage. A list of titles that met this criterion was generated by collection services, and staff from all branches came to help mark
the books to be removed. Each "tipper" was provided with a list of books
to turn spine-side up; these books were then packed and transferred to
the storage location by a moving company. This phase of the merger was
particularly challenging to organize as it required over 300-person hours
to complete and involved massive coordination of staff.

In addition to preparing the print materials for removal, 40 years of
accumulated papers, old office supplies, and other discarded items had to
be cleared from the staff and storage areas of the library. This was a mon-
umental task that was not factored into the planning of the timeline. This
work was done by librarians and library assistants whenever they had a
free moment and thus ended up being one of the last tasks to be completed. Physical removal of furniture and the staff's personal effects had to be
coordinated with moving the staff to their new office space. Modular furniture and cubicles had to be deconstructed and then reconstructed in the
new space, leaving the staff without desks for a few days.

The integration of materials into the Schulich Library had its own coordinator, though she also worked with the LSL coordinator to answer any

questions. Though the LSL journals continued to be a separate collection in Schulich, the integration process was complicated by issues resulting from incomplete journal lists from collection services. Some journals went into storage that should have been kept in Schulich and vice versa, and incomplete space was allotted for subscriptions still being received in print. As a result, the journal collection had to be shifted several times. For the LSL monographs to fit into Schulich, the entire Schulich collection had to be rearranged. Most of the LSL books are classified in NLM (National Library of Medicine), and as such, needed to be shelved at the end of the Schulich collection (classified in Library of Congress [LC]). However, the LSL collection also includes biology materials, which are classified in LC, meaning that space had to be made for these books. (A detailed description of the Schulich Library project can be found in Badia, Chapter 11.)

Staff and librarians started in their new location on the first day of the academic year, a typically busy time that was made more difficult by delays in phone and electricity work in their new office space. It was challenging to learn how to manage a new configuration of two locations as the librarians provide on-call reference in both locations and they have to be extra clear when arranging to meet with students to avoid someone being at the wrong location. It is also a challenge for the librarians to remain connected to the students and faculty they serve as they are no longer in the midst of the daily comings and goings of these users. The new location has provided the LSL librarians with the opportunity to work more closely with their colleagues in the Schulich Library, and new collaborations have formed from this proximity.

User reaction has been mixed. Some faculty and students have commented that they miss having the library and the librarians so close to their offices and classrooms. Other faculty and students may actually be better served by the new location as it is closer to their workspaces. Still others do not perceive any difference as they mainly use the library remotely or make individual appointments with librarians. The user experience of the merged libraries will continue to evolve as the librarians and the users adapt to the change.

Howard Ross Library of Management

The Howard Ross Library of Management was a small branch serving the Desautels Faculty of Management as well as the management programs associated with the School of Continuing Studies. Embedded in the Faculty of Management complex, the library operated primarily to serve the 4500 full- and part-time students and 120 faculty and lecturers affiliated with the faculty. At the time of its closure in 2010, it had on staff one head librarian, two liaison librarians, one manager, and four library assistants and was open approximately 75 hours a week, including weekends. Despite being relatively small, the library was visited almost 250,000 times per year. Beyond the typical collection of books, journals, etc., the library also housed three specialized resources not available elsewhere on campus: Bloomberg, Datastream, and Morningstar.

There had been plans to completely renovate the library for several years prior to the merger. Minor refurbishments had been undertaken previously in 2007 and 2008 which included painting, new furniture, carpet, and an updated service desk. However, as the Faculty of Management began renovating spaces throughout its building, the library space stood out as dated and in need of more significant attention. A joint project between the library and the faculty began in 2010 to fully renovate the space. This process began with the development of a joint vision document and meetings with the University Planning Office. As questions about resources were finalized (both the faculty and the library would contribute funds), an architect was selected, and decisions about floor plans and designs were finalized.

It was eventually determined that the renovations would require that the library (as well as other non-library spaces on the second floor) be closed for eight months. Library materials were moved in December 2009 to the nearby Humanities and Social Sciences Library in anticipation of the renovations beginning in January 2010. The library staff were also relocated to the Humanities and Social Sciences Library at this time. The library would maintain a small temporary service point within the Desautels Faculty of Management for the duration of the renovation. This space would include high-use items such as course texts, DVDs, and Bloomberg, Morningstar, and Datastream terminals as well as the most popular journals and newspapers. This space would include a small lending area staffed by one library assistant as well as an information desk that would be staffed by a management librarian.

By February 2010, the former library had been completely demolished. Work on the new floor was to begin in March with an expected September reopening. This short completion schedule was possible as the new library design had very few walls. At approximately the same time, the university announced that there would be budget reductions in the coming fiscal year and a new dean of libraries began her term. After a meeting between the new dean of libraries and the dean of management on the new project, a decision was made not to rebuild the library. Rather the floor would be developed primarily into student space. There were several reasons that this became an attractive option for both the faculty and the library. These included

- the growth of the Faculty of Management and its need for additional space,
- budgetary concerns,
- increasing availability of library resources online, and
- the Faculty of Management's proximity to the Humanities and Social Sciences Library (located across the street).

Although it was decided that the management library would not reopen after the renovations, the temporary library service point was maintained throughout the remainder of the term and that summer.

Even though the decision to close the library was made in February 2010, an announcement to students and faculty did not occur for several months as the library and the Faculty of Management worked closely to address anticipated concerns. To determine what these concerns might be, an associate dean of the faculty and the head librarian met immediately with key faculty and student leadership. From these meetings it was determined that some aspects of the library's services would need to remain within the management building. These included a librarian office (to be staffed as the librarians' schedules permitted) and course reserves.

Also from these meetings, a list of FAQ was developed and a number of operational decisions were made. When the announcement was eventually made, this key information was included in the communications.

Reaction to the eventual announcement was tempered by the fact that it occurred at the end of term when many students and faculty were engrossed in year-end activities and that the library space had already been demolished. It became clear in the fall that many had missed the announcement entirely. In the fall, the university was also experiencing a staff strike and the news of the library closing was overshadowed by this campus-wide disruption.

By the time the majority of students realized that there would no longer be a library in the complex, the new space had debuted. This new space maintained many of its former library attributes that were important to students: quiet study space, group study rooms, and computers. A librarian office was also set up in the space. A combination of all these factors (delayed announcement, space closed during renovations, new space included library attributes) meant student reaction to the closure was minor.

Among faculty the reaction was mixed. For some who only used online resources and librarian services via email, the decision to consolidate library services in the main library less than 100m away made a great deal of sense. There were also faculty who were concerned. Some felt it reflected badly on the Faculty of Management not to have a dedicated library. Additionally, some faculty members expressed concerns about students' research skills and abilities suffering without a library presence in the building. Occasionally, faculty displeasure with the closure of the management library is still mentioned at faculty meetings and in conversation with the management librarian. It continues to show up in comments submitted through the annual LibQUAL survey. Despite concerns, there were no Facebook campaigns or demonstrations, and the consolidation was completed very peacefully.

For additional discussion of the Howard Ross Library of Management including measurements of circulation, instruction, and service quality statistics before and after the closure, see Lange, Lannon, and McKinnon (2014).

Analysis

All three of the branch mergers at McGill Library took place on the same campus within a relatively short time frame and with the same senior management team; however, the process unfolded in very different ways and were met with very different reactions. On one hand, all three mergers could be considered successful in that they were all completed. However, of the three mergers, the closure of the management library was met with far less negative reaction. It is possible that this difference could be attributed to the variances between the faculties involved. For example, one could conclude that professors and students in the Faculty of Management at McGill were less attached to their physical library than professors and students in the Faculty of Education or the departments served by the LSL.

Also the Faculty of Management building is much closer to its new library than is the case for the Faculty of Education and many of the departments served by the LSL, making the move less inconvenient. Though these may or may not have been factors, there were some important distinctions in the processes of the three mergers that likely contributed to the difference in user reaction and that can be learned from.

In the case of the closure of the management library, the head librarian and an associate dean from the Faculty of Management met individually with professors in advance of the closure announcement. In these meetings, they sought input on the closure process and on how best to mitigate any issues that would arise from it. From this they were able to develop a clear and easily understood message that was later rolled out to the wider audience. In the same way, the dean of libraries and the head librarian met with student leadership as well as library staff. These meetings gave a voice in the process to key people who otherwise might have become adversaries. In these meetings (where appropriate) emotions were addressed, and there was openness and honesty about the problems and feelings that would likely arise as a result of the merger. Wherever possible, the suggestions that were put forward were acted upon. Also, the merger was rolled out over a very long period of time. Additionally, the Faculty of Management had a very clear plan for the space that was vacated (student study space and group rooms), which was communicated broadly.

In the case of the Education Library and LSL mergers, almost the reverse occurred. An announcement was made that the libraries were being considered for closure, after which a consultation phase was initiated. In between the announcement and the consultation, there was both time and opportunity for adversaries of the change to control the message. Also, since these mergers were largely necessitated by staff retirements and budget cuts that had to be addressed within a relatively short time frame, the library was not able to allow the process to develop over the span of time that would have smoothed the transition.

Conclusion

Based on these variances, some best practices emerge for library mergers and closures in an academic context:

- Identify they key people affected by the change and get their input first. Doing this may prevent them from becoming adversaries.

- Have a plan in place for the vacated space. In cases where another unit will be taking control of the space, make every effort possible to ensure that a space plan exists before the merger or closure is announced.
- Drive the messages and the information—the communication must be clear and easily understood.
- Be honest about the problems and issues that necessitated the action.

Negative reaction to a library merger or closure can be oddly gratifying because it feels like a validation of the value that users' place on libraries and their services. Though this may be true to some extent, the long-term effect is often a user base that feels that the library does not have its best interests at heart. It is possible, however, to reduce negative reaction to a minimum. If this is accomplished, closing or merging an academic library can be, and be seen as, beneficial to both the library and the user community it serves.

References

CBC News. (2013, April 12). McGill may close 2 libraries in face of budget cuts. Retrieved from http://www.cbc.ca/news/canada/montreal/mcgill-may-close-2-libraries-in-face-of-budget-cuts-1.1390500

Lange, J., Lannon, A., & McKinnon, D. (2014). The measureable effects of closing a branch library: Circulation, instruction, and service perception. *Portal: Libraries and the Academy 14*(4), 633–651.

Low, B., & Winer, L. (2013, May 6). McGill's Education Library plays an essential role [Opinion]. *Montreal Gazette*. Retrieved from http://www.montreal-gazette.com/news/Opinion+McGill+Education+Library+plays+essen-tial+role/8349870/story.html

Save the McGill Education Library from Closure. (ca. 2013). In *Facebook* [Group page]. Retrieved October 15, 2014, from https://www.facebook.com/Save-McgillEducationLibraryFromClosure

Save the McGill Life Sciences Library from Closure. (ca. 2013). In *Facebook* [Group page]. Retrieved March 9, 2014, from https://www.facebook.com/savelifesciences

CHAPTER 9

One Hundred Years of History:
Closing and Consolidating the Scripps Institution of Oceanography Library

Amy Butros

THE SCRIPPS INSTITUTION of Oceanography (SIO) was founded in 1903, with the founding scientist's personal collection of books serving as the institution's library. In 1913 the first SIO librarian was hired, nearly 50 years before the campus of the University of California, San Diego, was established (Brueggeman, 2013). After 100 years of serving the SIO, the UC San Diego community, and oceanographers worldwide, the SIO Library closed its doors on June 29, 2012 with collections and staff consolidated into the UC San Diego's Geisel Library.

In 1960 the campus of the UC San Diego was founded, and at that time the SIO became a department of UC San Diego with noted oceanographic scientists and former Scripps directors, such as Roger Revelle, contributing to the founding of the campus. To help understand the complexity and impact of the Scripps Library closure, an understanding of the institution's size and reputation and its variety of programs and research areas is needed. A succinct description of the SIO appears on its website:

Scripps Institution of Oceanography is one of the oldest, largest, and most important centers for ocean, earth, and atmospheric science research, education, and public service in the world. Research at Scripps encompasses physical, chemical, biological, geological, and geophysical studies of the oceans, Earth, and planets. Scripps undergraduate and graduate programs provide transformative educational and research opportunities in ocean, earth, and atmospheric sciences as well as degrees in climate science and policy and marine biodiversity and conservation. (Scripps, 2014a)

The Scripps community consists of 415 professors, researchers, postdoctoral students, and other academics; 235 graduate students; and 822 staff members—a specialized community of over 1,470 people, not counting the approximately 630 volunteers and over 170 undergraduate students (Scripps, 2014b).

This chapter focuses on new library services and processes put in place after the closing of this important library.

Background

The Scripps campus, located approximately one mile west of the main UC San Diego campus, is fairly large with departments housed in over 20 buildings, spread out all around a hilly coastal area. The Scripps Library was located in the center of the approximately one square-mile of Scripps buildings. I had been the assistant director and instruction and outreach librarian of the SIO Library for nine years when the decision to close the library was announced. During my years working in the Scripps Library, the main goal of my outreach work was to connect with the Scripps community and be recognized as the person to contact for any library or informational needs. To accomplish this, I followed an outreach plan that included cold calling all current academics (faculty and researchers) and incentivizing graduate students to attend consultations with me for tailored one-on-one instruction sessions. In a typical year, the outreach program generated contact and meetings with 30–65% of Scripps academics and 50–80% of the incoming graduate students (percentages varied from year to year depending on incentives and frequency of emailed reminders). To augment and solidify contacts made from outreach, I attended many scientific seminars, departmental meetings, and presentations, and I participated in projects with faculty and the graduate program at the SIO. The end result was that librarian support was regarded as an essential service and one that would need to be maintained.

News of the planned library closure was met with disbelief and outrage from the Scripps community, and the various emotional responses persisted for months. A group of graduate students and faculty circulated a petition (Appendix 9A) in opposition to the Scripps Library closure soon after the first closure announcement. The petition garnered over 700 signatures. In addition, the Scripps graduate students' committee conducted a survey of all Scripps graduate students, faculty, staff, and alumni to ask them about which library services they valued most. The petition and survey were completed without the library's involvement, and the results were sent to the UC San Diego chancellor, director of Scripps, the university librarian, and two vice chancellors.

The user needs highlighted in the petition and the survey's responses (Figure 9.1), together with feedback from meetings between the university librarian and Scripps faculty and library administrators and Scripps managers, helped shape the resulting library service models that I proposed for the Scripps community.

Planning for the Scripps Library Closure and Consolidation

The announcement about branch library closures was disseminated to the UC San Diego campus in May 2011 in an email sent from the Office of the University Librarian to all academics, staff, and students, noting that the planned closure of the SIO Library would happen later in the 2011–2012 academic year after the closures of two other branch libraries. The main reason given for the closures was "recent and anticipated budget cuts," which were reported in local and national publications (Hayden, 2011).

Having several months lead time for the closure of the Scripps Library and the consolidation of the collections and services to the Scripps community served two purposes: Preparing library staff for the changes and alerting the Scripps community of the eventual closure of the library on its campus. In the months following the announcements, the Scripps Library

FIGURE 9.1
Scripps Graduate Students' Committee's Survey Results

SIO Student Response from Student Led Survey

- 66% of Graduate Students participated in the survey.
- The pie chart below represents a summary of the answers to the following question: *"We're going to have to make sacrifices, but we want to know what you value about the library so that we know what to push for and have data to back-up our claims when we talk with the UCSD administration. What services do you value most from the SIO Library? (Please choose only your top five and give them a ranking from 1–5)"*
- The services valued for the majority of the students that participated are:
  — Hard Copy Scientific Texts
  — Study Space
  — Knowledgeable Research Assistance

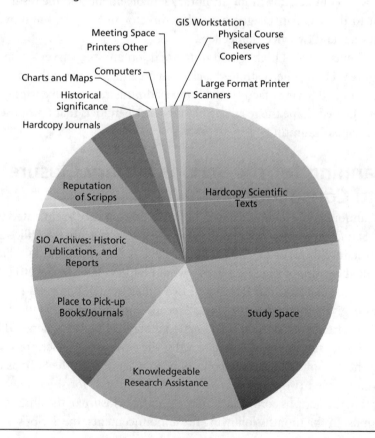

Committee had more frequent meetings with the Scripps Library director and assistant director to discuss the upcoming library closure and plans for services to Scripps after the closure and consolidation.

The Scripps Library Committee had been in existence for over 30 years and was created and run by the SIO Staff Council, with members appointed annually following the submission of interest forms and the chair selected by the SIO Director following recommendations from the SIO Staff Council and SIO Committee on Committees. The library committee is made up of 7–10 faculty members and includes representatives from the Scripps graduate office, a graduate student, and an ex-officio member from the library (formerly the Scripps Library director or assistant director and now the Scripps liaison librarian).. The Scripps Library Committee had many meetings leading up to the closure, mainly to discuss changes in service relating to borrowing policies and due dates; graduate course reserves processes and location; interlibrary loan; and collection issues such as the fate of the world famous oceanographic charts collection, terrestrial charts, atlases, special collections and archives, monographs, print journals, dissertations, etc. These discussions led to detailed recommendations on services and collections. My service proposals and collection disposition decisions were based on the responses from the university librarian to these recommendations, and the results of the meetings between the university librarian and director of SIO. In addition to meetings with the Scripps Library Committee and the Scripps graduate program manager, I had frequent meetings with other stakeholders including the associate university librarians (AULs) for user services, collections and technical services, and administrative services, and the managers and coordinators of impacted areas, such as facilities, collections, and access services.

I was appointed as the Scripps Library closure project coordinator at the end of January 2012. As project coordinator, one of my first tasks was to post and keep up to date a shared spreadsheet of all closure tasks. This spreadsheet detailed all aspects of the closure and consolidation, so library staff could view the progress notes and keep themselves informed. The Scripps director and university librarian jointly sent out a message (Appendix 9B) to the Scripps community detailing the plans for the library consolidation with a tentative timeline for the next steps that had been drafted, negotiated, and accepted by the university librarian, AULs, and the Scripps director. This message was sent out on February 6, 2012 and the timeline covered June 2012 through 2014.

Envisioning New Services after Library Closure and Consolidation

After I learned about the content of the Scripps community petition and survey, I planned meetings with the graduate program manager and library managers in impacted areas (access services for circulation, reserves, and interlibrary loan and facilities for collections moves and paging). Several meetings and messages over the course of four months resulted in detailed proposals for the three main service areas that were of concern for the Scripps Library Committee and the Scripps community in general: (1) collection access (local collection paging and delivery), (2) interlibrary loan (delivery of requested items), and (3) graduate course reserves. These areas were of major concern because the library closure meant that there was no convenient and close service point for the Scripps community as the Geisel Library, over a mile east of the Scripps campus, was the planned location for the collection move. In addition, the remaining four Scripps Library public services staff members were relocated to the Geisel Library and were not available to help monitor various service and collection issues in the closed library because they were tasked with other duties due to staffing shortages that had resulted from hiring freezes and retirements. There was a campus shuttle in place, but faculty and graduate students voiced concerns over use of the shuttle and the inconvenience of having services and collections (in particular print course reserves) in a remote location from their classes, research labs, and offices. To address these concerns, I drafted proposals for new processes for all of these services and met with the Scripps and library stakeholders to revise and refine the proposals to address all of their needs. The resulting three proposals, with some minor changes, have been in place for over two years and have worked well, with very few complaints for most of the people concerned.

The first proposal covered the process for enabling online requests of print material (any circulating item from the library's collection) and daily delivery of the material by library van to a designated room in the Scripps building staffed by graduate program staff. Developing this proposal was time-consuming and required multiple meetings with the Scripps Library's public services manager and with the main library's access services managers. It became clear early on that the book request and paging process could be complex, depending on the type of material patron was requesting (e.g., book, dissertation, print journal volume, atlas, map, etc.) and where the material was housed at the time (the closed library building, Geisel Library, remote storage facility, or in transition and undergoing re-cataloging or processing). A flowchart was drafted to help library staff visualize the steps involved (Figure 9.2).

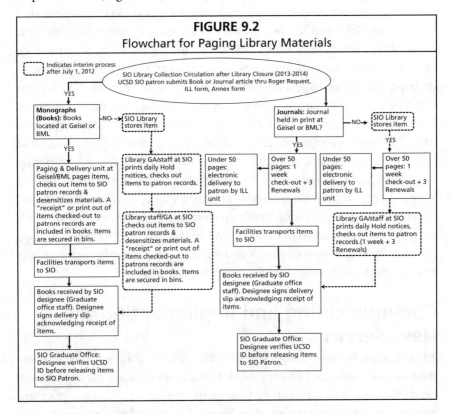

FIGURE 9.2
Flowchart for Paging Library Materials

For the protection of patrons and library material, a waiver form was created (Appendix 9C) with advice from the library's legal council. Requesting patrons must agree to the terms on the waiver before items are checked out to them and delivered to the Scripps location.

Creation of a separate proposal for interlibrary loan was necessary due to the library's obligation to lending libraries to keep their material safe. I worked with the Scripps director for capital planning and space management to select securable bookshelves for this purpose. These secure cabinets were also used for the print reserve material that was requested by teaching faculty at Scripps for their graduate courses. Course reserves for Scripps graduate students were retained on the Scripps campus with the support of graduate program staff. Course reserves for any undergraduate class taught by Scripps academics would be housed in the Geisel Library or Biomedical Library buildings.

The final processes that were put in place for library materials, interlibrary loan, and course reserves required the Scripps graduate program staff to check people's identification cards before releasing the items to them, send email notices when items were delivered by the library to the Scripps office location, and receive returned items in preparation for the library van's pickup trips. Scripps managers offered a classroom in the historic Old Scripps Building to serve as the graduate course reserves and book pickup location. During the spring of 2012, the classroom was converted into a group study room that houses conference tables, chairs, three securable glass front book cabinets, two workstations supplied by the campus's Academic Computing and Media Services, and a large format printer that had been housed in the Scripps Library for creating and printing posters for conferences. This shared effort in planning, furnishing, and brainstorming processes for staff was very successful and helped respond to several of the main concerns the Scripps community voiced in its petition and survey: access to collections, course reserves, and a gathering place for graduate students.

Communicating and Implementing the New Services

After drafting the proposals, I shared them with the library and Scripps Institution stakeholders, key personnel in access services and its department head, reserves and interlibrary loan departments, the Scripps graduate program manager, and the assistant director for capital planning and space management. I collected feedback from these stakeholders, revised the proposals accordingly, and sent the revised version of all proposals to the AUL for User Services for approval to proceed with announcing and implementing these new services. The approved proposals were implemented in time for the Scripps Library closure, Friday, June 29, 2012 and put into action the following Monday, July 2, 2012.

To help with the emotional responses still being received from the Scripps community, and to respond to questions about future services and access to resources, I sent invitations to an open house for the last afternoon that the Scripps Library was open; many faculty, staff, and students dropped by for refreshments and souvenirs (Scripps Library promotional pens, mugs, posters, etc.). They also shared their favorite library stories and, more importantly, asked about what would be happening next. I was able to personally explain the new services, how to access resources, and how to schedule my services of reference and research assistance and instruction. I was also able to use an office in the closed library space on the first floor for a brief period of time as Scripps contractors renovated and converted the first floor's north side to office space. During this time, I oversaw some collection details, mainly the weeding of the reference collection; responded to Scripps community needs; and prepared for the move to my new office in the Scripps Administration Building.

Office space is at a premium on the UC San Diego campus, especially at Scripps. For a non-Scripps employee such as me, being given office space on the Scripps campus demonstrated my work's value to the Scripps community and to library management. When I moved into my new office, I sent the Scripps community a message about my new location with reminders about the new library services and access to the collection and an invitation to drop by with any questions they might have. I was able to adapt and evolve my reference and instruction services from library based to remote location based, creating a new role as an embedded (Kvenild & Calkins, 2011) or integrated librarian, holding reference office hours and one-on-one consultations in my office and instructing groups in departmental conference rooms.

Collection Consolidation Decisions

It took over a year to move the large Scripps Library monograph and serial collections from the closed library to the Geisel Library. At that time the Scripps collections were over 210,000 volumes, 700 print serial subscriptions, and around 400 media and CD titles. The new compact shelving in the lower level of the Geisel Library needed to be completed and other collections shifted before most of the Scripps Library collection consolidation commenced.

The third floor of the former Scripps Library building remains part of the UC San Diego Library, housing the large Scripps archives collection and special collections material important to the Scripps community (e.g., rare books, rare serials, and expedition reports). Access and use of these collections is by appointment only and managed by the library's Special Collections & Archives program.

A major project that took over four months to complete was moving the huge bathymetric chart collection and weeding and transporting the large terrestrial map collection. Following input from stakeholders, several meetings with the Scripps Library Committee, and considerable work from the map librarian and the government documents librarian, the terrestrial map collection (geographic, geologic, and topographic maps) was moved to the Geisel Library, and the bathymetric and ocean charts collection was left on the first floor of the former Scripps Library due to the number and weight of the charts' cases and to provide easier access for Scripps community. Over 100 chart cabinets (totaling around 350 full map drawers) with over 35,000 charts were moved from the north side of the first floor and secured in the southeast side, with access by appointment. The resulting model of having terrestrial maps located in the Geisel Library and ocean charts in the former Scripps Library's first floor has been working well for all parties involved.

The second collection project involved the weeding and moving of the Scripps Library reference collection, which encompassed over 1,300 monographic titles. Since the collection would be remote to its primary users, titles from the collection that would be of interest to Scripps faculty, researchers, or graduate students were moved to the circulating collection to allow for online request and delivery. Four hundred and forty-seven titles were moved and consolidated into the Science & Engineering Library's reference collection located in the Geisel Library, and then after a year, the titles were consolidated into the general reference collection when the Science & Engineering Library closed in June 2013. In addition, many print reference titles, mainly encyclopedias and handbooks, were not retained in reference when the electronic versions were purchased, which further accommodated the needs of the remote clientele.

After the Closing of the Scripps Library Doors

I experienced a large influx of virtual reference questions after the Scripps Library closed its doors. Most of these questions were about locating and requesting books, and some were more complex research questions or concerns about library closure. A number of questions were referred to me from other reference providers because they were oceanographic-related topics (marine sciences, geosciences, or atmospheric sciences) or came from Scripps patrons. These queries were usually received through the library's ask-a-librarian (QuestionPoint) service but also came by phone and in person as a result of the signage placed on the closed library doors directing people to the Geisel Library's phone number and website. The number and frequency of these questions declined with time, particularly when the collection moved from the closed building to the Geisel Library's compact shelving area and when it was eventually integrated and consolidated with the Geisel's collections. In addition to signage around the former Scripps Library building, I frequently updated the Scripps Library website, prominently displaying the closure information, detailing the collection consolidation, and explaining procedures for locating and requesting material, including links to an online catalog guide and the necessary patron waiver form.

My new Scripps office was adjacent to the graduate program's offices and the room designated for book pickup and course reserves, so I could drop by frequently and check how the new services were working for Scripps patrons and staff (mainly the staff member hired to work in that room). Services, such as book delivery time, were adjusted and revised depending on feedback received. I routinely communicated any changes to services or collection locations to the Scripps community via email. Preservation, digitization, and weeding projects to protect and streamline the collection, such as sending to remote storage facilities; scanning unique titles; and dealing with outdated media collection, older serials, duplicate titles, and oversized atlases are still underway.

Overall, it took almost one year to have the process of collection access and paging settle into a routine. The main challenges were the collection location changes and the need to frequently remind patrons to use the online catalog's automated request feature and fill out the waiver form before requesting items as well as monitoring and facilitating any communication issues between the two library units, access services, and facilities, which jointly manage the book delivery process.

Library Presence without Library Space

At this writing it has been a little over two years since the Scripps Library closed its doors and one year since the collection was consolidated into the main campus library, the Geisel Library. The collection paging service and the processes for requesting appointments to view archival and special collections and to meet with me, the Scripps liaison librarian, for a consultation have been working very well.

I attribute the relatively smooth transition from locally available library space, resources, collection, and services to a remote collection, virtually available services, and locally available librarian to frequent meetings with impacted stakeholders before and after the closure and consolidation. The frequent communication with the Scripps community and regular meetings and email consultations with library administrators and stakeholders made the transition to the new model more accepted and adopted by all parties concerned. There were some complaints, from both Scripps community and library staff for the added workload. This was inevitable, but I believe that these infrequent and usually easily addressed complaints were very few because the impacted community and library staff were informed and involved in the planned closure and consolidation.

Conclusion

Walter Munk, Scripps emeritus research professor of geophysics and one of the world's most famous and oldest living oceanographers, stated in a 2012 interview, "If my hopes are fulfilled, then the closure will be an inconvenience but not a major setback. I do understand the financial strains on UCSD have been very severe and something had to be done" (Showstack, p. 291). This statement from a concerned and involved member of the Scripps community underscores the importance of involving the impacted community in planning services and collection decisions, which is essential for the success of any major library transition, closure, or consolidation.

Over two years have passed since the Scripps Library closure, and the new services and remote procedures implemented after the closure and consolidation have been working well, and most have become a routine part of the library's service offerings. All of these efforts to include stakeholders, keep a librarian available in the impacted campus area, and maintain frequent communication and outreach resulted in a community that can rely on dependable library services and easily accessible resources, even if it does not have a library building in its vicinity.

References

Brueggeman, P. (2013). *Scripps Institution of Oceanography Library history.* [Collection of papers]. Retrieved from http://scilib.ucsd.edu/sio/hist/BrueggemanSIOlibrary.pdf

Hayden, E. (2011). Budget woes sink marine archive. *Nature, 471*(7336), 18. doi:10.1038/471018a

Kvenild, C., & Calkins, K. (2011). *Embedded librarians: Moving beyond one-shot instruction.* Chicago, IL: Association of College and Research Libraries.

Scripps Institution of Oceanography (2014a). About the Scripps Institution of Oceanography. Retrieved from https://scripps.ucsd.edu/about

Scripps Institution of Oceanography (2014b). Mission and quick facts. Retrieved from https://scripps.ucsd.edu/about/mission-and-quick-facts

Showstack, R. (2012). With Scripps Library closure, university tries to minimize impact. *Eos, Transactions American Geophysical Union, 93*(30), 291. doi: 10.1029/2012EO300003

APPENDIX 9A. Petition by Scripps Institution of Oceanography Community

Petition in Opposition to the Closure of the SIO Library Building

To:

Tony D. Haymet
Director, Scripps Institution of Oceanography

Marye Anne Fox
Chancellor

Suresh Subramani
Senior Vice Chancellor, Academic Affairs

Gary C. Matthews
Vice Chancellor, Resource Management/Planning

Brian E.C. Schottlaender
University Librarian

Miriam Kastner
Chair, SIO Library Committee

As members and colleagues of the communities of Scripps Institution of Oceanography (SIO) and the University of California, San Diego, it has come to our attention that university officials have recently proposed to close the SIO library building for the 2011–2012 fiscal year, as outlined in a publicly available letter Mr. Schottlaender wrote, dated February 11, 2011.

We, the undersigned, wish to express our opposition to the proposed closure of the SIO library building. The historical value and legacy of the SIO library is unparalleled. We hold that its continued existence is essential to preserving, organizing, and providing access to the robust knowledge base of ocean, climate, and the earth sciences and the capacity of SIO scientists to perform meaningful and world-class research. Indeed, in our view, ensuring the operation of a library with such a profound history and rich pool of academic resources—as that at SIO—is key to maintaining a high quality, bustling research institution.

We find many concrete uses for the SIO library, including, but not limited to, access to: 1) SIO archives, publications, and course reserves; 2) scientific texts, literature, and journals; 3) charts and maps; 4) computers, printers, copiers, and scanners; 5) ample study and meeting space; and 6) an invaluable, informed, and engaged source of knowledge, librarian Amy Butros.

Lastly, we understand that budget constraints are forcing those in charge of the allocation of funds to make difficult, hard-thought decisions. However, we firmly and wholeheartedly believe that the proposed closure of the SIO library would be an unwise decision in the face of deep budget cuts—one that seems to consider neither its direct impact on students and faculty nor its inevitable long-term consequences on the status of SIO as a research institution.

Sincerely,

The Undersigned

APPENDIX 9B. Message from the Scripps Director and the University Librarian

February 6, 2012

Dear Scripps Community,

As most of you are aware, in early 2011, in response to continuing budget cuts, the UC San Diego Libraries initiated a consolidation process that will soon result in four physical library locations. These efforts are similar to consolidations undertaken by many of our peer institutions. The four library locations, which will be available to members of the Scripps community, include the Geisel Library, the Biomedical Library, the Trade Street storage annex, and the Scripps Archives and Library Annex.

The newly named "Scripps Archives and Library Annex", housed in the Eckart building on the Scripps campus, will be operated jointly by Scripps and the UC San Diego Libraries. The Libraries will continue to provide access to the Scripps Archives, by appointment, for all campus and off-campus users. The Scripps Library Annex will soon house accessible student course materials and—after minor renovation—will serve as the pick-up point for library materials delivered from the other campus library sites. Temporarily, these services will be provided in the Old Scripps Building (OSB)/Scripps Department (starting approximately July 1, 2012) until the UCSD Libraries staff can vacate space on the first and second floors of the Eckart building and any minor modifications to the space can be completed by Scripps. The large-scale printer utilized by Scripps students also will be relocated temporarily to the OSB, with support/access provided by the Scripps Department.

The first and second floors of the Eckart building will then provide approximately 18,000 square feet of study and meeting space for students, as well as space to support expanding instructional and research programs at Scripps. The third floor of the Eckart building will be managed by the UCSD Libraries and will provide archive and special collection services for Scripps. The Archives at Scripps house a wide range of historic materials about Scripps and UC San Diego and will continue to be accessible by appointment, M-F, 9-5.

The timeline for these changes—attached below—remains tentative as planning and discussions among the Libraries, Scripps faculty, and students continue. We appreciate your many constructive suggestions over the last 11 months, and your ongoing interest in the library services that are so vital to the education and research missions of Scripps. The Libraries' Amy Butros will provide regular updates to the community as the timeline below unfolds.

Tony Haymet
SIO Director

Brian E. C. Schottlaender
The Audrey Geisel University Librarian

Tentative timeline:

- June 29, 2012 – Scripps Library closes to the public

- June 30, 2012 – Area on first floor north will be cleared of library furnishings

- Scripps would like to start renovation of first floor by July 2, 2012

- July 2, 2012 – Scripps Archives open to the public, M-F, 9-5, by appointment

- Beginning Mid-summer 2012 – Scripps journals begin to be relocated to Geisel Library

- Beginning Mid-summer 2012 – Relocation of all other Scripps collections except Archives begins

- October 2012 – OOI move into renovated space

- Late 2012/early 2013 – Relocation of Scripps journals to Geisel completed

- Late 2012/early 2013 – Disposition and relocation of all Scripps collections, excluding Archives but including Hubbs and Map collections, completed

- Mid-to late 2013 – Libraries completely vacate first and second floors of Scripps Library building and transfer space to Scripps

- Fall 2013 – Scripps would begin any renovations deemed necessary to repurpose the space on the first and second floors.

- Early 2014 – Scripps occupies space on the first and second floors.

APPENDIX 9C. Patron Waiver Form

Waiver Form to Update Library Account and Allow Remote Check-Out of Library Items

I, (Your Full Name) hereby give the UCSD Library permission to access my library patron record and to allow the UCSD Library staff to:

1. Check-out library materials to my Library account in my absence using the barcode number in my library account (UCSD ID barcode) after June 29, 2012.
2. Issue a receipt that includes my full name and title of library materials checked-out to my library account.
3. Deliver library materials to the designated pick-up location administered by SIO Department Graduate Office at the SIO campus. Staff at the SIO Department Graduate Office will check my UCSD Photo ID prior to releasing library items to me. My acceptance below indicates that I understand that the UCSD Library reserves the right to charge me for the repair/replacement cost of materials if they are damaged or lost while loaned to me.

(Note: To view your Library account on-line, please visit: https://roger. ucsd.edu/patroninfo)

Instructions: Please mark the box next to "Yes" to have your library materials delivered to SIO campus. Mark the box next to "No" if you prefer to pick up library materials at the Geisel Library Building on upper campus.

Please select one:	☐ YES	☐ NO (I will pick up my books at Geisel Library Bldg.)

Please return the completed form by e-mail or campus mail as soon as possible.

E-mail to: abutros@ucsd.edu
Campus Mail: c/o Amy Butros, Library, 0175-E

CHAPTER 10

Using Data to Make Collections Decisions:
A Case Study from University of California, Berkeley

Susan Edwards and Hilary Schiraldi

THE UNIVERSITY OF California, Berkeley, like many research universities, is experiencing increased competition for limited campus space, serious financial pressures, and changes in patterns of research and scholarship. Adding seismic safety concerns for one of the buildings into this mix created a perfect storm, necessitating a radical restructuring of three subject specialty libraries. The Business Library has transitioned to an (almost) all-digital library, the Education Psychology Library is scheduled for decommissioning by the end of 2016, and the Social Welfare Library is transitioning into the Social Research Library with a high use collection, tightly focused in applied social research from education, psychology, social welfare, and public policy.

This chapter will describe the conditions that created the need for change, the process that was used to determine how to best meet research and teaching needs given the fiscal reality, and the data that was used to make very difficult decisions.

The University Library: Changing Budgets, Changing Research Methods

State funding to the University of California system began to decrease in the early 2000s, and by 2013 made up only 12% of UC Berkeley's total budget, down from 28% as recently as 2009 (state support was over 50% in the 1980s and '90s). The university library was not immune to budget cuts, and by 2008 implemented a hiring freeze in order to spare the collections budget. The library avoided layoffs by reducing staff by attrition and retirement incentives.

By 2012, the library employed 20 fewer librarians and 60 fewer staff than in 2008, and it was becoming clear that this budget environment would continue. In response, the library administration convened two internal study teams as part of the Re-Envisioning Library Services Initiative. In their reports, the teams presented several potential models for reducing staff workload and making more efficient use of human resources by consolidating the number of separate service locations on campus (University of California, Berkeley, 2012). The study teams also felt that changes in the way scholars conduct research today, particularly the increased use of online rather than print journals, meant that a larger number of volumes could be held in off-campus storage without inconveniencing patrons. The university librarian and other library administrators visited deans and department chairs around campus to present the re-envisioning reports and gauge support.

Meanwhile, a number of faculty members on campus expressed discontent with the study teams' recommendations. A petition was circulated, signed by 150 faculty members, asking that no changes to library services be made until the Academic Senate had had a chance to examine the financial and scholarly issues and submit its own recommendations. In fall 2012, UC Berkeley's executive vice chancellor and provost convened the Joint Administration and Faculty Senate Commission on the Future of the UC Berkeley Library. The commission report, released in fall 2013, concluded that "some consolidation of Subject Specialty Libraries or service points, and modification of some services at those over two dozen service points, may be appropriate" (University of California, Berkeley, 2013). The report recommended that the library administration work together with deans, department chairs, and faculty in the relevant areas to identify libraries where different operating models, including consolidation of print collections, would still serve faculty and student needs.

The Haas School of Business: New Programs, New Curricula

The Haas School of Business houses six degree programs and numerous centers and institutes as well as a large non-degree granting Center for Executive Education. The number of faculty and staff needed to support all these initiatives has grown in the 20 years since the school moved into its three-building complex on the eastern edge of the UC Berkeley campus. In fact, for several years Haas has rented additional office space in downtown Berkeley.

There have been major changes in the MBA and business curricula since the buildings were opened in 1995. There is a greater emphasis on collaborative projects and experiential learning, which require reservable, private group study rooms. The Haas School was built with eight of these rooms within the library, but some of Haas's peer institutions with newer buildings have many more. Some of the newer degree programs also require special spaces, such as the finance lab used by the Masters in Financial Engineering (MFE) Program, which has been located within the Business Library for several years. Having the group study rooms and MFE Lab located within the Business Library caused friction when students needed access outside of the library's normal operating hours. Finally, the Haas School is involved with online learning initiatives on campus, which require specialized classrooms and studios.

Due to all of these factors, along with the Haas administration's willingness to be an early adopter of new campus initiatives, the Business Library was identified early on as a potential partner for the library in implementing a new service model. The Haas dean's office sent a survey to faculty asking about their use of the Business Library's 80,000 on-site print volumes, and though the response rate was low (only 20 responses out of more than 200 tenure track and professional faculty), over 90% said they wouldn't mind if the print collection were housed remotely. In addition, surprising new data from the Library Systems Office (LSO) showed that books in the Business Library were checked out by other campus departments much more than by business faculty and graduate students (more detail on this circulation data is included in the next section). A citation analysis of bibliographies of business dissertations completed at Berkeley from 2008–2012 reinforced this finding. Business students overwhelmingly cited articles; only 17% of the citations were to books (Schiraldi &

Dorner, 2014). In fall 2013, the university librarian and Haas dean circulated a call for comments proposing that the Business Library become an all-digital library, with the vast majority of the print collection moved elsewhere (aside from a small reference collection and a few periodicals). Librarians would remain on-site to provide reference and instruction; circulation services would be limited to course reserves and books paged from other libraries; and access to the group study rooms, MFE Lab, and study space would be available outside the library's operating hours. After a six-week comment period, which generated no negative feedback from the Business School, the university librarian and Haas dean instructed the library to implement this new service model.

Tolman Hall: Seismic Concerns

Tolman Hall, constructed in 1962 near the northwest corner of the UC Berkeley campus, is the home of the Graduate School of Education, the Department of Psychology, and the Education Psychology Library. In 1997, a review by the University of California Office of the President (UCOP) found that Tolman Hall's seismic rating was poor. In spring 2014, UCOP formally recommended that Tolman Hall be demolished and replaced with a new building in downtown Berkeley. The new building will not have space for book stacks, so the 112,000 volumes in the Education Psychology Library will need to find new homes. Collection analysis (both the dissertation citation analysis and circulation data by major for graduate students and by department for faculty) showed strong synergies between social welfare and psychology and education and psychology. Books in the Social Welfare Library have very low circulation numbers, but the library itself is beloved by the faculty and students. It is located in Haviland Hall, home of the School of Social Welfare, and is part of the "classic core" of the Berkeley campus. Designed by architect John Galen Howard, the space is under architectural preservation. The school was eager to partner with the library to design a space and a collection that better meets current needs. The remodel includes relocating the school's computer lab into the library, adding glass doors into a seminar room for group study and classes, lending students high-end laptops with statistical software, and having a small high use collection supporting social research theory and practice. To accomplish the space remodel and to accommodate the staff and books moving in from the Education

Psychology Library, the current collection of 19,000 volumes had to be dramatically reduced to 2,000.

Data-Informed Decision Making

Once the decision has been made to close or consolidate a library, librarians must make difficult choices about how to deal with the existing print collections. Data is necessary to make patron-centered decisions about whether to withdraw, store, or retain items. But determining which data is most helpful—and then obtaining and interpreting the data—is challenging. The UC Berkeley library administration created a Large Scale Collection Review Committee in 2012 to develop practices and procedures for rationalizing the collection across campus libraries, with the goal of developing a shared sense of what materials should be kept on campus, shelved remotely in off-site storage, and withdrawn. The committee identified opportunities for new data to help with decision-making and worked with the LSO to provide this data.

Library Usage by Discipline

UCB's integrated library system (ILS) currently provides detailed statistics on circulation by library and by patron type (undergraduate, faculty, alumni, etc.), but provides no information about which department or school a particular patron is from. As one of the main reasons to keep a subject library's print collection close to the discipline it serves is usage of that collection, it was necessary to know who was using what in order to make decisions about which subject libraries should remain. Berkeley's LSO was able to create snapshots of print item lending by major (or department) for graduate students and faculty with information drawn from the patron address file. Unfortunately, this data is not available for undergraduates whose affiliations are not included in the ILS. The information for graduate students and faculty has been invaluable in visualizing which collection mergers would have the least negative impact on departments and where they may even offer advantages to disciplines drawing heavily on books from a broad range of subjects. For example, Figure 10.1 shows that individuals from many departments are borrowing books from the Business Library, with a relatively low (19%) usage by business faculty and graduate students.

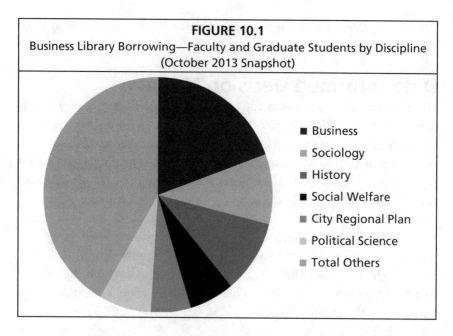

FIGURE 10.1
Business Library Borrowing—Faculty and Graduate Students by Discipline (October 2013 Snapshot)

- Business
- Sociology
- History
- Social Welfare
- City Regional Plan
- Political Science
- Total Others

Figure 10.2 shows usage at the Social Welfare Library to be the opposite—books are borrowed almost exclusively by members of the School of Social Welfare.

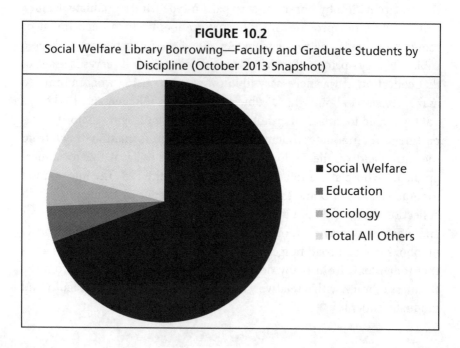

FIGURE 10.2
Social Welfare Library Borrowing—Faculty and Graduate Students by Discipline (October 2013 Snapshot)

- Social Welfare
- Education
- Sociology
- Total All Others

Usage Measures

Usage is the key factor in deciding whether to keep an item on campus, move it to storage, or withdraw it when it is not eligible for storage. The library was interested in an item's total historic circulation, and most importantly, the circulation that the item had received in the past five years. Fortuitously, Berkeley had implemented a new ILS in 2009, so staff were able to easily determine the total circulation of each item and the number of times it circulated since 2009. Having information about historic total circulation *and* relatively recent circulation has been essential in determining which items in the downsized collection should remain on campus. Librarians considered using the date of publication as an additional factor, but a recent dissertation citation analysis for education, psychology, and social welfare showed that students were using older material much more heavily than expected. The median age of books cited was 14 years for psychology, 13 years for education, and 11 years for social welfare (Edwards & Jones, 2014). Given this finding, publication date was not used.

Berkeley is fortunate to share two off-site storage spaces, the Northern and Southern Regional Library Facilities (RLFs), as part of the 10-campus University of California. Due to serious space constraints in the RLFs, a non-duplication policy mandates that only one copy of a monograph or serial can be stored system-wide at either RLF. The LSO has developed a tool that checks to see if a monograph is already stored in either RLF, providing tremendously useful information for these large projects. Librarians may request a list of titles by location with total circulation and circulation over the past five years as well as whether the item is already in an RLF. Other data items that have proved helpful to include in collection review spreadsheets are listed in Appendix 10A.

Limitations of Local Data

Are all circulations equal? Or should the number of circulations necessary to earn a space on campus be affected by the size of the user population, or the need for print browsing by that discipline? For a very small school like social welfare, for instance, the number of circulations required for an item to remain on campus might be lower than for a larger discipline that has more usage but also many more books. We have not yet developed a good and equitable weighting factor for this element.

Another challenging question facing research libraries is what constitutes "enough" copies of a particular monograph or serial to ensure long-term access (and re-digitization if necessary) to withdraw the local copy. As Schonfeld and Housewright (2009) explored in "What to Withdraw: Print Collections Management in the Wake of Digitization," it is important to have print versions available for re-digitization when the digital copy is found to have missing or unreadable content or images that have not been adequately reproduced. The question of "How many copies are enough?" is especially high stakes for research libraries that are assumed to be the repository of long tail scholarship—but that face the same challenges as other libraries of budget and space constraints, making it difficult to pay the high cost of ensuring long-term access to low-usage material. Berkeley adopted Schonfeld and Housewright's methodology for determining what JSTOR titles could be withdrawn, but outside of JSTOR it was not possible to determine X (the number of copies necessary to ensure long-term access) or to generate a list of all the monographs or serials under review that had fewer than X copies nationally. Even if this were possible, one would also need to know whether the libraries holding these items were making a long-term commitment to their preservation. For UC Berkeley's projects, there is still enough space in the RLFs to handle all non-duplicative material that cannot remain on campus. However, this might not continue in the future as the RLFs approach capacity. A less complex factor, but one that would be very useful at a large library with multiple locations, is whether a given book is held in other libraries on campus. Berkeley's ILS wasn't able to provide that data for the first phase of this project, but we hope to have it as future projects move forward.

Additional issues included items with missing or incomplete data such as low-level serials records, unanalyzed series, and replacement volumes (since the circulation history doesn't migrate to the new record). The UC Berkeley Library has not found a way to automatically match serials holdings to determine whether the volumes have already been stored at one of the RLFs, so these titles require a time-consuming manual comparison of the holdings records. In-house usage was another missing factor—the previous ILS did not track in-house usage data for each monograph. Currently all libraries are collecting this data so that in-house usage can be added to loans data as the library plans future projects.

Books without meaningful circulation data such as reference and special collections need to be considered individually. Ideally, another level of scrutiny would include questions of provenance and condition (Is it in better shape than the copy in the RLF?) as well as the number of copies available nationally.

Final Parameters and a Methodology

Once librarians know the target size of the reduced collection, the final parameters can be identified. These were different in each location. For example, in the Education Psychology Library, high circulation monographs were defined as those that had circulated in the past five years and were cataloged at least three years ago. These are being moved to the newly established Social Research Library, while books with mid-level circulation are being moved to the main library on campus and low-use items eligible for storage are being moved off-campus. Low-circulation books not eligible for storage (i.e., duplicates) were placed with a used book dealer with any money from sales returning to the library. In the case of the Business Library, monographs with no circulation in the last seven years were moved to off-campus storage, with the remaining higher-use books transferred to the main library. Figure 10.3 documents the decisions and workflow that we went through for each book.

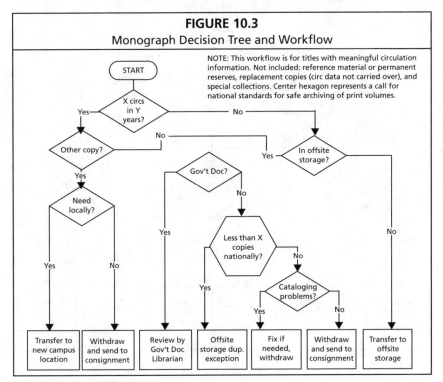

FIGURE 10.3
Monograph Decision Tree and Workflow

Serials, as mentioned earlier, present their own challenges and opportunities. The challenges include low-level cataloging and holdings records that need to be manually compared, but the advantage is that in general UC Berkeley Library users prefer e-journals to bound journals. Bound journals moved to off-site storage can have articles scanned and emailed on request, and paper duplicates not needed to fill gaps in the JSTOR archives can be recycled. With a few exceptions, the default decision at both the Education Psychology Library and the Business Library was to move serials to off-campus storage. Figure 10.4 and 10.5 outline the decision and workflow for serials.

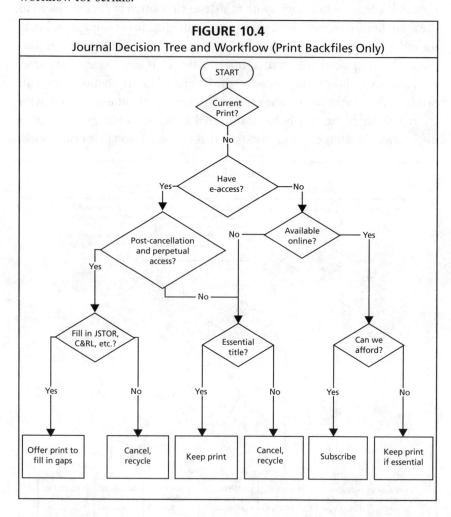

FIGURE 10.4
Journal Decision Tree and Workflow (Print Backfiles Only)

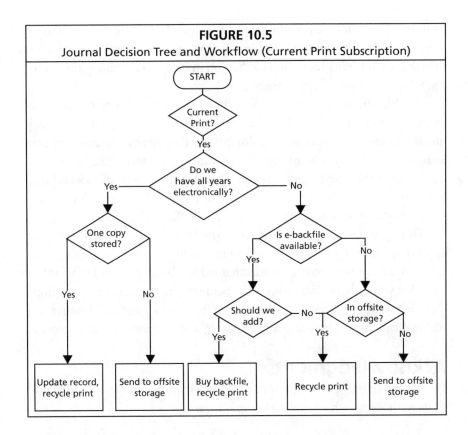

FIGURE 10.5
Journal Decision Tree and Workflow (Current Print Subscription)

Conclusion and Lessons Learned

In the case of UC Berkeley, librarians found themselves having to make major collections decisions on a short timeframe with limited data. It took close collaboration with the LSO to identify what metrics were available, followed by more work between the LSO and the circulation and technical processing staff in the affected libraries to produce the data for the librarians to use. We hope that the decision trees included here will be helpful to colleagues in similar situations at UC Berkeley and other research libraries.

It became clear that although data is essential for user-informed decisions, sometimes other factors come into play. The Education Psychology Library staff carefully analyzed usage data, worked with the affected departments and schools, and shared information with the entire campus community while also providing an opportunity for input. Librarians were therefore caught totally off guard by the vehemence of the opposition to the (misinformed) idea that the library was eliminating the revered children's literature collection. Students began a campaign and a Change.org petition to save the Children's Literature Collection in its own separate space within the Education Psychology Library.

The librarians met with the petition organizers and a group of interested students to explain that although some downsizing was necessary due to the decommissioning of Tolman Hall, they were evaluating the collection carefully. By establishing shared values, they were able to reassure the students that the library was not eliminating valuable works and that librarians were balancing the needs of the users with campus and library space realities and struggling to make those difficult decisions.

Finally, we were most dismayed by the lack of data on the number of copies of a given item held in libraries nationwide, which raises major preservation concerns. Since the trends that led to library consolidation at UC Berkeley will only be increasing worldwide in the coming years, we hope that OCLC, the Association of Research Libraries, or another organization will make gathering this data and releasing it in a usable format a priority.

Acknowledgments

We wish to thank Jeffery Loo for generously lending his data visualization skills to these flowcharts and other graphics.

References

Edwards, S., & Jones, L. (2014). Assessing the fitness of an academic library for doctoral research. *Evidence Based Library and Information Practice, 9*(2), 4–15. Retrieved from https://ejournals.library.ualberta.ca/index.php/EBLIP/article/view/21601

Schiraldi, H., & Dorner, J. (2014, August). *Collection assessment for the social sciences at UC Berkeley.* Poster session presented at the Association of Research Libraries Library Assessment Conference, Seattle, WA. Retrieved from http://escholarship.org/uc/item/6z69958p

Schonfeld, R., & Housewright, R. (2009). *What to withdraw: Print collections management in the wake of digitization.* Retrieved from http://www.sr.itha-ka.org/research-publications/what-withdraw-print-collections-management-wake-digitization

University of California, Office of the President. (2014). *Action item to the members of the committee on grounds and buildings: Approval of the budget and approval of external financing, Tolman Hall seismic replacement, Berkeley campus*. Retrieved from http://regents.universityofcalifornia.edu/regmeet/mar14/gb1.pdf

University of California, Berkeley, Commission on the Future of the UC Berkeley Library. (2013). *Report of the Commission on the Future of the UC Berkeley Library.* Retrieved from http://evcp.berkeley.edu/sites/default/files/FINAL_CFUCBL_report_10.16.13.pdf

University of California, Berkeley, Library Service Models Self-Study Team. (2012). *Library Service Models Self-Study Team overviews.* Retrieved from http://www.lib.berkeley.edu/AboutLibrary/re_envision_LSM_Overviews.pdf

APPENDIX 10A. Elements in Spreadsheet for Decisions

Sort order
Catalog item number
Call number
Volume number
Copy number
In-house usage
Total checkouts
Checkouts from past 5 years
Last check out date
Location (or sub-location)
Record creation date
Barcode
Catalog bib number
OCLC number
245 Title
260$c Date of publication
RLF status

CHAPTER 11

Everything Must Move:
Coordinating the Implementation of a Large Collection Merger

Giovanna Badia

MOVING A LIBRARY collection is a large undertaking that involves numerous details and impacts a significant number of individuals. The literature on library collection moves is abundant, mostly consisting of authors' reports of what happened at their institutions. In her classic how-to textbook on this topic, *Moving Your Library: Getting the Collection from Here to There*, Elizabeth Chamberlain Habich (2010) lists 200 articles published from 1929–2006 that describe library collection moves, and more accounts have been published since then (e.g., Bridges, 2009; Czechowski et al., 2010; Sharpe, 2012). However, only a few articles provide details of the personnel involved in the move and how they participated (e.g., Baumann, 2006; Calderhead, 1997; Czechowski et al., 2010; Snow, 2004). The purpose of this chapter is to describe the human logistics involved in implementing the move and integration of library collections, specifically the organizational structure required for efficient implementation and the different roles performed by a move coordinator. This chapter will draw from the literature and from my recent experience as a move coordinator for the integration of two large print collections in an academic library system. It will also discuss issues that can arise during the cleanup phase that occurs after implementing a large-scale project.

Background

The McGill Library, located in Montreal, Quebec, is a system of 14 branch libraries and reading rooms. It serves McGill University, a large research-intensive institution with undergraduate and graduate programs and a population of approximately 38,500 students. In 2013, the McGill Library merged its education and life sciences collections with two of its other branch libraries. The education collection, housed in the same building as the Faculty of Education, was moved and incorporated into the Humanities and Social Sciences Library. The life sciences collection, located in the same building as the Faculty of Medicine, was transferred and integrated into the Schulich Library of Science and Engineering. This chapter will focus on the move of the life sciences collection and its integration into the Schulich Library.

The moves were not simple transfers from points A to B. Some items in the education and life sciences collections were sent to the library's storage location due to space constraints. The moves to storage happened during the same time period as these collections were being moved to another branch. Life sciences books not borrowed in the past five years (approximately 45,000 items), some life sciences journals, and existing books in the Schulich Library that had not been borrowed in the past 10 years (approximately 62,000 items) were sent to storage in order to accommodate the merged life sciences, physical sciences, and engineering collections at the Schulich Library. Before the move of the life sciences collection, staff across the McGill Library system tipped forward on the shelves all the items in the Life Sciences Library and Schulich Library that were destined for storage. Circa 30% of the life sciences collection and 30% of the physical sciences and engineering collection were tipped and sent to storage. At both locations, movers pulled the tipped books from the shelves, packed them in boxes, transported them to storage, and shelved them there. At the Schulich Library, the movers also shifted the remaining items. This was done one floor at a time. Boxes, containing materials from the life sciences collection in call number order, arrived in batches to the Schulich Library. These batches usually contained the items that needed to be integrated on a specific floor and were shelved according to their call numbers by library staff or movers within a span of a few days after they arrived. Every book and journal at the Schulich Library was moved to a new floor or shelf to incorporate the life sciences collection. The boxes of tipped books at the

Schulich Library were transported to storage and unpacked there after the move and integration of the life sciences collection was finished. The movers were divided into teams, with different teams working simultaneously in each of the locations; for example, as a group of three to four movers were boxing tipped books, shifting, or unpacking life sciences items at the Schulich Library, another team of three to four movers was packing up the collection at the Life Sciences Library.

The process for integrating the life sciences collection at the Schulich Library can be summarized as follows: (1) physical sciences and engineering books not borrowed in 10 years were selected for storage and tipped forward on the shelves by library employees; (2) movers packed the tipped books and put the boxes aside; (3) movers shifted the remaining items on the shelves and, with assistance from library staff, unpacked boxes of life sciences items and shelved them; and (4) movers brought the boxes of tipped books to the library's storage location, built shelves, and unpacked them. Steps 2 and 3 were frequently done consecutively on a specific floor before moving to the next floor and repeating the process.

Management Support

The planning and implementation of the collection moves and integrations was a large-scale project that had to proceed swiftly from conception to completion in just four months. Support from the library's senior administration, enough manpower, and a clear objective communicated widely and repeatedly to library personnel were some factors that led to its completion in a timely manner. The importance of factors such as these is reflected in the literature. In her study on how library employees in Ontario manage projects, Horwath (2012) mentions that researchers in the project management literature in general agree that "[m]anagement support for and involvement in the project, adequate staffing for the project, a project plan that details goals, timelines, budget and staff, a clearly defined mission for the project, project monitoring to ensure plan targets are being met, and clear communication channels" contribute to a positive outcome (p. 17). Over half of the 92 participants (about 55%) in Horwath's study indicated that "management support for the project" was a "very important" factor for its success.

Management support was an important project success factor for the move and integration of McGill Library's education and life sciences collections. Full hands-on support from the Dean's Cabinet (McGill Library's senior administration group) helped keep the project on schedule. The Dean's Cabinet is composed of the dean of libraries and a mix of associate deans, directors, and administrative support staff. The library's senior director of planning and resources, a member of the Dean's Cabinet, was the lead project manager for the education and life sciences collection moves. There were also move coordinators on each site to provide directions to the movers. The move coordinators were library staff members who, for the duration of the project, reported directly to the senior director for this project, thereby skipping a level or two in the library's organizational hierarchy. This flattened reporting structure made it possible for the move coordinators to rapidly acquire human or material resources when faced with obstacles or laborious tasks that would have slowed the project down. For instance, additional library personnel were needed to shelve materials when life sciences books started arriving at the Schulich Library in batches of 50 and 100 boxes. One of the move coordinators approached the senior director about obtaining additional manpower. On the same day, the senior director contacted head librarians across the McGill Library system to ask them to send one or two of their staff members to shelve for 90-minute shifts. Additional help was thus quickly obtained, with staff from other branches shelving at the Schulich Library the very next day.

Access to sufficient human resources was a factor that worked in tandem with support from upper management to assist in keeping the project on track. The final decisions to move the education and life sciences collections were made at the end of June, and the target completion date for tipping the books at the Schulich Library was set for July 31. The senior administration planned for the majority of the moving to occur during the summer months in order to minimize the impact on the McGill community. Tipping the approximately 62,000 books destined for storage at the Schulich Library was a labor-intensive task that took an estimated 350 hours and necessitated the involvement of staff from multiple branches and departments in the library system to complete it on schedule. Schulich Library staff (12 individuals) tipped half of the books during the last week of June and the first three weeks of July. During this same time, staff from other libraries were at the Life Sciences Library helping to tip the materials that were going to storage. The remaining items would be moved to the Schulich Library. The dean of libraries and the senior director of planning and resources each made periodic calls for volunteer tippers during that summer. The request was made at the weekly managers' meetings, when the dean, directors, head librarians, and department supervisors meet to discuss issues across the library system; it was also included in the summary of the managers' meetings that the library's communications officer sends to all library staff. On the afternoon before the July 31 tipping deadline, the dean of libraries sent an email to all head librarians and department supervisors asking that they send as many volunteers as possible to help finish the task. This call helped to double the number of volunteers for the day, and the tipping was finished on time.

Through their words and actions that summer, members of the Dean's Cabinet clearly communicated to all library employees that moving the education and life sciences collections was the top priority. Dean's Cabinet members volunteered their time to tip materials in all the affected libraries. Tipping was presented as a vital service to the whole library system. Depending on their supervisor, some employees were told to volunteer, what some people jokingly referred to as "voluntold," and others were asked. Regardless of how they were approached, the majority of tippers showed up with a positive attitude. Each supervisor ensured that there was adequate service desk coverage at the branch while some of his or her staff were away tipping. In total, 37 paraprofessionals and administrative staff and 21 librarians came from other branches in the McGill Library system to help tip books at the Schulich Library. These individuals contributed 170 hours to the project during the last eight working days in July. Including Schulich Library staff, 40% of the entire library workforce was involved. This participation rate would be considerably higher if it were adjusted to account for the availability of volunteers since there were many library staff members away on summer vacation during that period. To show her appreciation and thank everyone for their collaboration and goodwill, the dean hosted a free pizza lunch for library staff, which was held a week after the tipping was completed at the Schulich Library.

Roles of a Move Coordinator

During the tipping phase of the project, move coordinators at the Schulich Library organized the scheduling of the volunteer tippers, showed them what needed to be done, assigned sections of the collection to tippers at appropriate times so that individuals did not bump into each other in the aisles while working, and answered any questions raised. This is just one example illustrating some of the tasks that the move coordinators performed.

A move coordinator is a library staff person who interacts directly with the movers during a collection move, representing the interests of the library, and participates in planning the move with the library's senior administration or move committee. Both library professionals and movers state in the literature that there should be a designated person(s) giving directions to the movers in order to avoid transmitting conflicting information (Baumann, 2006; Tanner, 1993). The library's move coordinator should give orders to the movers' supervisor, who communicates it in turn to the movers (Tanner, 1993). In her article about the transfer and incorporation of a university's chemistry library into its main campus library, Calderhead (1997) explains that "the term 'coordinator' was used rather than 'leader,' because it was assumed all parties knew their particular task better than any other party. However, the well-being of the library was the 'boss' or 'leader.' Generally speaking, a librarian knows the library better than the contractors, even if libraries are their particular specialty" (p. 73). Library staff and the library's community of users are the ones who live with the consequences of a move after the contractors leave; therefore, the onus is on the library's move coordinator to ensure that the move is executed correctly. The move coordinator is involved in more daily supervision if a general moving company is hired to do the job rather than a company that specializes in moving libraries (Snow, 2004). In a survey of 82 ARL member libraries about moving collections, "over 62% of libraries utilized trained library movers over any other collection transport method, even though this was likely more expensive than other options available to them" (Atkins & Hain Teper, 2005, pp. 75–76). For the education and life sciences collection relocations, McGill Library hired the university's preferred moving company, which the library had a previous working relationship with from moving other collections.

There were two move coordinators at the Life Sciences Library and another two at the Schulich Library during the relocation of the life sciences collection, which enabled the co-coordinators to divide the labour, support one another, and ensure that the library's interests were always represented when one coordinator was away. The Schulich Library's circulation supervisor and I, a liaison librarian, were Schulich Library's move coordinators. The head of the Schulich Library at the time of the move had formulated the collection layout floor plans that showed what a merged collection would look like, with call number ranges indicated on the plans for each of the shelving units in the library. We used these floor plans as a guide when managing the implementation of the move. We shared an office during the project, making it easier to work together and keep each other informed of any updates that occurred in the other's absence. In addition to overseeing the work of the movers and volunteer tippers, we were also responsible for sending daily updates to library staff about the integration of the life sciences collection into the Schulich Library, which the communications officer then quickly posted on the library's website. We also supervised the work of four library student workers on the project, which included shelving, shifting, shelf reading, sign making, and inventory, and we worked closely with librarians and library support staff in other departments to update the catalogue, the library's floor plans, and the website.

As the move coordinators, we took on the following roles to accomplish the tasks required of our position:

- **Troubleshooter:** Solving any problems that arose with the project—we made space where there was none by using study carrels, carts, and tables as temporary shelving units to allow library staff to shelve incoming life sciences materials at the same time as movers were packing tipped books or shifting items.
- **Implementer:** Executing the merging of the collections—we frequently met with the movers' supervisor to create and revise step-by-step plans for how the items would be shifted, whether the shifting would be performed backwards or forwards on a part of a floor or on the entire floor, how much space to leave empty on the shelves in certain call number ranges on a particular floor, etc.
- **Teacher:** Training the movers—we explained how call numbers functioned and the reasoning behind the shelving arrangement in the library.
- **Advisor-critic:** Providing objective advice to senior administrators—we reported directly to the senior director of planning and resources, which gave us a greater opportunity to provide advice on other projects that affected the move at the Schulich Library, such as recommending that another moving company be hired to move the life sciences librarians' office furniture into the Schulich

Library so that the process of integrating the life sciences collection would not be halted for the week-long office move.

- **Environmental sensor:** Foreseeing future problems and acting to prevent them—the Dean's Cabinet initially decided to list the collections at the Life Sciences Library and the Schulich Library as "temporarily unavailable" in the library catalogue while the life sciences collection was being relocated. We recommended that the existing collection at the Schulich Library not be labeled with this message since the materials would always be accessible to the community during the move; they would just have been shifted to a different shelf in the building. Listing the Schulich Library materials as "temporarily unavailable" would have caused unnecessary delays for patrons and more work for library staff who would have had to retrieve the items off the shelves. Rather, temporary signs indicating call number ranges were updated on a daily basis to reflect the shifting that had been completed in that area.

The troubleshooter, implementer, teacher, advisor-critic, and environmental sensor roles are also described by internal consultants to explain what they do (Kelley, 1979). Internal consultants are staff members within the organization who perform similar functions to traditional external consultants, such as problem solving, advising the head of an organization, interpreting research, and implementing new programs, and are directly accountable to their sponsor. Consultants, whether internal or external, will often work on projects that either require them to provide possible solutions to a problem or to implement a solution. The two are not mutually exclusive, but the focus of the consultants' work may be on one or the other (Harrison, 1974). A move coordinator can be seen as an internal consultant, both in terms of the equivalent roles that the coordinator plays and his or her unparalleled access to senior administration during the duration of the project. It may be useful to view the functions of a move coordinator from this perspective to better understand what skills and relationships with upper management are needed for a move coordinator to be successful. Coordinating a move is more than just interacting with moving staff on the library's behalf; it also means advising the library's senior administration or move committee on decisions about the move. It requires seeing the larger picture and making it happen—keeping track of all the parts of the move and visualizing what the end result will look like in order to create a detailed, step-by-step method for transforming an abstract, such as floor plans showing a merged collection, into reality (Fortriede, 2010; Tucker, 1999).

Cleanup

The process of moving and integrating the life sciences collection into the Schulich Library started at the end of June 2013 and finished with the last batch of life sciences books being unpacked and shelved on October 8, 2013. Though the major work of the relocation was finished, the cleanup phase had just begun. Tasks common in a cleanup include shelf reading, updating stack signage, re-shifting parts of the collection to distribute growth space more evenly, and correcting errors in the work completed (Habich, 2010). The majority of errors in the life sciences collection move consisted of mis-shelving and misdirected items (some materials were transported to McGill Library's storage location instead of the Schulich Library branch and vice versa). Habich (2010) recommends making a list of cleanup tasks, also known as a "punch list;" assigning specific individuals or groups to finish each task; and identifying deadlines for completing each task. She states that the resolution of punch list items may take several months to accomplish depending on the number and complexity of the items on the list (Habich, 2010). The majority of items on Schulich Library's punch list were completed in the year that followed. The time period for cleanup can be shortened if the punch list is created immediately after the moving is over and support from upper management is obtained for assigning additional human resources to tackle the jobs on the list. A move is considered truly finished when all the items on the punch list have been done.

Conclusion

Moving library collections is a detailed and intensive enterprise that requires the participation and goodwill of numerous individuals, at all levels, both inside and outside of the library, to make it happen on schedule. The move coordinator manages the daily logistics of the move and is just one example of the multiple players involved in this large operation. Active involvement and continuing support from the library's senior administration is necessary to encourage as many staff members as possible to participate. Library employees will more likely be encouraged to contribute if they see their superiors working in the frontlines of the move.

References

Atkins, S. S., & Hain Teper, J. (2005). A survey of library practices in planning and managing temporary moves. Collection Management, 30(4), 59–84.

Baumann, K. (2006). Using a transition team to facilitate library building moves. Colorado Libraries, 32(1), 13–17.

Bridges, J. (2009). Moving a hospital library. Medical Reference Services Quarterly, 28(1), 77–87.

Calderhead, V. (1997). An operations research approach to a chemistry library relocation: Measure often, move once. Science and Technology Libraries, 16(1), 61–80.

Czechowski, L., Barger, R., Fort, M., & Maxeiner, G. (2010). Letting go: Closing a branch library of the Health Sciences Library system, University of Pittsburgh. Library Resources and Technical Services, 54(3), 153–163.

Fortriede, S. C. (2010). Moving your library: Getting the collection from here to there. Chicago, IL: American Library Association.

Habich, E. C. (2010). Moving library collections: A management handbook. Santa Barbara, CA: Libraries Unlimited.

Harrison, K. (1974). Managing the internal consultant. International Studies of Management & Organization, 4(3), 35–45.

Horwath, J. A. (2012). How do we manage? Project management in libraries: An investigation. Partnership: The Canadian Journal of Library and Information Practice and Research, 7(1).

Kelley, R. E. (1979). Should you have an internal consultant? Harvard Business Review, 57(6), 110–120.

Sharpe, P. A. (2012). The big shift: How the University of Houston libraries moved everything. Journal of Access Services, 9(2), 66–79.

Snow, R. (2004). How not to move a library: Misadventures in moving. Collection Management, 29(2), 53–67.

Tanner, S. (1993). Help the removal company to help you. Aslib Information, 21(1), 18.

Tucker, D. C. (1999). Library relocations and collection shifts. Medford, NJ: Information Today.

CHAPTER 12

When Libraries Combine:
Creating a Georgia Regents University
Libraries Website

Virginia Feher and Kim Mears

SUCCESSFUL ACADEMIC LIBRARY website design is crucial for providing convenient, effortless, and rapid discovery of information and scholarly
resources. The design of a webpage along with the clarity of the terminology affects how various elements are discovered as well as perceived, determining if users are able to easily find the information they need when
quickly scanning a webpage. Successful design requires not only choosing
the correct elements to include but also combining them skillfully so that
the visuals support, rather than impede, information delivery. In addition, a
well-organized website provides clear pathways to information. Because of
the abundance of services and information academic libraries offer, library
websites have the potential for offering too much information, looking cluttered, and confusing the user. Nielsen (2000) argued that "people are extremely goal-driven on the Web. They have something specific they want to
do, and they don't tolerate anything standing between them and their goal"
(p. 380), while Holtze (2006) pointed out that "web designers in libraries
face a particularly difficult challenge: selecting only a few salient pieces of
information to highlight since each patron's desired outcome differs" (p. 96).

When two universities with disparate user populations consolidate, the challenges of combining their respective library's websites into a cohesive and effective website can increase exponentially, especially when employees face increased workloads and time constraints related to consolidation. Reconciling the differences requires teamwork and the willingness to compromise. Because each library may place emphasis on different resources or services, it is equally challenging to reconcile similarities, such as a shared online catalog or a database aggregator. One library may heavily promote a shared resource while the other prefers to keep it less visible. Combining two very different library websites requires detailed planning and implementation so that the final product fulfills each library's purpose and retains its unique identity while communicating a unified presence. This chapter outlines the challenges and the opportunities that library employees encountered while combining the Reese and Greenblatt Library websites into a unified web presence: the Georgia Regents University Libraries website.

Background

In January 2012, the University System of Georgia (USG) announced consolidation plans for eight of its thirty-five institutions. In a news release announcing the consolidations, Hank Huckaby, chancellor of the USG Board of Regents, explained that the benefits of consolidation would include "increased administrative efficiencies and greater economies of scale through the creation of larger institutions" (USG, 2012). Consolidating universities was viewed as a cost-saving measure for the USG with the goal of a "more educated Georgia" (USG, 2012).

As part of this cost-saving plan, two institutions located less than three miles apart—Augusta State University (ASU) and Georgia Health Sciences University (GHSU)—were designated by the USG Board of Regents for consolidation. Though closest in physical proximity of the institutions chosen for consolidation, they could be considered the farthest apart with regards to institutional mission and student populations. An access institution with a focus on the liberal arts, ASU served a mainly undergraduate population of approximately 7,000 students and employed 250 faculty. (An access institution provides learning support and other services for students who might otherwise not attend college because of admissions or financial challenges.) GHSU offered professional degrees in the health sciences to 2,500 students and employed 950 faculty (Heck et al., 2013). On January 8, 2013, the Board of Regents officially approved the consolidation of ASU and GHSU, and the combined institutions became Georgia Regents University (GRU), a comprehensive research university with a focus on the health sciences.

Between January 2012 and January 2013, work groups, teams, and sub-teams consisting of employees across the campuses participated in consolidating the two universities. The ASU-GHSU Consolidation Working Group consisted of representatives from both campuses as well as the Augusta community and acted as an oversight committee, guiding the consolidation process. The Consolidation Action Team, consisting of key leaders from each institution, governed day-to-day consolidation activities. In addition, multiple teams and sub-teams across both campuses worked on reconciling policies and procedures, such as promotion and tenure, faculty governance, and human resources (Augusta State University & Georgia Health Sciences University, n.d.).

In the new organizational structure, ASU Reese Library and GHSU Robert B. Greenblatt, M.D. Library became GRU Libraries. While each library provides access to resources for undergraduate and graduate students, faculty, researchers, staff, and community users, the libraries differ in their target user groups. Reese Library serves a broader user group within multiple disciplines, mainly undergraduates, while Greenblatt Library serves a health professional community and the GRU Health System. The Library Work Team (LWT), with members from both Reese and Greenblatt, guided the libraries through the process of reconciling the differences to combine the two libraries into one administrative unit. The LWT was also responsible for overseeing and approving the work of sub-teams as well as for ensuring the libraries' continued compliance with selected Southern Association of Colleges and Schools Commission on Colleges (SACS-COC) accreditation standards. In "Consolidation: A Tale of Two Libraries," Heck et al. (2013) offer an overview of the libraries' consolidation, describing the sub-teams' charges and accomplishments, including a brief summary of the Libraries' Consolidated Website Sub-team (CLWS), which was formed in June 2012 and "tasked with designing and implementing a new consolidated website for the University Libraries" (p. 7).

Planning for a Consolidated Libraries Website

The CLWS consisted of librarians and staff from Greenblatt and Reese libraries, with five members at the outset. Greenblatt Library members included the virtual services librarian, an access services staff member who transitioned to the nursing information librarian faculty position while serving on the sub-team, and the clinical information librarian. Reese Library members included the user engagement librarian and a library systems staff member. In October 2012, the newly hired Reese Library government information librarian joined the CLWS. This addition resulted in equal representation from the two libraries.

The CLWS members recognized the challenge of making a cohesive website given the numerous differences between the two libraries' user populations and website needs. For example, while both libraries utilize Voyager, the statewide integrated library system, they direct users to different versions of the online public access catalog (OPAC), called GIL and GIL-Find. The Reese Library academic community primarily uses GALILEO, the statewide database interface that provides a web scale discovery tool, offering users a "single search box providing a Google-like experience" (Vaughan, 2011, p. 7). The Greenblatt Library website provided the most popular databases in a quick links menu on the homepage and a webpage with an alphabetical list of resources, linking users to subject-specific databases. To find solutions for reconciling these differences, the CLWS members established a process that included gathering website design literature, creating and distributing a survey to Reese and Greenblatt library users, reviewing peer and aspirational academic and health sciences library websites, and performing a card sort exercise on both campuses. The Greenblatt Library director requested that they gather information derived from the end-user perspective in order to make data driven decisions. This approach greatly assisted in facilitating compromise as the sub-team members had divergent and strong viewpoints based on individual experiences.

In searching the literature, the CLWS members found several useful books on website design for libraries. In a guide produced by the Library and Information Technology Association, Lehman and Nikkel (2008) reviewed the complete process for curating a user-friendly web presence. The types of usability assessments and their real-world applications are covered as well as techniques for documenting and communicating the results. Davidsen and Yankee (2004) provided guidance on overall website design targeted at library users, including the need to establish phases and tasks by setting goals and completing a thorough analysis of the design before implementation. Norlin and Winters (2002) emphasized the importance of conducting usability testing to create a quality website and provided concrete examples for replication. Additionally, the CLWS members reviewed several scholarly articles. Cobus, Dent, and Ondrusek (2005) discussed a usability study a web committee conducted at the Hunter College Libraries with 28 users. The web committee conducted testing in two stages with different participants for each stage, revising the website based on the first round of testing and then evaluating the changes during the second round of testing. The authors provided sample task-based usability questions, included participants' comments and suggestions, and outlined website revisions as well as potential future changes. Cockrell and Jayne (2002) reported on an article-finding website usability study they conducted in order to determine if search behavior patterns existed in participants who were unsuccessful in the task, if educational status (undergraduates, graduates, or faculty) factored into success, and if successful participants "were discriminating about their choice of index and citation" (p. 123). Tolliver et al. (2005) described various usability testing strategies that the library conducted, including sector interviews, card sorting, tasked-based usability testing using a paper prototype, and task-based usability testing with a finished prototype. The CLWS members also conducted online searches to identify and review other library's usability test questions (MIT Libraries, 1999) and website survey questions (Fairleigh Dickinson University, 2007; Coahoma Community College, n.d.). This multiphase research process provided valuable information for determining website redesign best practices, including information for conducting a website survey and performing usability testing.

With approval from the GHSU Division of Institutional Effectiveness, the CLWS members created and distributed separate surveys to Reese and Greenblatt library users. The surveys included similar questions but were customized based on campus differences. For example, Greenblatt Library offered a customized database list on the library's website while Reese Library directed patrons to the statewide database system GALILEO. In addition, the Greenblatt Library's survey included the user category "clinical" while the Reese Library's survey included "community user" to better reflect each library's user populations. The purpose of the surveys was to determine users' opinions of and experiences with the current websites as well as to discover what features, content, or improvements users desired. According to Robbins, Esposito, Kretz, and Aloi (2007), "soliciting user feedback in the form of surveys, focus groups, and task-based analysis has proven a valuable method of ensuring that any redesign will reflect the needs and thought processes of the end user" (p. 4). The surveys were valuable for demonstrating the needs of both user populations. The results showed that Reese Library users always or often go to the library's website to access GAILEO databases (always, 26%; often, 37%), GIL-Find (always, 21%; often, 34%), and the electronic journal locator (always, 15%; often, 30%). The results also showed that Greenblatt users always or often go to the library's website to access specific databases (always, 44%; often, 41%) and the eJournal navigator (always, 29%; often, 45%). Additionally, Greenblatt users rarely (22%) or never (38%) access GIL from the website. Notably, many of the survey participant's comments indicated a pressing need to redesign both websites.

To identify trends and useful features, the CLWS members looked at existing library websites that represented both an academic library and a medical or health sciences library, including the University of Kentucky Libraries and the University at Buffalo Libraries. The committee also reviewed the library websites of university peer and aspirational institutions, such as the University of Alabama, Birmingham. Trends that emerged included a horizontal navigation menu with drop-down links, a prominent tabbed search box for searching databases and/or the online catalog, and a social media dashboard. Another trend that the committee identified was a main page, or portal, for institutions with more than one library, which serves as a gateway to the different library homepages. The CLWS members agreed that the portal approach could serve as a unifying presence, both functionally and symbolically, as the consolidated homepage would not just provide library users with a central point of access but also would provide a virtual collaborative space for the two libraries. Additionally, the page would provide pathways to information about both libraries and also direct users to each library's unique website.

The CLWS members decided that applying a horizontal navigation menu on the libraries' webpages—encompassing the portal page, Reese Library website, and Greenblatt Library website—would serve as a unifying element while still allowing each library to retain its own web identity on its homepage with unique design and content. To gather user data that would assist them in choosing categories and links for the horizontal navigation bar, the CLWS members performed a card sort exercise on both campuses. A card sort exercise is one method for determining users' expectations with regards to both the structure of a webpage and its terminology (Kitalong, Hoeppner, & Scharf, 2008; McHale, 2008; Robbins et al., 2007; Whang, 2008). Card sorts use index cards in addition to writing implements and are not automated; they can be open or closed. Some studies described an open card sort in which participants were provided with predetermined terms on index cards that they were asked to organize into logical groupings, and then choose a category heading name for each grouping (Kitalong et al., 2008; McHale, 2008; Robbins et al., 2007). Whang (2008), however, described an open card sort in which the participants were provided with blank index cards and told to choose their own terms as well as category headings. McHale (2008) described a closed card sort in which participants were provided with the category headings and asked to group the cards with predetermined terms under the headings. Nielsen (2004) recommended using 15 participants for a card sort exercise because this results in a 0.90 correlation, providing optimal information, while using more than 15 participants results in "diminishing returns" (para. 9).

The CLWS members chose to perform a closed card sort, asking participants to organize index cards that had a resource or service name already provided into groups under a predetermined category heading. At the end of the sorting exercise, the card sort moderator asked the participants to suggest alternate names and categories and asked a series of follow-up questions, including how they would order the cards in a list, such as alphabetically or by importance. The CLWS members hoped that the card sort exercise data would further assist in reconciling the differences between the disparate user groups—health professionals and a mainly liberal arts commuter community—and identify services and resources appropriate for both user groups. Data from the card sort, however, was difficult to analyze and apply given that subjects tended to group unrelated items under the same heading, seemingly forcing items into disparate groupings. Brucker (2010) contended that with a closed card sort "there is a real danger of skewing the results, guiding users into categories that might not actually make any sense to them, or categories they never would have created on their own" (p. 43). Despite these difficulties, the card sort was useful in identifying confusing terms and also provided rich qualitative data from the participants' comments and suggestions.

Based on the survey results, the card sort activities, and meeting discussions, the CLWS members developed a draft mockup of the consolidated libraries homepage. The members agreed that the following features should be present on the mock-up: a prominent search box, a live chat box, links to individual library websites, a horizontal navigation menu, an RSS blog feed, and social media links. Several meetings were dedicated to determining which categories and drop-down links to include in the navigation menu. The CLWS members wanted to ensure that the information provided would be applicable to both user groups without overloading the drop-down menus. Accomplishing this goal was a challenge given that library technologies were not fully integrated, including electronic journal locators and OPACs. The CLWS members resolved differences in terminology by providing separate links in a tabbed search box on the portal page with vocabulary based on campus vernacular or library name—Health Sciences Campus for

FIGURE 12.1
Navigation Menu Proposed to Library Work Team

Find Resources	Services	Get Help	Libraries & Collections	About Us	Contact Us
Catalog (GIL)	For Students	A-Z Index	Greenblatt Library (Health Sciences)	Floor Plans	
eBooks	For Faculty & Staff	Ask Us!	Reese Library (Summerville)	Give to the Libraries	
eJournals	For Clinicians	Liaison/Subject Librarians	Curriculum Center	Maps & Directions	
GALILEO Databases	For Community Patrons	LibGuides	Government Information	Organizational Chart	
Health Sciences Databases	For Patrons with Disabilities	Off-Campus Access	Historical Collections (Greenblatt)	Policies	
Mobile Resources	Borrowing & Renewal	Research Consultation	Special Collections (Reese)	Staff Directory	
	GIL Express	Tutorials		Strategic Plan	
	Interlibrary Loan				

Greenblatt Library and Summerville Campus for Reese Library. Although these decisions strayed from the CLWS's original vision for the consolidated libraries homepage, providing separate access points was necessary to maintain easy access to resources and meet specific population needs.

In late November 2012, the CLWS members agreed on the structure and content for the horizontal navigation menu and distributed a draft of the menu to all library employees, asking them for comments and suggestions. Once the CLWS members finalized the navigation menu (Figure 12.1), they completed the consolidated homepage mockup (Figure 12.2) and reported their findings to the LWT in early December 2012. The LWT recommended multiple changes to the order and content of the drop-down menus and shared several concerns about the mockup, ultimately requiring major revisions to the design.

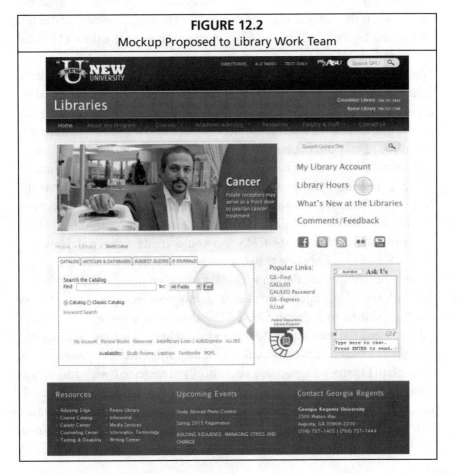

FIGURE 12.2
Mockup Proposed to Library Work Team

Implementing a Consolidated Libraries Website

In late December 2012, the LWT disbanded the CLWS and assigned the responsibility of implementing the combined web presence to a team of two librarians: Virginia Feher, a government information librarian at Reese Library, and Kim Mears, a nursing information librarian at Greenblatt Library (the authors). This team structure ensured representation from both libraries and removed the task of website consolidation from a committee environment, thus accelerating planning and implementation. We effectively streamlined the project and developed a revised graphical mockup of the consolidated homepage that addressed the concerns of the LWT. This mockup was based on a template that the Office of Communications & Marketing (OCM) developed, which was not yet approved or available for editing in the content management system (CMS). Because we did not have access to the CMS on the GRU staging server at the time of official consolidation in January 2013, we proactively contacted the OCM for assistance with presenting a unified library web presence and asked for a rudimentary landing page that would link to the existing ASU and GHSU library websites. In hindsight, a simple "under construction" page with links to the respective library's homepages would have been a better solution as the library did not have the permissions to edit the temporary page, necessitating multiple requests for changes and corrections to the content.

At a meeting with the OCM in mid-June 2013, we learned that the Reese and Greenblatt websites had to be migrated to a new server to meet an early July SACS-COC deadline. By this time, the libraries had gained access to the template in the CMS and could create webpages. However, the CMS provided only one template with limited flexibility in design, including the inability to offer a horizontal navigation menu—the key feature that both the CLWS and us worked diligently on developing. The priority was then shifted to meeting SACS-COC deadlines, even with pages that did not meet the sub-team's design and usability expectations. Since the Greenblatt Library website existed within the same CMS environment, the Greenblatt Library's pages were successfully transferred with minor updates. The Reese Library's pages had to be reconstructed due to compatibility issues, resulting in quick decisions regarding organization and content with little input from Reese Library staff. Fortuitously, much of the Reese site linked to content on outside servers, such as LibGuides, GALILEO, and the OPAC, reducing the number of pages that we had to reconstruct, and thus decreasing the time spent on completing the task.

We had reservations about the design and restrictions of the university template and believed that it would interfere with our goal of a robust and visually pleasing libraries website. Peterson (2006) stated that "the library Web site is unique due to the wide range of services and content available" (p. 217). We wanted a unique consolidated homepage that would look professional and polished and not have the look of a secondary page. Connell (2013) found common themes when reviewing case study articles about libraries that implemented an institutional CMS for their website, including "the issue of lack of control and problems of collaboration between academic libraries and the campus entities controlling website management" (p. 44). We faced similar circumstances, so we met with the director of libraries to discuss options.

Because the university template offered little flexibility in design, including the lack of a horizontal navigation menu, we and director of libraries decided to pursue other avenues to create a libraries website that met our needs. With support from the vice provost, we worked with an outside contractor to design and implement the consolidated libraries homepage. We provided the revised mockup to the contractor, who created a draft page that retained the elements but provided an alternative design. After several revisions with refinements to the design and content, the page was approved by us and LWT. We then faced a significant challenge due to an extremely brief timeline set by university administration to go live with the consolidated homepage. Several of the secondary pages for the links in the navigation menu had not yet been created and the tabbed search box was missing content. Though not ideal, we opted to launch the page in phases, with the navigation menu removed for the first launch. This decision expedited the timeline, and the libraries finally had a unique consolidated homepage on July 29, 2013. With subsequent phases, we reinserted an updated navigation menu (Figure 12.3) with links to newly created pages that (mainly) represented both libraries and added an OPAC search feature in the tabbed search box. Even with the consolidation of the OPACs and GALILEO databases, the two campuses are still divergent in how they access resources. For example, the Summerville Campus remains wedded to GALILEO and its discovery tool, while the Health Sciences Campus uses an alphabetical linked list of resources.

		FIGURE 12.3 Final Navigation Menu		
Resources	**Services**	**Get Help**	**Libraries & Collections**	**About Us**
Databases A–Z	Students	Ask Us!	Greenblatt Library (Health Sciences)	Maps & Directions
eJournals	Faculty & Staff	Liaison/Subject Librarians	Reese Library (Summerville)	Organizational Chart
Health Sciences eBooks	Clinicians & Researchers	LibGuides	Government Information	Policies
Catalog (GIL-Find)	Community Users	Off-Campus Access	Historical Collections & Archives (Health Sciences)	Staff Directory
GALILEO		Research Consultation	Special Collections (Summerville)	Strategic Plan
			Scholarly Commons	Give to the Libraries

To retain local control and update information quickly, we decided to maintain the Greenblatt and Reese Library websites within the CMS environment and forego the navigation menu as a unifying element across the websites. The consolidated homepage (Figure 12.4) remains the only page with the horizontal navigation menu. Library staff edit the page outside of the CMS, and the OCM staff upload revised files as library staff do not have server access. Though not ideal, we considered it a necessary compromise so that the libraries could provide a unique portal page that positively represents the combined libraries but also ensures that we could easily maintain the Reese and Greenblatt websites.

During the project, the GRU director of libraries asked us to propose a slogan representing the libraries' vision that they could feature on the consolidated homepage. This request provided the opportunity for us to solicit feedback from staff in both libraries, encouraging consensus building. We compiled a list of possible slogans and then distributed a survey to all library employees, asking them to choose or nominate a slogan. The winning slogan "Connect, Discover, Collaborate" was approved by the director of libraries and is now featured prominently on the consolidated homepage. The slogan is also available for use on libraries' promotional materials, such as flyers and posters.

FIGURE 12.4
Final Consolidated Libraries' Homepage

Conclusion

The website project occurred within a fast-paced environment in which staff across both campuses were responsible for many tasks related to consolidation in addition to their day-to-day responsibilities. This, among other factors, made the process of developing a consolidated web presence a challenge. Leading up to and immediately after consolidation, library staff did not have access to the staging server within the CMS, meaning that they had to wait for OCM staff to provide access and also rely on them to create and update the temporary consolidated homepage. The OCM was focused on launching the main GRU webpages, resulting in delays for the libraries. Despite gaining access to the CMS, compulsory SACS-COC accreditation deadlines forced us to focus on completing tasks (quantity) within time constraints rather than focusing on quality. We had to alter planned features, such as the navigation menu, and we also could not include the chat box since both libraries had not yet implemented the service. Further complications resulted from delays in the consolidation of information technology systems across both campuses, which necessitated that the libraries maintain different authentication methods for accessing subscribed resources off-campus. Greenblatt Library used a single sign-on method and Reese Library used a common university password that was changed and redistributed at the beginning of each semester. Libraries information technology staff implemented a work-around so that both campuses could use a single sign-on method, but since the Health Sciences Campus does not utilize the discovery tool, we have not added the search box. Thus the consolidated homepage search box still includes different links for Greenblatt and Reese patrons, which emphasizes the campus differences.

Though challenging, the project had many positive results. It afforded us the opportunity to develop professional relationships with the OCM staff, which will facilitate future collaboration on website projects to benefit library users, such as a robust A–Z databases page (currently a static HTML page that is difficult to maintain). Collaborating with the OCM also made it easier to request additional links to the GRU Libraries' homepage on university webpages, increasing the libraries' visibility to the campus community. In addition to links featured on the GRU Academics and Students homepages, a Libraries link is available in the footer of the majority of the university's webpages. Most importantly, the project resulted in unification of the libraries' web presence and fostered consensus building between the two libraries.

More than a year after official consolidation, the intensity of efforts has waned. However, websites require continuous maintenance and revisions, and libraries' administration has requested an expansion of our web team to ensure representation from departments across both libraries. Thus, the web team has expanded into a Libraries Web Group (LWG). The group is charged with working on short- and long-term projects with tangible results. In the short-term, the LWG implemented mobile sites for the consolidated homepage and the Reese Library homepage and redesigned an existing Greenblatt mobile site (for consistency in design). The LWG also implemented a redesigned Reese Library homepage and a redesigned Greenblatt Library homepage. Future long-term projects include a dynamic A–Z database page and additional webpages that link to resources for specific subject areas. These ongoing projects are aimed at providing a robust GRU Libraries web presence while still providing direct access to customized resources for both user populations.

Acknowledgments

We would like to thank the GRU Libraries employees who assisted in the web project, particularly Owen Angleton, Lindsay Blake, Veronica Corradino, Tom Cutshall, Kathy Davies, Autumn Johnson, Melissa Johnson, Dr. Brenda Seago, Fay Verburg, and Lisa Workman.

References

Augusta State University & Georgia Health Sciences University. (n.d.). ASU-GHSU consolidation: Creating the next great American research university. Retrieved from http://asughsu.org/work-teams

Brucker, J. (2010). Playing with a bad deck: The caveats of card sorting as a web site redesign tool. *Journal of Hospital Librarianship, 10,* 41–53.

Coahoma Community College. (n.d.) *Coahoma Community College Library web site survey.* Retrieved from http://216.79.145.2/library/forms/Library%20Website%20Survey.html

Cobus, L., Dent, V., & Ondrusek, A. (2005). How twenty-eight users helped redesign an academic library web site. *Reference & User Services Quarterly, 44*(3), 232–246.

Cockrell, B. J., & Jayne, E. (2002). How do I find an article? Insights from a web usability study. *Journal of Academic Librarianship, 28*(3), 122.

Connell, R. (2013). Content management systems: Trends in academic libraries. *Information Technology & Libraries, 32*(2), 42–55.

Davidsen, S., & Yankee, E. (2004). *Web site design with the patron in mind: A step-by-step guide for libraries.* Chicago, IL: American Library Association.

Fairleigh Dickinson University. (2007). *FDU Library website survey.* Retrieved from http://view.fdu.edu/files/surveysummary.pdf

Heck, J. J., Davies, K. J., Verburg, F. L., Brown, M., Loveless, V. L., Bandy, S. L., & Seago, B. L. (2013). Consolidation: A tale of two libraries. *Library & Leadership Management, 28*(1), 1–14.

Holtze, T. L. (2006). The Web designer's guide to color research. *Internet Reference Services Quarterly, 11*(1), 87–101.

Kitalong, K. S., Hoeppner, A., & Scharf, M. (2008). Making sense of an academic library web site: Toward a more usable interface for university researchers. *Journal of Web Librarianship, 2*(3), 177–204.

Lehman, T., & Nikkel, T. (2008). *Making library web sites usable: A LITA guide.* New York, NY: Neal-Schuman.

McHale, N. (2008). Toward a user-centered academic library home page. *Journal of Web Librarianship, 2*(2/3), 139–176.

MIT Libraries. (1999, March). *MIT Libraries web usability test: A observer comment form.* Retrieved from http://web.mit.edu/hennig/www/presentations/simmons/testA.pdf

Nielsen, J. (2000). *Designing web usability.* Indianapolis, IN: New Riders Publishing.

Nielsen, J. (2004). Card sorting: How many users to test. Retrieved from http://www.nngroup.com/articles/card-sorting-how-many-users-to-test/

Norlin, E., & Winters, C. (2002). *Usability testing for library websites: A hands-on guide.* Chicago, IL: American Library Association.

Peterson, K. (2006). Academic web site design and academic templates: Where does the library fit in? *Information Technology & Libraries, 25*(4), 217–221.

Robbins, L. P., Esposito, L., Kretz, C., & Aloi, M. (2007). What a user wants: Redesigning a library's web site based on a card-sort analysis. *Journal of Web Librarianship, 1*(4), 3–27.

Tolliver, R. L., Carter, D. S., Chapman, S. E., Edwards, P. M., Fisher, J. E., Haines, A. L., & Price, R. M. (2005). Website redesign and testing with a usability consultant: Lessons learned. *OCLC Systems & Services, 21*(3), 156–166.

University System of Georgia. (2012). Newsroom: Eight USG institutions recommended for consolidation [Press release]. Retrieved from http://www.usg.edu/news/release/eight_usg_institutions_recommended_for_consolidation

Vaughan, J. (2011). Web scale discovery services. In D. Freeman (Series Ed.), *Library Technology Reports: Expert Guides to Library Systems and Services, 47*(1).

Whang, M. (2008). Card-sorting usability tests of the WMU Libraries' web site. *Journal of Web Librarianship, 2*(2/3), 205–218.

CHAPTER 13

Hidden from View:
The Role of Organizational Culture in Collegiate Restructuring

Lynn N. Baird

ADMINISTRATORS IN HIGHER education are frequently challenged to seek synergies, achieve efficiencies, and deliver effective educational experiences in an environment of declining resources. Presidents and provosts continually seek that spot where engaged student learning occurs at a reasonable cost. The academic library often becomes an area of interest for administrators because of high operating costs, perceived waning use by patrons, and the absence or ineffective use of standardized metrics to communicate contributions to the education and research missions of the institution. Library administrators may find their provost and decanal colleagues lack an appreciation for the managerial and communal processes that define librarianship. In environments where respect for this special disciplinary knowledge is lacking, library leaders may find their libraries vulnerable to external pressure to restructure and reshape their programs.

One strategy to reduce costs is to streamline operations to achieve efficiencies with fewer staff. This chapter examines how one institution launched a merger of the library and its information technology unit with a vision of finding efficiencies and building synergies. This case study will be useful to library administrators, higher education administrators, and others contemplating organizational mergers. Through an analysis of events, readers will develop an understanding of organizational culture and how leaders must manage cultural expectations during periods of change.

Case Study

In 1987, Patricia Battin promoted a blending of libraries and information technology (1987). This hybridization proposal illuminated the revolutionized world of academic libraries, a response necessitated by the dawning of the information age (Molholt, 1985). Disruptive computing technologies forced the library profession to reexamine its core principles as it sought to address changing user expectations for service (Baron, 2010). The shift was so sudden that libraries lacked both the entrepreneurial culture and human capacity to serve these new demands. Thus, blending information technology with libraries as merged units was seen as a model to expedite the advance of revised library missions. Several such organizational mergers yielding various levels of success were prompted by Battin's concept (Bolin, 2005; Massis, 2011). The institution that is the center of this case study had several conditions converge to determine proposed merger's fate. External factors pressed upon university leadership: declining revenues, a worsening economy, unexpected competition for reputation resulting in fewer student enrollments, and a loss of political influence. University leadership resolved that dramatic moves were needed to reestablish its focus.

Mergers of libraries and IT occur for many reasons (Hirshon, 1998); in this case, there was growing dissatisfaction with the library's ability to quickly respond to user demand for technology. This university's president was enamored with the promise technology offered to both the learning enterprise as well as the institution's reputation. He wanted to be sure no other in-state competitor could match the technological infrastructure offered by his institution. As with most institutions of higher education, limited resources were available to build this infrastructure.

The president decided to find funding through a prioritization process. Campus groups were identified to explore organizational changes that would result in efficiencies and synergies. These groups were organized into "clusters"—the library was included in the Information Management Services Cluster. The report for this cluster identified three alternative organizational structures to "enhance focus, efficiency and synergy" (Abraham et al., 2001, p. 1). All three structures featured the library as the hub, either by maintaining status quo, adding an information commons, or developing a virtual library.

Within two months of receiving the cluster reports, the president announced his decision to reorganize the university by eliminating colleges, separating units, and combining the library and Information Technology Services (ITS) into a single unit, Library and Information Technology (LIT). Given the small universe of changes considered in the cluster report, university faculty members were stunned by the magnitude of the changes. These changes were unveiled at a town hall meeting of faculty and staff; little opportunity for questions or input was offered as these decisions were made and final. Faculty opinions would not change these decisions as leadership viewed them as merely administrative, not impacting the curriculum that was clearly under the purview of faculty.

Library faculty members were particularly dumbstruck by their new unified structure as they received new leadership. They were now under the direction of the vice provost-chief information officer (CIO). The library faculty expressed their discontent to the president by noting that "the realignment... de-emphasizes the library's role as an academic program" (Faculty of the University of Idaho Library, personal communication, March 15, 2002). The position of dean was made part of a sub-unit and was thus no longer a direct leadership position (University of Idaho, President's Office, personal communication, July 10, 2003). This was, perhaps, the crowning blow and appeared to confirm the library faculty's growing concern that the president viewed the library as irrelevant and library faculty as particularly outdated in their mastery of their content area. The president championed information technology, not the library, as the future for access to resources and often remarked how he had visited a law practice where the firm had abolished its library's print holdings for online access. He suggested that libraries were obsolete and would soon be replaced by computers (R. Hoover, personal communication, 2003). He was not alone in this opinion. During this time, information technology services became a campus focus in the ongoing competition for advantage and distinction among colleges. As other institutions were cementing their public reputations by being included in the "Best Colleges" list in *US News and World Report*, this institution pursued a different strategy to gain recognition. It was recognized as one of *Yahoo! Internet Life* magazine's most wired universities in the country ("A Presidential Transition,"

2003, p. 7), a badge of honor and a signal of progressive investments in future technology.

Since the library had been, de facto, subsumed by ITS, its faculty was no longer represented in university leadership activities. The dean had not been terminated; however, he was limited in his authority and oversight of the library, and he no longer was a part of university leadership groups (University Council, Dean's Council, etc.). The LIT leader saw an expansion of the CIO role, moving beyond being merely the head of ITS and responsible for technology as a utility, to a new role where information technology would have an academic role in partnership with library resources. External perceptions were different. University faculty saw the library had been placed under ITS, an entrepreneurial entity that was perceived to be more involved in generating revenue than in serving people. Morale among library faculty was seriously compromised; the inability to communicate directly with the president or provost ensured that bitterness pervaded the library's climate. The lack of respect felt by library faculty was compounded by a quantifiable steady decline in support for library resources, evidenced by a 26% reduction in library faculty and staff during this period. While the provost championed the new organizational structure as a means to "develop new strengths through a strategic partnership" and assured the faculty that strategic investments in IT infrastructure would benefit future library development (B. Pitcher, personal communication, March 26, 2002), the library faculty was not appeased.

The climate in the library did little to aid merger activities. ITS unit leaders knew that library faculty had petitioned against the merger, and library faculty were unwilling to work in a merged environment. From ITS' perspective, library faculty rejected them and it felt personal. With this as context, the LIT Leadership Team was formed.

The team met regularly and recognized that they needed to make progress, regardless of personal feelings. During meetings, it became clear that participants made radically different assumptions about organizational issues and leadership based on their respective organizational cultures. This lack of shared perspective significantly delayed operations, erected invisible barriers, and made the process of participants arriving at an understanding about the content and context of working together much more difficult. However, when group members became cognizant, through frank conversations in meetings, of the existence of multiple organizational cultures, transformative learning occurred. Members of the two cultures became aware that they were not seeing problems from the same perspective and needed to share information differently in order to achieve goals.

The LIT, as a concept and a working structure, ended with a change in the university presidency and subsequent retirements of the formal leaders of LIT: the CIO, director of ITS, and the dean of the library. During its three-year existence, ITS saw strategic benefits of aligning with academic programs as it became an integral part of the academic mission. The library benefitted from having strategic partnerships with ITS as new technology and services were launched in this era. However, the library became less visible to academic faculty during this period.

Four Frames Analysis

The case study offered here illustrates an outcome of cultural clashes within a higher education environment and how such cultures can impede organizational change unless managed in a thoughtful manner. In order to examine and better comprehend the forces of organizational culture in a change process, I will employ an analysis based on Bolman and Deal's (2013) framework. In this work, the authors develop four separate lenses, or frames, by which organizational culture can be perceived, and they explore organizational culture through an organization's structure, its approach to labor, how it operates to compete for scarce resources, and how it embodies and acts upon its values.

Other authors have posited explanations for higher education culture (Bergquist, 1992; Bergquist & Pawlak, 2008), but Bolman and Deal's four frames provide a method for rich description of organizational culture by considering its interdependence with organizational structure. The four frames—structural, human resources, political, and symbolic—will be used to illustrate how organizational cultures collided in this case. Each of these frames will be discussed as a means of demonstrating differences that occurred.

Structural Frame

The structural frame, as envisioned by Bolman and Deal (2013), helps describe an organization through its organizational charts, its lines of authority, and its rules and policies. Through this orderly fashion, an organization

sets goals and deploys resources to achieve goals. In the case study presented here, several differences emerge in an examination of this lens (Table
13.1). The ITS organization was designed to address and resolve problems
with great speed and needed to have clear lines of authority, while the library had a deliberative and administratively flatter organization, designed
to reach consensus in decision making. This structural difference has been
noted in other cultural studies of libraries and computer science mergers
(Baron, 2010; Cain, 2003).

Table 13.1		
Structural Frame in the Context of the Case Study		
DESCRIPTION	**ITS**	**LIBRARY**
Division of work: Who does the work?	Professional staff; technology specialists; classified staff	Library faculty; classified staff
Leadership: Who directs the work?	Assistant provost; director of ITS; department heads	Dean; associate dean; department heads
Organizational structure: How is work accomplished?	Divisional form; chain of command	Professional bureaucracy; faculty governance
Communication and decision making: How do we talk?	Based on need for quick solutions; direct lines	Use of consensus; inclusive communications
Planning and control systems: How are goals set and measured?	Performance control	Action planning

Human Resource Frame

Organizations are formed by groups of people who take on roles that
are designed to accomplish feats that no single person could achieve in-
dependently. Among organizations, rules for who does what work, how
employees are rewarded or compensated, and the conditions under which
employees labor can be very different, based upon assumptions about the
nature of human behavior. These factors help identify the organization's
culture and establish conditions that employees measure when considering
their personal fit or compatibility with an organization.

This case study illustrates a number of differences between the ITS and library units with regards to human resources. One of the most obvious is a comparison of market value between most computer science/technology and library positions. Technology jobs frequently garner higher salaries and rewards (Katz & Salaway, 2004, p. 4). There is a perceived shortage of excellent programmers, systems administrators, etc. that results in high mobility and steep competition for salary and other forms of benefits (Goldstein & Pirani, 2008, p. 10). Librarians and library staff workers historically have been viewed as employees in a feminine profession (Fleming-May & Douglass, 2014; Williams, 1992), doing work that is not as highly skilled or valued by higher education administrators as reflected in the low wages for this segment of the academy. At this university, these human resource factors related to salary were institutionalized. As a result, the ITS staff was predominantly young, male, and well paid, with relatively short careers; the library faculty and staff were predominantly female, paid at less than market value, and had a long tenure with the university.

The level of organizational investment in professional development support for ITS relative to investment in library staff was also an obvious area of difference. The IT professionals were expected to keep current in their skills, and there was plenty of support for conference travel and other trainings. The librarians were, by contrast, given release time, and travel costs were shared between the participant and the institution. Despite the significant upheavals in the library profession brought about by the increased emphasis on technology, no additional funding was provided to ensure librarians were developing new approaches to integrate technology with their practice.

The two units approached work from different perspectives. Within ITS, the work was divided into functional units and these units operated in teams to meet their production goals. The library work units were broader and more inclusive. The work was less focused on task but on process, looking at a continuous improvement of the process. When the two groups began meeting to do shared work, this orientation to what work would be accomplished and how the work was to be accomplished was initially mystifying to all parties because the rules of engagement were not clearly understood. The new LIT organization provided both the ITS and library staff with a very different organization, one where all employees needed to reevaluate their compatibility with the university.

	Table 13.2 Human Resource Frame in the Context of the Case Study	
DESCRIPTION	**ITS**	**LIBRARY**
Mobility: Are employees place-bound or free agents?	Employees in highly competitive market; staff recruited and rewarded	Faculty, staff with long tenure due to lack of other opportunities
Rewards: Are salaries and other remunerations competitive?	Across university, highly paid; salaries slightly below market	Across university, lowest paid professionals; salaries well below market
Professional development: Is there investment in training?	Unit-funded professional development and networking	Partial funding for professional development and networking
Autonomy and participation: What are the roles of employees in directing their work?	Team approaches	Faculty planning and autonomous governance

Political Frame

Politics, power, and leadership share the dubious honor of being terms that are widely distrusted, used to describe others and not ourselves. Bolman and Deal acknowledge this negativity, yet suggest that such a view disadvantages an understanding of organizational effectiveness and the roles individuals play in achieving goals: "Viewed from the political frame, politics is the realistic process of making decisions and allocating resources in a context of scarcity and divergent interests" (2013, p. 183). Politics within higher education institutions are no different; they are rooted in competition for scarce resources. This case illuminates tensions between legacy and futuristic programs, a constant struggle between what is perceived to be essential to academia (e.g., foundation courses) in contrast to innovative or popular courses or degrees (e.g., visual technology and design or zombie studies). This struggle often goes unresolved, and universities try to support both innovation and traditional programs. Universities attempt to "satisfice" parties in this way until such actions are insupportable, requiring realignment of resources with institutional priorities. In this particular case, administrators decided to develop a robust IT structure at the expense of library materials and staff.

Relationships are key to the political frame. The politics of higher education rest upon the many extensive and complex coalitions that form in the struggles to acquire resources and prestige. In this case, many such coalitions existed. Some were new, stemming from the institution's recent decision to adopt responsibility centered management, a budgeting model that seeks to reward those departments that attract students and allows costs and revenues associated with delivering classes to be allocated to these departments. The cost-recovery model was used by ITS while the library was supported through central administration. In other words, ITS services were available to those departments that had money (either returns from sponsored grants or high enrollments) while others were unable to support their technology needs. In terms of political power, those disciplines that traditionally did not have a high research activity component also did not have much to invest in technology at a time when this investment would have helped attract more students and thus secure more resources.

The scientific disciplines and professional colleges were much more successful in grants and therefore, had a strong affinity with ITS as they were able to invest in technology for classrooms and research. Those faculties who lacked resources perceived this fee-for-service model as one that limited their professional success. They often found unauthorized processes to implement technology, establishing servers and systems that threatened the security of official networks. This fee-for-service model did not endear ITS to the academic side of the house. The library, on the other hand, had developed new systems to support academics that were available free of charge. Such services as electronic reserves and the growing list of electronic databases were seen as valuable assets to faculty, saving them time and money in delivering instruction. The library was perceived to be a highly valued partner to the faculty.

LIT's leadership recognized the political capital that both ITS and the library brought to this new partnership and saw the merging of units to be critical to overcoming the university's digital divide. However, because the CIO's native organizational home was perceived as being located in ITS, he was not trusted and unable to sufficiently make this case to the academic side of the organization. Had either of the two sub-unit leaders shared the CIO's vision, or if the CIO had been able to identify and support informal leaders, the fate of the merger may have had a different outcome.

Table 13.3		
Political Frame in the Context of the Case Study		
DESCRIPTION	**ITS**	**LIBRARY**
Scarce resources: How are priorities set? What shapes the arena for competition?	A commodity worthy of investment for future benefits, including reputational gains	A public good that is waning as a community need
Alliances: With whom and how are relationships developed and nurtured?	Faculty and students are customers (fee for services rendered)	Faculty and students are partners in the educational process
Power distribution: Is authority concentrated or diffuse?	Authority is concentrated in the central administration of the unit	Authority is diffused through faculty governance

Symbolic Frame

Looking at organizations through the symbolic lens is more easily done by those standing outside the circle as "our own cultural ways are often invisible to us because we see them simply as the way things are—and ought to be" (Bolman & Deal, 2013, p. 244). The symbolic frame captures an organization's values and beliefs, its stories, its way of life. The symbolic frame embodies the organization's culture. The symbolic frame may be, for all organizations, the most important: It is the defining frame, giving each organization its unique shape. Culture shapes the organization's structure, its human resources, and how it negotiates the political realm. Culture may find its beginnings as an informal presence, elements of an organization's climate that becomes institutionalized over time.

Organizational Culture versus Climate

Understanding the role of culture in organizations is vital to analyzing this case because it was this lack of cultural knowledge that led to a failed change initiative. Indeed, as a participant, it was when awareness emerged of the existence of multiple realities that real learning and cooperation ensued. Turning to the literature, one finds extensive writings on leadership but fewer on organizational culture. Yet, blending leadership theory with theories of organizational culture and climate highlights how humans in groups behave and how this behavior is a collective force.

Culture and climate are located in the domain of leadership as Schein (2004) explains,

> On the one hand, cultural norms define how a given nation or organization will define leadership—who will get promoted, who will get the attention of followers. On the other hand, it can be argued that the only thing of real importance that leaders do is to create and manage culture; that the unique talent of leaders is their ability to understand and work with culture; and that it is an ultimate act of leadership to destroy culture when it is viewed as dysfunctional. (p. 11)

This is echoed by Denison (1996) as he notes, "One of the most important contributions a manager or executive can make is the culture they create… Culture management is a long-term strategy and a difficult asset to cultivate" (p. 194). Other theorists embraced a concept of "strong culture" to define leadership's domain. Deal and Kennedy (1982) claim "strong culture" creates a more effective workplace because it inspires people to commit more of themselves to their work as the employees find it personally rewarding. This view was embedded in managerial literature (Bennis, 1989; Ouchi, 1982; Peters & Waterman, 1982) to the point where causation statements concerning strong cultures result in effective corporations had been accepted as an unquestioned law of organizational theory (Kotter & Heskett, 1992, p. 18). Kotter and Heskett challenged the idea that strong cultures result in effectiveness, finding that such existing cultures "can actually lead intelligent people to behave in ways that are destructive—that systematically undermine an organization's ability to survive and prosper" (p. 142). Their study showed that such cultures could be change resistant and thus could lead to disaster when environmental conditions called for adaptive measures. Regardless of conclusions, these authors are united in acknowledging the importance of organizational culture and a need for leadership to both have an awareness of its existence and ideas for how to affect cultural change.

Climate

The conflation of climate and culture in organizational studies is quite common, and scholars have taken efforts to establish differences between these concepts. Ashforth (1985) explained climate as the employees' attempts to understand the organization. Litwin and Stringer (1968) approached climate as a socially constructed and subjective reality of the "total configural environment" (p. 196) that managers create in order to "manage motivation" (p. 167) so they are more effective in their roles.

Another distinguishing feature between climate and culture is the temporal dimension of climate. Climate is a characteristic of the present that clearly directs perceptions and actions of employees, while culture is a highly enduring characteristic (Moran & Volkwein, 1992; Reichers & Schneider, 1990). As Reichers and Schneider (1990) explain, "Culture researchers make a distinction in the definition of culture between culture as something an organization *is* versus something an organization *has*" (p. 22). Thus, while organizational culture may be deep, unrecognized, and unyielding, an organization's climate is malleable, a social construction by employees, and can be managed by leadership. The leader can introduce new symbols, structures, human resource policies, and political alliances during a change initiative; it will be a matter of time before these elements become integrated into the organization's culture and reflected in its very structure.

Through multiple meetings in this case, librarians and ITS staff were provided opportunities to view the culture of the other. Librarians noted the corporate tone of how business operations were handled, from the formatting of memos and reports to the way in which meetings were scheduled and conducted. ITS staff viewed the library faculty as complaining and change resistant, entrenched in traditional programs and unwilling to see advantages presented in new opportunities. Librarians constructed the ITS narrative to reflect overabundance: for the library, ITS was wealthy (with "owned" expensive equipment), had access to all-expense paid travel, provided service for the elite, and maintained adequate numbers of staff with high salaries. ITS constructed a library narrative that reflected deprivation, the noble poor: For ITS, the library was shabby, in need of staff and salaries, generally proud but needy. The library could be a drain on ITS resources. Another major area of cultural conflict was rooted in the concept of service. To ITS staff, the focus of service is to solve a problem with technology; it is problem-focused. To librarians, service is to help people become more proficient in helping themselves; it is process-focused.

Table 13.4		
Symbolic Frame in the Context of the Case Study		
DESCRIPTION	**ITS**	**LIBRARY**
Plans, meetings, report: What were the purpose, appearance?	Corporate forms, strategic	Academic, plans made to address user needs
Narrative: What were the perceptions of the units?	Highly paid staff; well-equipped; future orientation	"Noble poor;" mission-driven; rooted in historic traditions
Service orientation: What are the goals of service?	Users want technology answers to problems: problem-focus	Users want to be independent learners: process-focus

Lessons Learned

This close examination of one case provides a postmortem on a failed merger. While it is not possible to reconstruct what the actors were thinking and feeling during this process, it is known that the participants were highly educated and well respected. Their knowledge, however, was insufficient armor against the forces of culture. At the end of this experiment, it can safely be assumed that none of the merger's anticipated benefits were realized: There were no savings in operational costs (in fact, costs associated with reorganization were probably real and considerable in terms of lost revenues and increased expenditures), and there were no new synergies that improved academics. Morale was decreased because the human resource frame was nearly ignored. Bolman and Deal note that restructuring organizations is not for the faint of heart, to wit: "Restructuring is a challenging process that consumes time and resources with no guarantee of success" (2013, p. 86).

Hindsight offers readers the opportunity to view this case from a multifaceted perspective. In this case, selected aspects of the structural frame were considered with little or no regard to the other three frames. This merger might have succeeded had there been an acknowledgment of the organizational cultures of these two units.

For this case to have seen a different ending, leadership would have to have been aware of each unit's cultural differences. The disenfranchisement of a dean in an academic unit where the faculty feels neither respected nor rewarded is unlikely to result in a group of willing participants. Had leadership acknowledged and addressed the group's concerns, it would have created a narrative that spelled out how each individual would benefit from a new organizational structure. Leadership would also have facilitated an opportunity for this group to engage in a period of mourning, leading to acceptance of the new order. Personal and professional relationships would have been nurtured; recognition of past contributions would have been honored. Also, a new shared vision between the sub-unit leadership of how the library and ITS could become better partners in teaching and learning would have been offered and encouraged (how this new unit would have political advantages over previous structure, for example). Human resource planning would have produced a revised rewards system. This was a particularly complex restructuring because rather than a straight reorganization within a single organizational culture it blended two distinct cultures. In society, we have many examples of how this type of cultural integration is difficult, if not impossible. World leaders have been stymied by the complexity of blending cultures; it is therefore not unexpected that this particular merger was unsuccessful.

The nature of case study research is to provide rich description of a particular situation and the knowledge that emerges should not be considered to be generalizable. Adding to the existent literature (Baron, 2010; Fulton, 2001), certain cultural observations of this case resonated with other cases. However, the primary lesson of merging cultures can be writ more broadly across the literature of leadership: Organizational culture is a factor that holds weight in any decision-making scenario.

Change management demands leaders take a holistic approach to their organizations when contemplating organizational realignments. Thus, planning must include schema that addresses the organization's structure, its human resource talent and psychological needs, its political arena, and its heart: the organization's culture. While much exists in the literature on each of these topics, successful change is realized only when each of these different organizational pillars is given deep consideration. Using the four-frame model as a vehicle for planning will ensure that leaders contemplating merging units will look beyond the organization chart in the development of their approach to change.

References

Abraham, T., Baird, L., Bolin, M., Force, R., Hughett, H., Lanham, K.,... Christiansen, J. (2001). *Information management services cluster organizational structures*. Unpublished report, University of Idaho, Moscow, ID.

Ashforth, B. E. (1985). Climate formation: Issues and extension. *Academy of Management Review, 10*(4), 837–847.

Baron, S. B. (2010). *Employee perspectives of library and information technology mergers: The recursiveness of structure, culture, and agency* (Doctoral dissertation). Retrieved from ProQuest Dissertations and Theses. (UMI No. 3433635)

Battin, P. (1987). The electronic library. *Collection Management, 9*(2/3), 133–141.

Bennis, W. G. (1989). *On becoming a leader*. Reading, MA: Addison-Wesley.

Bergquist, W. H. (1992). *The four cultures of the academy: Insights and strategies for improving leadership in collegiate organizations*. San Francisco, CA: Jossey-Bass.

Bergquist, W. H., & Pawlak, K. (2008). *Engaging the six cultures of the academy: Revised and expanded edition of the four cultures of the academy*. San Francisco, CA: Jossey-Bass.

Bolin, M. K. (2005). The library and the computer center: Organizational patterns at land grant universities. *Journal of Academic Librarianship, 31*(1), 3–11.

Bolman, L. G., & Deal, T. E. (2013). *Reframing organizations: Artistry, choice, and leadership* (5th ed.). San Francisco, CA: Jossey-Bass.

Cain, M. (2003). The two cultures? Librarians and technologists. *Journal of Academic Librarianship, 29*(3), 177–181.

Deal, T. E., & Kennedy, A. A. (1982). *Corporate cultures: The rites and rituals of corporate life*. Reading, MA: Addison-Wesley.

Denison, D. R. (1996). What is the difference between organizational culture and organizational climate? A native's point of view on a decade of paradigm wars. *Academy of Management Review, 21*(3), 619–654.

Fleming-May, R. A., & Douglass, K. (2014). Framing librarianship in the academy: An analysis using Bolman and Deal's model of organizations. *College and Research Libraries, 75*(3), 389–415.

Fulton, T. L. (2001). *Integrating academic libraries and computer centers: A phenomenological study of leader sensemaking about organizational restructuring* (Doctoral dissertation). Retrieved from ProQuest Dissertations and Theses. (UMI No. 3036035).

Goldstein, P. J., & Pirani, J. A. (2008). Leading the IT workforce in higher education. *ECAR Key Findings*. Retrieved from http://net.educause.edu/ir/library/pdf/EKF/EKF0807.pdf

Hirshon, A. (1998). *Integrating computing and library services: An administrative planning and implementation guide for information resources.* Boulder, CO: CAUSE. Retrieved from http://net.educause.edu/ir/library/pdf/PUB3018.pdf

Katz, R. N., & Salaway, G. (2004). Information technology leadership in higher education: The condition of the community. *ECAR Key Findings.* Retrieved from http://net.educause.edu/ir/library/pdf/EKF/ekf0401.pdf

Kotter, J. P., & Heskett, J. L. (1992). *Corporate culture and performance.* New York, NY: Free Press.

Litwin, G. H., & Stringer, R. A. (1968). *Motivation and organizational climate.* Boston, MA: Harvard University Press.

Massis, B. E. (2011). Academic libraries and information technology. *New Library World, 112*(1/2), 86–89.

Molholt, P. (1985). On converging paths: The computing center and the library. *Journal of Academic Librarianship, 11*(5), 284–288.

Moran, E. T., & Volkwein, J. F. (1992). Cultural approach to the formation of organizational climate. *Human Relations, 45*(1), 19–47.

Ouchi, W. G. (1982). *Theory Z: How American business can meet the Japanese challenge.* Reading, MA: Addison-Wesley.

Peters, T. J., & Waterman, R. H. (1982). *In search of excellence: Lessons from America's best-run companies.* New York, NY: Harper & Row.

A presidential transition. (2003 Fall). *Here We Have Idaho,* 6–7.

Reichers, A. E., & Schneider, B. (1990). Climate and culture: An evolution of constructs. In B. Schneider (Ed.), *Organizational climate and culture* (pp. 5–39). San Francisco, CA: Jossey-Bass.

Schein, E. H. (2004). *Organizational culture and leadership* (3rd Ed.). San Francisco, CA: Jossey-Bass.

Williams, C. L. (1992). The glass escalator: Hidden advantages for men in the "female" professions. *Social Problems, 39*(3), 253–267.

CHAPTER 14

Branch Mergers at the University of British Columbia Library:
A Case Study in Communication

Simon Neame

THE DECISION TO merge or consolidate library branches is often a complicated one, driven by a combination of factors including shrinking budgets, changing service models, and evolving patron use of collections and facilities. The type of communication needed at various stages of the process is often just as complex, requiring a balance between logistics and the broader messages that help provide the context for decisions. Although these types of changes are often unpopular with those campus stakeholders and library staff directly impacted, they are nonetheless an opportunity for the library to demonstrate a proactive rather than reactive response to broader trends in both the academic and higher education environments.

This chapter will focus on communication practices in the context of branch mergers and consolidations and the development of specific messages for key stakeholders including students, faculty, library staff, and the broader community based on recent experiences at the University of British Columbia (UBC) Library. Particular themes to be explored will include framing these changes in the context of institution-specific drivers, includ-

233

ing budget, as well as the opportunity to message the broader trends in public services and collection management in academic libraries. Ideas around timing and specific modes of communication will also be addressed.

Background

This case study will draw on experiences at the UBC Library related to the consolidation and closure of several branches on the UBC Vancouver campus and at two hospital locations over a two-year period. In May 2012 the UBC Library announced a series of branch mergers and consolidations as part of a broad reorganization of public services. These changes formed a key component of a three-year budget realignment and deficit reduction plan. Branch consolidations included merging the Science and Engineering Library with the Woodward Biomedical Library to form the Woodward Library and merging the Music Library into the Art, Architecture and Planning Library to form the Music, Art and Architecture Library. In addition, a review of the three off-site libraries in teaching hospitals recommended the closure of two physical sites and the transition to a new service model for the teaching hospitals, with one physical site remaining at the Vancouver General Hospital.

These changes triggered a series of collections moves as well as relocation of staff and service points. Since the changes were announced in May 2012, all physical moves have been completed, and new service models are either under development or currently being assessed. Although the timing for these changes was largely influenced by budgetary issues, each individual decision was based on a number of factors including patron use of physical locations and collections and the opportunity to bring synergistic collections and services together. Communication with library staff and users played a role in implementing these changes, and many lessons were learned along the way, a number of which will be shared as part of this chapter.

The main campus of the UBC is located in Vancouver, BC, with a second regional campus located about 400 miles northeast in the Okanagan Valley and a smaller presence in downtown Vancouver. UBC enrolls approximately 48,000 undergraduates and 10,000 graduate students between the two campuses. Of the total student population, almost 10,000 are international students. In 2013–2014 UBC attracted almost $519 million in research funding across all disciplines (University of British Columbia,

2014). The university maintains strengths in a number of disciplines, including applied and health sciences, and delivers medical education at teaching hospitals across the province in partnership with several other BC universities. Despite the applied research focus, UBC also has a large Faculty of Arts and is home to several well-known cultural institutions, including the Chan Centre for Performing Arts and the Museum of Anthropology.

The UBC Library is one of Canada's largest academic libraries, with a total FTE of almost 300 staff, including 80 FTE professional librarians. The collection includes almost seven million items, including 1.4 million e-books and over 200,000 serial titles (University of British Columbia Library, 2014). The library is organized into 12 units spread over eight physical locations, including off-campus libraries at the Vancouver General Hospital and the UBC Okanagan campus. UBC Library's current strategic plan is based on the priorities of the university and focuses on key areas such as student engagement, digital collections, and supporting research. The library also has a strong community engagement mandate managed through the Irving K. Barber Learning Centre.

Like many academic and research libraries, the challenges of meeting new demands for services and collections with stagnant or shrinking budgets has meant taking a hard look at resource allocation. Many of the changes described in this chapter were a result of decisions to reallocate funding from areas with lower impact or activity levels to areas that the library felt represented future growth opportunities, both in collections and new services. Factored into these decisions was the knowledge that the library had broken ground on a large storage facility at the south end of the UBC Vancouver campus. This facility, known as Library PARC (Preservation Archives), is based on the Harvard model of modular storage, with the first module having a capacity for 1.6 million volumes. The library viewed this project as an opportunity to take a tiered approach for print collection access with active and medium use collections remaining on open stacks or in the automated storage and retrieval system located in the Barber Learning Centre and very low use collections located at the PARC facility. These collection moves provided the opportunity to rethink the physical arrangement of library collections and services with a focus on the Vancouver campus.

Finally, it is worth noting that the UBC Library maintains a dedicated communications and marketing department, consisting of a director, manager, and two full-time staff. This department provides system-wide communications support for the library and works closely with members of the library's administration on specific projects, including the branch closures and mergers described in this chapter.

A Coordinated Approach

Since the UBC Library was planning to implement a number of moves and mergers simultaneously, a coordinated approach was needed to support both implementation and communication. To oversee and direct changes at both the strategic and operational levels, a Change Management Team was formed consisting of members of the library's leadership team with responsibilities for collections, public services, communications, human resources, finance, and facilities. This team identified the importance of communications at all stages of project implementation, and the library's director of Communications and Marketing took the lead in developing a communications strategy to support the work of this team (L. Ong, personal communication, May 23, 2014). The communications plan included a formal chain of command based on the organizational structure of the library and university, along with a growing number of less formal communications such as websites, blogs, and social media tools.

In the case of the UBC Library, the top of the communication structure is the university librarian, who would communicate directly to deans as well as members of the University Executive, including the provost; associate university librarians would communicate directly to branch and unit heads; and heads would provide information directly to their units. Although the university librarian regularly sent broadcast emails to all library staff, the Change Management Team acknowledged that a more proactive and integrated approach was required to ensure that information reached all stakeholders. Branch and unit heads in particular had considerable impact on how staff would perceive the changes, and this group was an essential part of the communication network.

In most organizations, formal communication channels are where the process begins, but it is only the start of a more extensive plan. Under the guidance of the Change Management Team, UBC Library Communications and Marketing went to work developing a comprehensive public information campaign branded "Library Changes." This title was deliberately simple and set the tone for further communications that highlighted the many ways that the library was evolving across almost every area. Communications staff developed a series of key messages around why changes were being made and specifically why the UBC Library was choosing to close or merge branch locations as part of its budget realignment plan. These messages focused on many factors, including but not limited to, the increasing use of electronic collections, changing use of library spaces, the shift in the roles of liaison librarians, and the need for the library to redirect finite resources to new and emerging areas.

The campaign started with an internal focus on how the changes would impact library staff. Although some conversations had taken place with the specific branches and units that would be directly impacted, most library employees first heard about the planned changes at the all-staff forum in May 2012. At this forum the leadership team set the context for what was happening broadly in academic and research libraries across North America, and then moved to the specifics of UBC Library's budget situation, strategic priorities, and operational changes. Detailed information about the budget and how the planned branch changes would help redirect funding to support strategic priorities was shared with staff. The forum also gave the leadership team an opportunity to gauge firsthand the reaction of staff to the plans, and while not all staff were happy with the news, many appreciated hearing the messages in person as well as the opportunity to ask questions and voice concerns. Once the mergers and consolidations had been made public, the Change Management Team began the next phase of the communication plan.

Internal Communications

The internal communications strategy included a mix of technology-based and in-person communications. In addition to the town hall event, communications staff created an FAQ list based on questions and concerns from staff. This list was added to over the course of the project and available to both staff and members of the university community. Library staff were also kept up to date about the mergers through regular updates in the library's weekly staff newsletter as well as emails sent to an all-staff list. The Change Management Team anticipated that concerns related to job security, changing roles, and a number of other personnel issues would be items of high priority to many staff. The library's Human Resources staff was essential in helping shape the messages and timing around conversations with staff, especially those working in locations impacted by the planned branch closures and mergers. In addition, HR played a key role in liaison with various union and association representatives at UBC, who maintained a strong interest in how the changes would impact their members. This part of the communication process will vary by institution and the types of collective agreements in place, but time invested in keeping these stakeholders informed was a worthwhile investment in the case of UBC Library.

UBC Library is a fairly large organization with staff located across the Vancouver campus and several remote sites. The Change Management Team was very conscious of how the planned changes could have a negative impact on staff morale across an organization already struggling with many issues related to change management. With this in mind, the team felt it was important to meet with all staff face to face to discuss how the changes would impact individuals at the unit level. Although this approach represented a significant investment in time, the team recommended a series of branch and unit visits by the university librarian, deputy university librarian, and the associate university librarian responsible for a particular area. In this phase, every library unit was visited, even those that had been visited before the May staff forum. This became an opportunity to follow-up with the individuals and units who were most affected by the changes. During these visits the tone was deliberately kept as informal as possible, and staff were encouraged to ask questions and express any concerns they had about the changes. Overall the feedback from staff about the process was positive, and many expressed their appreciation for the chance to talk about issues and concerns in these smaller, more informal settings. Not only were these in-person visits helpful for staff, but they also allowed the leadership team to understand concerns at a more individual level, and the visits were a positive step toward building trust, something that can be a challenge across a large and distributed organization.

Engaging the Campus Community

Soon after the internal communications began, the Change Management Team started reaching out to the broader campus community. Since the UBC Library was implementing changes across a number of different disciplines and subject areas, key messages were needed to speak to the interests of students and faculty from a variety of faculties and schools. This approach also gave the team an opportunity to learn more about what a particular community of students and faculty considered important about the library. For example, off-campus hospital staff expressed concerns about changes in access to the library's online resources, while students and faculty at the School of Music were dismayed with the relocation of physical collections and reference staff from the Music Building to the Music, Art and Architecture Library at the Barber Learning Centre. There was very little concern expressed by the users of the Science and Engineering Library regarding the merger with the Woodward (Life Sciences) Library, partly due to the fact that the Woodward Library is located closer to the engineering precinct on campus than the previous location at the Barber Learning Centre. Also, the science and engineering librarians and staff already had a history of working closely with their students and faculty, often travelling to their classrooms and facilities and communicating with them virtually, so a change in physical location was less of a concern for these groups. It was important for the communications plan to allow for these differences in priorities and interests of various subject areas and disciplines.

On the advice of the library's director of Communications and Marketing, the Change Management Team reached out to other campus communications staff, in particular those representing departments whose students and faculty would be directly impacted by the changes in collections and services. These conversations were an important opportunity to strengthen relationships and create allies and ensure that the library and the faculties were putting forward consistent messages to the broader campus community. The library also needed to be cautious when framing communications in the context of university priorities and aspirations. Although the timing for many of the changes was related to pressing budget issues, it would have been misleading to suggest a lack of support from senior university administration for the library. University administration was in fact very supportive of the library and valued its contributions to the university's mission. To make this clear, several key announcements were issued jointly with the library and the Office of Provost and Vice President, Academic, to which the library reports. Similarly, the library worked closely with staff at the School of Music and the Faculty of Medicine on a number of jointly issued announcements. Even with these coordinated efforts, the library struggled at times to control the message. For example, the School of Music posted several lengthy communications on its departmental website that summarized the relocation of the Music Library from its perspective, and while not inaccurate, strongly reflected the school's own interests and concerns. As well, the Change Management Team was not always able to control the timing of some of the jointly issued announcements, and in the case of the Faculty of Medicine, the timing around the closures of the hospital libraries had to be adjusted due to a communications delay.

The library also benefited from the expertise and support of UBC Public Affairs, the central department that manages external communications. In particular, this unit provided advice and training for those individuals selected to speak on behalf of the library to external media. This training was invaluable in helping spokespeople convey information clearly and respond to questions in a consistent way. The benefits of this support were evident in several articles that were published about the changes happening at the UBC Library and how these changes were connected to broader trends in academic libraries and the post-secondary education sector. In the fall of 2012 the UBC student newspaper, *The Ubyssey*, featured an article, titled "Turning a Page: The Changing Role of the University Library," that examined how the library was evolving to meet user needs and expectations in the digital environment (Bates, 2012). The overall tone of the article was positive and reflected the proactive approach the library was taking to balance budget challenges with evolving user needs. An earlier article from *The Ubyssey* covered a public forum sponsored by the UBC School of Music to discuss the plans for relocating the Music Library to the Barber Learning Centre (Wong, 2012). The tone of the meeting was tense, with both faculty and students voicing their concerns about the planned changes and the potential negative impact it would have on the school and its programs. The article presented a fair coverage of the meeting, and it also allowed ample opportunity for the library to present its point of view. An additional article appeared the same month in the arts and entertainment weekly *The Georgia Straight*, providing an additional opportunity for the School of Music and the library to present their perspectives on the changes (Thomson, 2012). Staying on topic with points that are brief, focused, and easy to quote helped to influence how key messages were presented in the broader media.

Communication Tools

At the centre of any communications strategy are the tools used to convey the story. The Change Management Team felt that keeping the university community up to date on changes to services and collection relocations was a top priority. A dedicated website (http://about.library.ubc.ca/changes/) to accompany the "Library Changes" campaign included information about the timing for various branch closures and mergers as well as detailed information about collection moves and service changes. This website quickly became a central location for library staff and users and also functioned as the official access point for public documents related to the various move and merger projects. For example, several documents were made available from the work of the UBC Hospital Libraries Models Working Group, which was jointly established by UBC's dean of medicine and the university librarian to identify potential new sustainable service delivery models. These documents included the "UBC Hospital Libraries Usage Survey," the "UBC St. Paul's Hospital Library at St. Paul's 2012 Fact Sheet" (Figure 14.1a and b), and the "UBC Hamber Library at BC Children's & Women's Hospital 2012 Fact Sheet."

Confidential documents, such as those including potential staffing models and cost reduction strategies, were not shared online. Documents like fact sheets, presented in an easy to read info-graphic format, conveyed key data and information about user behavior, such as a 120% increase in online database use or librarian expertise as one of the top three services valued by users. These documents were made publicly available in the spirit of transparency and because they reinforced the fact that decisions were based on specific data. The website also included prominent links to comment forms and email addresses, thereby encouraging library users to provide feedback. The responsibility for answering questions in a timely and consistent manner was assigned to a member of the library communications department.

In addition to the website, the library communications staff created several print-based items including posters, postcards, and bookmarks that could be distributed at service points as well as at locations directly impacted by the changes.

A consistent look helped library users recognize these items as a source of information about changes to collections and services. The use of a template allowed posters and other signage to be easily updated, especially

---

FIGURE 14.1a
UBC St. Paul's Hospital Library at St. Paul's 2012 Fact Sheet

---

UBC St. Paul's Hospital Library at St. Paul's Hospital

St. Paul's Library at a glance

In 2011/12

St. Paul's Library is used most often by residents, graduate students, researchers, UBC teaching faculty, and hospital staff.

In-person visits 19,221
Loans 1,706
Reference transactions . . 1,949

Staff (FTE) 2.6
Open days/week 5.5
Open hours/week 50
Seating 41
Computer terminals 6

From 2007 to 2012

Delivery from other branches 55%

Borrowing print items 70%

In-person visits 30%

Online database searches (CINAHL) [1] 120%

Focus group with St. Paul's Library users[2]
Participants discussed what they value most and future directions

Collections

Online journals
Improved network access

Services

Librarian expertise
Technical help
Book/article delivery

Spaces

Quiet & comfortable
Group study spaces
Self-serve 24/7 access

FIGURE 14.1b
UBC St. Paul's Hospital Library at St. Paul's 2012 Fact Sheet

2012 fact-sheet

UBC Hospital Library Usage Survey [3]

In an August 2012 survey about the importance of library services to their UBC research and work, 119 respondents (22%) identified St. Paul's as the library they are most likely to use.

62% of those respondents are affiliated with the UBC Faculty of Medicine and a further 21% with the School of Nursing and Faculty of Pharmaceutical Sciences.

Who responded?

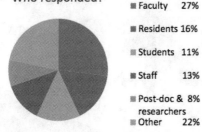

- Faculty 27%
- Residents 16%
- Students 11%
- Staff 13%
- Post-doc & 8% researchers
- Other 22%

Survey comments stressed the importance of online journal collections and the need for librarian/staff support.

Student respondents identified study space and self-serve 24/7 access as high priorities:

"24/7 access to libraries is a common theme in other parts of the country. As a world-leader, UBC deserves to have 24/7 access to libraries as well."

What do they value most?

#1 Book & article pickup
#2 Librarian expertise
#3 Computers for access to online journal articles

1. CINAHL database searches reflect library-wide use.

2. St. Paul's Hospital Library focus group organized and facilitated by the UBC Faculty of Medicine, Evaluation Studies Unit.

3. Survey administered jointly by the UBC Faculty of Medicine and UBC Library.

Jeremy Buhler, UBC Library Assessment Office - September 2012 when informing library users about collection moves or the relocation of a service point. All of the print-based materials alerted users to check the library's website for the most up-to-date information and also invited them to connect with the library through various social media (Figure 14.2).

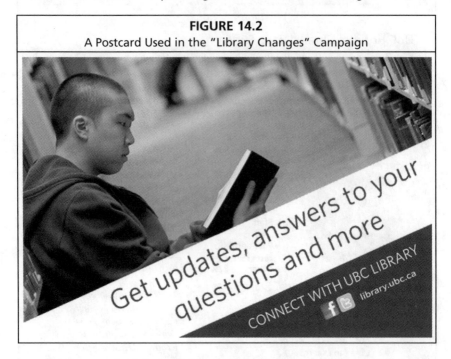

FIGURE 14.2
A Postcard Used in the "Library Changes" Campaign

UBC Library has been active in social media for several years. At the time of implementing the changes described in this case study, the library had an active presence on Facebook and Twitter as well as several blog platforms, most notably WordPress. No doubt in the near future there will be new tools added to the list. While no longer a new frontier, libraries need to be aware that whether they choose to participate in social media or not, both library users and staff will be active in discussions and debate around decisions. The library's Communications and Marketing assigned a dedicated staff person the responsibility for monitoring the library's social media presence, including user and staff comments directly related to the branch closures and mergers. In addition to the official UBC Library Facebook, Twitter, and WordPress accounts, various branches and individual library staff are also active on social media. Given the importance of academic freedom in the university context, communications staff were careful to comment only on posts if incorrect information was being provided. Individuals monitoring social media maintained a positive and somewhat neutral tone when commenting on blog posts, tweets, and other types of online commentary and did not engage in opinion or take a defensive tone when correcting misinformation. Twitter, in particular, is one of the most active forms of social media, and any announcements regarding changes to library spaces or services were often quickly redistributed beyond official library channels.

The Change Management Team found social media to be an additional source of feedback from both library users and staff. In the case of UBC Library, some of the messages developed by the Change Management Team caused confusion among some users and were also seen negatively by staff. These messages reflected a desire to maintain a positive tone, deemphasizing branch closures and instead focusing on the realignment of staff and collections to other locations. Receiving feedback via social media from both users and staff helped the Change Management Team adjust future messages and also address staff concerns directly, in the spirit of open dialogue. Staff reacted positively to the shift in messages and felt the library administration was listening to their concerns. Based on the experiences with social media and the "Library Changes" campaign, the library communications department is exploring whether it makes sense to have fewer official social media accounts across the system, recognizing that individual staff will always be able to maintain their own social media presence.

Conclusion

Though the decision to close or merge branches and relocate library staff, collections, and services is a difficult decision for libraries to make, the reality of the post-secondary sector makes these types of decisions more common, especially as academic libraries realign funding and services to meet new user needs and demands. The changes announced in May 2012 at UBC Library were ambitious and required a coordinated approach, including a communications strategy. The library decided to use the changes as an opportunity to develop a public information campaign called "Library Changes." While many of the traditional communication channels were utilized, social media played a far greater role in communicating with library users and staff than previously anticipated, although a careful balance had to be established between academic freedom and the need to ensure the distribution of accurate information. Social media also allowed staff and users to provide useful feedback on the communications plan that ultimately led to changes in how library administration presented some of its key messages. Ultimately the commitment made to a series of in-person meetings with library staff as well as key stakeholders proved the most beneficial in understanding the important issues as well as building trust among all those involved in implementing the changes.

References

Bates, A. (2012, October 24). Turning a page: The changing role of the university library. *The Ubyssey*. Retrieved from http://ubyssey.ca/features/turning-a-page-the-changing-role-of-the-university-library/

Thomson, S. (2012, September 26). Plan to relocate UBC's music library opposed. *The Georgia Straight*. Retrieved from http://www.straight.com/article-788306/vancouver/ubc-library-plan-opposed

University of British Columbia. (2014). UBC Overview and Facts. Retrieved from http://www.ubc.ca/about/facts.html

University of British Columbia Library. (2014). UBC Library Facts and Figures. Retrieved from http://wiki.ubc.ca/Library:About_UBC_Library

Wong, M. (2012, September 19). Music community gathers at town hall to keep library in-house. *The Ubyssey*. Retrieved from http://ubyssey.ca/news/ubc-music-library-566/

About the Authors

Editors

Sara Holder is an associate librarian and head of the Schulich Library of Science & Engineering at McGill University in Montreal, Quebec. She has edited and contributed to monographs and has coauthored journal articles on subjects including librarian training and development, library assessment strategies, academic library management, information literacy, and collection development. She is active in ALA, ACRL, and LLAMA, and she is a frequent reviewer for *Library Journal*. Sara received her MLIS from Dominican University in River Forest, Illinois and her BA from Vassar College.

Amber Butler Lannon is an associate librarian and head of the Humanities and Social Sciences Library at McGill University. She has coauthored several articles and book chapters on a variety of topics including e-book usage, library closures, library management, and dog therapy in libraries. She is an active member of the Academic Business Library Directors Group and a founding editor of *Ticker: The Academic Business Librarianship Review*. In addition to her MLIS from Dalhousie University, she has an MBA from the University of British Columbia.

Chapter Authors

Mary Beth Allen is an associate professor emerita and served over 20 years as the applied health sciences librarian at the University of Illinois Library at Urbana-Champaign. She is author of *Sports, Exercise, and Fitness: A Guide to Reference and Information Sources*, published in 2005 by Libraries Unlimited, and numerous journal articles.

Blair Anton is associate director for clinical informationist services at Welch Medical Library. She came to Johns Hopkins as a clinical librarian in 2006 and was promoted to her current position in 2009 after a 16-year clinical career in behavioral health care.

Giovanna Badia is an engineering and physical sciences librarian at McGill University. Her professional interests include citation analysis, database comparison and evaluation, information literacy, and marketing. She also summarizes and critically appraises research articles for the journal *Evidence Based Library and Information Practice*. Giovanna received her BA and MLIS from McGill.

Lynn N. Baird has served as the dean of University of Idaho's University Libraries since 2007. She co-facilitates the university's Leadership Academy, a program designed to develop faculty and staff. Her doctoral work compared leadership strategies of library and academic, deans and her research interests are centered on organizational culture and leadership.

Jill T. Boruff serves as the liaison librarian for rehabilitation sciences at the McGill University Library. Her research interests include teaching information literacy skills to health sciences students and expert searching for systematic reviews.

Will Bryant is the associate director of finance and administration for the Welch Medical Library since 2000. He has held a series of successive positions with the library and Johns Hopkins University for 27 years. He has a BS from Towson University and MBA from the University of Baltimore.

Margaret (Peg) Burnette is assistant professor and biomedical sciences librarian at the University of Illinois at Urbana-Champaign. Peg's current research explores the convergence of knowledge management and academic librarianship, particularly as it relates to tacit knowledge capture and sharing and researcher profiles.

Amy Butros is the earth and marine sciences librarian and the Scripps Institution of Oceanography liaison librarian at the University of California, San Diego Library. Amy received her MLIS from the University of California, Berkeley, and her BA from UC San Diego. As liaison librarian for earth and marine sciences, Amy enjoys exciting challenges in collection development, instruction, outreach, and real and virtual reference. She also enjoys working with her colleagues in the library's Academic Liaison Program.

James T. Crocamo is operations and undergraduate coordinator for the Science & Engineering Division at Columbia University Libraries, where he oversees access services in addition to providing undergraduate library instruction. He has a BA in English from Temple University and earned his MLIS from the iSchool at Drexel University.

Tomalee Doan is associate professor and head librarian for Humanities, Social Science, Education, and Business Division, Purdue University Libraries. She received the 2013 Special Libraries Association Center of Excellence Award. In 2010, she received the Dean's Award **for Significant Advancement of a Libraries Strategic Initiative.** Her scholarship focuses on higher education learning spaces.

Susan Edwards is head of the Social Sciences Division of the University of California, Berkeley Library and is intrigued by the ways that good data can help us make user-centered decisions about library collections and services.

Virginia Feher is head librarian for the University of North Georgia Libraries, Oconee Campus. She co-chaired the Georgia Regents University Libraries Website Redesign Team while working as the Reese library government information librarian. Virginia has an MLIS, an MFA in painting, and over 15 years of website design experience.

Robert Gresehover was the interim director of the Welch Medical Library (2013–2014) and head librarian of the R. E. Gibson Library and Information Center, Johns Hopkins Applied Physics Laboratory (1986–2013).

Katherine Hanz is a liaison librarian for the Humanities & Social Sciences Library at McGill University. She holds an MLIS from McGill University and an MA in English literature and theatre studies from the University of Guelph.

Cindy Ingold is the gender and multicultural services librarian in the Social Sciences, Health, and Education Library at the University of Illinois at Urbana-Champaign. She serves as departmental liaison to the Asian American and Gender and Women's Studies Departments and to the American Indian Studies and Women and Gender in Global Perspectives Programs. She also provides outreach and services to several cultural centers on the campus.

JoAnn Jacoby is an associate professor of library administration at the University of Illinois at Urbana-Champaign, where she serves as head of research and information services. She was the New Service Model program coordinator at Illinois from 2008–2012.

Maya Kucij is the coordinator of McGill's Education Curriculum Resources Centre and has worked as an education liaison librarian since 2008. She received her MLIS from McGill University in 2008 and her BA from Bard College in Annandale-on-Hudson, New York. She is the immediate past-chair of the Special Library Association's Education Division.

Jeffrey Lancaster is the emerging technologies coordinator for the Science & Engineering Division of the Columbia University Libraries. He earned a PhD in chemistry from Columbia University and now oversees the Digital Science Center where he facilitates the use of technology among students, faculty, and staff for research, teaching, and learning.

Jessica Lange completed her MLIS in 2009 and has since worked as a management liaison librarian at McGill University in Montreal, Quebec. Her research areas include information literacy and space planning in libraries.

Joe Lenkart is the international reference librarian and the manager of the Slavic Reference Service at the University of Illinois at Urbana-Champaign. His research focuses on access to vernacular language research resources, user studies, and environments in relation to area studies and Russian, East European, and Eurasian Studies.

Kelly A. McCusker is a research and instruction librarian at Auraria Library serving the University of Colorado Denver, Metropolitan State University of Denver, and Community College of Denver. Previously, she was the behavioral sciences librarian at the University of Illinois at Urbana-Champaign.

Mary McNeil is associate dean at Purdue University Libraries, where she has oversight of 12 libraries, archives and special collections, and technical services and collections. She is the author of *Fundamentals of Library Supervision* (2005 and 2010) and coedited *Advocacy, Outreach & the Nation's Academic Libraries: A Call for Action* (2010) and *Human Resource Management in Today's Academic Library* (2004).

Kim Mears is the scholarly communications librarian at the Georgia Regents University (GRU) Robert B. Greenblatt, M.D. Library where she assists faculty and students in the creation, dissemination, and preservation of their scholarly works. She co-chaired the GRU Libraries Website Redesign Team while working as the nursing information librarian.

Simon Neame is the associate university librarian for learning and engagement and the director of the Irving K. Barber Learning Centre, University of British Columbia (UBC) Library. Simon is responsible for student and community engagement, teaching and learning programs, and several public service branches at the UBC Library. Simon is a graduate of UBC's School of Library, Archival and Information Studies (iSchool) where he was an adjunct instructor from 2003 to 2010.

Nancy P. O'Brien is Professor and Head of the Social Sciences, Health, and Education Library at the University of Illinois at Urbana-Champaign. Her publications focus on the history, organization, and preservation of education resources in libraries. Her professional committee service includes the American Library Association and U.S. Department of Education.

Ellie Ransom is the Research Services coordinator for the Science & Engineering Division, Columbia University Libraries, where she is liaison to engineering, math, and statistics and organizes workshops for graduate students. She earned her MSLIS from Pratt Institute, SILS; MS in applied mathematics from Georgetown; and BS in mathematics from NC State.

Nancy Roderer is a professor emerita of Johns Hopkins University School of Medicine. She retired from positions as director of the Welch Medical Library and the Division of Health Sciences Informatics in 2013.

Linda Rose is operations manager for the Humanities, Social Science, Education, and Business Division, Purdue University Libraries. She creates position descriptions; hires, trains, and supervises division staff; and oversees customer service and collection transfers. Rose coauthored an article in *The B&F Bulletin* (newsletter of the SLA Business and Finance Division) on the winner of the 2013 Special Libraries Association Centers of Excellence Award.

Rebecca Rose is head librarian at University of North Georgia's Cumming Campus library. With over 20 years' experience working in libraries, Rebecca has served in multiple roles including online instructor, ILS system and electronic services administrator, library instruction and program coordinator, LibGuides aficionado, and Literacy Forsyth board member.

Lynne M. Rudasill is Associate Professor, University Library, and is embedded as the Global Studies Librarian at the University of Illinois at Urbana-Champaign. She is also the subject specialist for political science and provides services for the European Union Studies Center in her association with the International and Area Studies Library.

Hilary Schiraldi is head of the Thomas J. Long Business Library at University of California, Berkeley's Haas School of Business, where she has been working since 2008. Before coming to Berkeley she was a librarian at Credit Suisse in New York, where she conducted company and industry research for investment bankers, research analysts, and other staff. She has also worked at Forbes Magazine and at an independent brokerage, where she earned her Series 7 license. Hilary has a MLS from Pratt Institute and a BA from Columbia.

Stella Seal is associate director for the Welch Services Center at the Welch Medical Library, a position she has held since 2006. She has worked at the Welch Library her entire professional life, rising through the ranks from her beginnings as a circulation assistant in 1987.

Susan E. Searing is the interim associate university librarian for user services at the University of Illinois at Urbana-Champaign. As former head of the Library & Information Science Library there, she led its transition from a physical library to a new service model based on embedded librarianship and online resources.

Beth Sheehan is assistant professor and social sciences research services librarian at the Social Sciences, Health, and Education Library (SSHEL), University of Illinois at Urbana-Champaign. As a member of the SSHEL Implementation Team and Public Services Working Group, she developed and coordinated the new public services model and training program.

Claire Twose is the associate director for informationist services to the Johns Hopkins Bloomberg School of Public Health and the basic sciences at Johns Hopkins Medical Institutions. She is also directly responsible for services to several departments in the Schools of Public Health, Medicine, and Johns Hopkins Hospital.

Steve Witt is associate professor and head of the International and Area Studies Library at the University of Illinois at Urbana-Champaign. His research focuses on international developments in library and information science, placing global trends in librarianship and knowledge production in the context of wider social and technological developments.

Sue Woodson is the associate director for collections at the Welch Medical Library of Johns Hopkins University. She manages a collection that is essentially all electronic and is responsible for the interlibrary loan service. In 2010 she chaired the National Network of Libraries of Medicine SE/A Ad Hoc Committee on Print Collection Retention and Access.